Saving Cinnamon

Saving Cinnamon

The Amazing True Story
of a Missing Military Puppy
and the Desperate Mission
to Bring Her Home

Christine Sullivan

ST. MARTIN'S PRESS ☙ NEW YORK

Some names have been changed.

SAVING CINNAMON. Copyright © 2009 by Christine Sullivan. All rights reserved.
Printed in the United States of America. For information, address St. Martin's
Press, 175 Fifth Avenue, New York, N.Y. 10010.

www.stmartins.com

Library of Congress Cataloging-in-Publication Data

Sullivan, Christine.
    Saving Cinnamon : the amazing true story of a missing military puppy and
the desperate mission to bring her home / Christine Sullivan.—1st ed.
        p. cm.
    ISBN 978-0-312-59628-6
    1. Dogs—Afghanistan—Anecdotes. 2. Feffer, Mark. 3. Afghan war, 2001—
Personal narratives. I. Title.
    SF426.2s85   2009
    636.7092'9—dc22

                                                                2009016490

Originally published in the United States by New Hope for Animals, LLC,
2007, in different form as *44 Days Out of Kandahar*

First St. Martin's Edition: October 2009

10   9   8   7   6   5   4   3   2   1

In Loving Memory of
Richard L. Feffer, Sr.
1934–2008

The adventurer before me,
my silent safety net and unsung hero.

For Reggie, Maxie, Tyler, Spirit, and Brunswick,
I'll always love you.

And for Rose,
You will live on in my heart forever.

You must do that which you think you cannot do.

—Eleanor Roosevelt

ONE

THE MORNING BEGAN like most of my days at that time. I opened my eyes, thankful that I didn't have to get up that early. The ski season was long over. That winter I had taught skiing to three- to six-year-olds at a local ski resort. I had risen out of bed at 4:30 A.M. each morning. It was a necessary evil that allowed me to take care of things at home and still get to the mountain on time for work. There I'd endeavor to inspire little people to venture into the cold and attempt incredible feats of physical acts almost beyond their abilities. It was a lot to take on, but I had to admit getting up early had been enjoyable in unexpected ways.

You see, it seemed not much of the rest of the world was awake at that hour. Often during the winter, there was a new snow-fall overnight that made the morning especially quiet and serene. Spirit, my very energetic four-year-old Shepherd/Husky/Collie mix, required a long walk at least every morning, which kept her somewhat calm during the rest of the day. So we'd venture out, just the two of us, into the dark, peaceful morning, exploring and enjoying the winter wonderland while most everyone else slept.

Most important, though, getting up early that winter had afforded me the ability to chat live with my brother, Mark, through instant messaging. That's not so earth-shattering, until you factor in that he was halfway around the world in Afghanistan, serving his tour of duty in the war that raged on. For months I worried about him day and night. I was thrilled when we learned he had set up a computer and installed Instant Messenger. I could IM with him if I was lucky enough to catch him online. As it happened, because of the time difference, our schedules lined up in such a way that I was starting my day about the time he was ending his. The time was ten hours ahead in Afghanistan. For weeks, we chatted online first thing in the morning, giving me comfort knowing that he was safe another day.

It was June now, and I was no longer working at the mountain. The 4:30 A.M. wake up was a thing of the past. I could sleep in if I wanted to, but today I didn't. Instead, I popped out of bed, threw on my standard morning attire (sweatshirt and sweatpants) over my standard nighttime attire (whatever T-shirt was on top of the pile the night before). I stumbled down the stairs, readied Spirit to go out into the yard, and sent her on her way. I knew it was a poor substitute for our long, serene walks of the winter, but I was on a mission. I was headed to the computer.

Most days, I'm one of those poor souls who is compelled to turn on the computer before I start the morning coffee. To me it feels like worse than a bad habit, more like a sad habit. Today, though, it seemed acceptable. Today was different. Today, tomorrow, or maybe the next day there would be news—important news, and I had to have it as soon as it came and as soon as I could after waking.

The news I was waiting for would arrive in an e-mail from Mark. He was on his way home from Afghanistan, having been there for six months. I had treasured his e-mails each and every day. They were filled with the latest of what he was up to. The news he sent made his deployment seem less real, less dangerous, less threatening to the life and love that had come to mean so much. And we had gotten plenty of those e-mails throughout his time overseas. But these days I was waiting for an e-mail that would bring news of a different kind.

As my computer connected and I sent for my e-mail, I reflected on how lucky our family was. Mark had left home for training in late October 2005, with orders to spend a year or more overseas. But now he was coming home more than six months early, and his service up to this point was virtually uneventful. *Virtually.*

It was Mark's trip home that turned out to be far more eventful than his time in Afghanistan. Mark was in the city of Bishkek, Kyrgyzstan, part of the former Soviet Union. He had been there for several days, having spent most of the past ten days on an in-depth search for something gone missing—something very important to him that he was desperate to find. Mark's final flight home to the U.S. was to leave in just four days. Should he depart Bishkek without finding what he had lost, when he arrived home the distance could make it impossible to locate, and he would have lost a part of him that could not be replaced.

The e-mails started to come in, and, as most people do, I quickly scanned for the ones I would open first. That's when I saw it, an e-mail from Mark.

I skipped over all the other e-mails, barely even noticing them. I opened his mail, scanned it, and reached the bottom in disbelief. I started over. I read it again. I tried to absorb what it said, but it wasn't really making sense, wasn't sinking in. What he wrote couldn't be true.

The room started spinning. I couldn't focus. I felt the blood drain from my face and my mouth go dry. My mouth dropped open as my hand slammed over it. I was having one of those out-of-body experiences. I could see my surroundings but felt completely detached from them. I was floating above myself. The room kept spinning.

I took a deep breath and forced myself to start over one more time, to read every word, making sure this time not to miss a thing, to digest every bit of information there on the screen. And there it was—what had sent me reeling, what I didn't want to believe: the final lines he had written.

At this point, all we'd want is some assurance that Cinnamon is OK and living a life that is better than the one she was living in Afghanistan. The peace of mind that information would bring us is immeasurable, but we aren't confident that we will ever hear more about her . . . Please pray and hope that Cinnamon is doing well and is happy. That is what we will do. That is what we wanted.

The lump in my throat choked off any air. My eyes welled, and the tears began to flow. I couldn't stop them or the sobbing that now took over. This couldn't be happening. We had come too far. She was almost home. My brother and his wife had been through far too much in recent times for Cinnamon's fate to end this way. She was too special. She meant too much—and so did he.

The words finally registered, but they were hard to accept. The puppy that had kept my brother company and had watched over him during his time serving in Afghanistan, that he helped raise and had come to love enough to adopt and bring home, had been lost on her way to the U.S., abandoned at a foreign airport seven thousand miles away by the dog handler entrusted with her care and who had agreed to bring her home.

It couldn't be happening. It couldn't be true. But there it was, plain as day. I'd read the words he'd written but still couldn't believe them. My mind raced, and the questions flooded in. Where could she be? Was she all right? How could the dog handler have done this? What will happen to her now? But none of it mattered. According to Mark's e-mail, the answers will probably never be found. I broke down and sobbed uncontrollably.

TWO

AT SOME POINT in my adult life, I started to dread the random, unexpected phone call from family. One of the effects, I suppose, of caller ID. You know who's calling before you answer, and in a fraction of a second you make all kinds of assumptions about why they are calling and if you want to talk to them.

We are a close family. I speak with my mother on average once a week, sometimes more. Knowing her as I do, there are times when I know she'll be calling and times when I know she won't. And when her number pops up on the caller ID when she shouldn't be calling, my heart races. *How will my world change today?* Perhaps worrying the way I do is a genetic trait I inherited from her. Perhaps I want my world to stay just as it is. I want my life to remain unchanged. Safe. Secure. Predictable.

So when the phone rang that fall day in October 2005 and her number popped up, I held my breath. *What now?* I picked up, "Hello?"

I waited to hear her tone. Would it be happy? jovial? somber? Or maybe it was my dad calling, in which case the news could be worse. I braced myself. Her tone was off. What life-changing news was she about to deliver? I wanted to know. No, I didn't. The memories of other phone calls like this one came flooding back. Like the 6:00 A.M. call when I was in college that my grandmother had died. Or another one, the same time of day, but years later, that my uncle had passed away unexpectedly the night before. Calls like these had come to mean death to me.

I tried to relax, but she could barely speak. *Here it comes. No, don't tell me.* Nothing could have prepared me for what she said.

"Your brother's been called up." She choked on her words.

"What?"

"He's been called up. Mark's going to Afghanistan."

What on earth was she talking about? Mark was forty-one. A reservist. A navy guy. A sailor, for God's sake.

"You have to be kidding. When?" I started shaking. My knees trembled. I didn't think they'd hold me. I couldn't focus, but I needed to know more.

"He's leaving at the end of October." That was less than three weeks away. "Eight weeks of training, then a year's deployment. With luck, he'll be home by next Christmas."

A flood of emotions came rushing in, like a freight train barreling through a station it wouldn't be stopping at. I couldn't stop them. I was standing on the tracks. I was about to be run over.

As it all sank in, fear and guilt took hold—fear of him being overseas in the middle of a raging war. Okay, at least he wasn't going to Iraq. That was good news, right? Fear of a navy guy being on the ground in the middle of a battle zone. He'd been deployed before, during the Gulf War. But during that tour, he had spent six months on an aircraft carrier in the middle of the Persian Gulf. He had told me there was no safer place to be at that time.

Mark's responsibilities consisted of keeping the ship's combat computer systems running and standing watch on deck. Hardly combat duty. Yes, it was war, but he was navy. He'd eaten surf and turf every Saturday night, slept on a mattress, watched movies, and enjoyed the air conditioning. This time would be different, a lot different. This time he'd be in the thick of it, on the ground, in a role he hadn't been trained for. A friend had recently served eight months in Afghanistan. He'd told us all about it. War was still raging all around.

Guilt engulfed me as well, for all the times I watched the military deployments on TV and saw the families who cried. I didn't understand. Why were they crying? Their loved ones were in the military. They were deploying to do their jobs defending our country. They were trained for it. Most lived for it. I implored them to pull themselves together and support their soldiers. They were going to defend our country, to defend our freedom. Somebody had to.

Before that phone call, I hadn't understood the emotion brought on by knowing that someone you love would be in harm's way defending our country and our freedom. Yes, it was what they signed up for, but now it was happening to me, to my family, to my brother—my kid brother. Now it was my turn to cry, and cry I did.

"What are we gonna do?" I asked my mother.

She merely replied, "I don't know."

The next few days were spent getting the details about Mark's deployment. What about his job? What about his wife, Alice? How long will he be gone? When does he leave? What about training? What will he be doing? When will he be back? The questions didn't stop. Perhaps in some way I thought that as long as I kept asking questions, he wouldn't be able to leave.

His preparations began anyway, and with them reality set in. Mark was going to Afghanistan. Mark was going to war.

Along with this stark reality came my vigil of worry. Worry like I had never known. It lasted day and night. I couldn't breathe a full breath. I wouldn't dare. I wondered who would protect my little brother. I'd wake up each morning with a start. It was real. He was going.

And so my vigil began, and it would last until he'd come home. Nothing else mattered. I finally understood the tears of all those other families.

Lieutenant Commander Mark Feffer was in the Navy Reserves. He was the commanding officer of a Navy Reserve Unit. One of his responsibilities was to receive and deliver news of any mobilization for the men and women in his unit. Mark had received such news several times in the past few months and delivered it. It was never easy. A call like that always meant that someone was being mobilized and sent to either Iraq or Afghanistan. Most of the men and women believed it was their duty to go. They'd accepted the possibility that they'd be mobilized. They signed up for it. Their families, however, felt differently. It was never good news for them.

On October 12, 2005, Mark received another such phone call.

"Sir, I am calling with an assignment for your unit."

Mark knew it meant another reservist would be deployed into the war zone.

"Who's it for?" he asked with unease. There was a brief but noticeable pause on the other end of the line. Mark swallowed hard.

"Sir, it's for you." In disbelief, he replied, "There's got to be some mistake. There's no way."

It was about a year before that Mark had gotten back into the Navy Reserves. He had been in and out of the Reserves a couple of times since his commission. He'd decided to try to get back in and serve enough years to earn retirement. The response he had gotten from the Naval Personnel Commander was not quite what he'd expected.

"Out of the eighteen years since your commission, only eleven are good years." Mark had been out of the Reserves a total of seven of the prior eighteen years. It meant only eleven years would count toward his retirement.

"I'm not letting you back in. Since you haven't been selected for commander, I'll have to kick you out anyway in 2006 when you reach twenty years."

He was disappointed and frustrated but not deterred. "But I could make commander in those two years, and then I'd have another eight years to make retirement."

"Yes, that's true." But he denied Mark's request to be reinstated anyway.

Mark pleaded his case. "I want to give it a shot. Worst-case scenario, if I'm not selected for commander on the next board, you kick me out anyway. I have eighteen months until the selection board meets."

The commander relented. "Unless you make O5 [commander], you cannot make retirement. You have been advised. In August of '06, we'll kick you out unless you make commander. You'll have one more promotion board before then."

He'd won his case. But was this the right battle for Mark to have fought? Time would tell.

Over the next few months, Mark did his best to prove that he was worthy of promotion to commander. He successfully requested that he be assigned to an interim command position for a newly created reserve unit. He believed that if he could impress the selection board with his capabilities, he'd have a better chance at being promoted. But after a year in command of this unit, Mark's future with the navy had been uncertain.

October 1, 2005, was the beginning of the new federal fiscal year, and orders were being given. A new commanding officer had been assigned the leadership position in Mark's unit. Mark had been the interim commander, knowing a selection board would meet to officially fill the slot. He was in the running and could have been chosen, but he wasn't. Now he had to find a new assignment.

During the weeks leading up to his relief of command, Mark looked for a new assignment. He'd found one in Washington, D.C., and contacted the personnel unit about making the transfer. In the meantime, the new commander took over, and Mark was without an assignment in his unit. Until he was transferred to his new position, the navy had to put him somewhere—on paper. They'd change his reserve status to IAP, In Assignment Processing.

"No way," Mark said. "I'm not going IAP. I'll get deployed." Mark knew that the first place that navy planners looked when mobilization requirements came up was on the IAP list. Technically, those on the list were not assigned to a reserve billet, a personnel position within the navy. To the planners it looked like these reservists had no job.

The personnel chief reassured him. "No. That won't happen. We'll change your service code, your Manpower Availability Status [MAS]. You'll show up as IAP, In Assignment Processing, but your service code will say that we are administratively separating you.

It will look as if we are kicking you out of the navy. It'll only be for three weeks. I'll complete the transfer as soon as I can. They won't deploy you."

Mark felt better, but just a little. "If you can tell me you are changing my MAS code, then do it." It was a decision he agreed to, but one that would come back to haunt him. And it happened all too quickly.

"There's no mistake, sir. I have the orders here. You're being mobilized. You have to report to Norfolk by November 1."

"But that's less than three weeks from now," Mark replied.

"I know, sir. I don't know what happened. We just received your orders this morning."

Mark's options raced through his head. He could try to get out of it. There were a variety of ways to do that. He could claim that he was injured or had a medical issue. Or that he was essential personnel at work and his company couldn't afford to let him go.

Mark knew there were other ways as well. He'd heard many of them over the years, but none of them felt right to him. For someone to invent a reason to be exempt from service was dishonorable. It was out of the question for him. While he would rather not go, Mark knew he would. He had always said he would. It had been a point of contention between him and his wife, Alice. They'd fought about it when he had signed back up a little more than a year earlier.

"Why are you getting back in now?" Alice questioned. "You know you'll be called up sooner or later. They'll send you to Iraq. I don't know if I could take that."

"Honey, you don't know that." Ever the skeptic. Mark rarely believes anything is going to happen until it actually does. "I'm forty years old. I'm a surface warfare officer. I have no special skills. Guys like me don't get called up to go overseas." He hesitated, then continued, "But if I do get called up, you know I'll go."

She had a valid point, but he wanted back in. He'd gone into the Navy Reserves as an officer following five and a half years of active duty to fulfill his commitment as a United States Naval Academy graduate. He'd spent five years in the Reserves, then he got out.

He had been bored with his assignment, and the time commitment had gotten in the way of their family life. He'd served so much time at sea, it was more than he and Alice could withstand.

But Mark liked the navy, and what went along with it—the camaraderie, the challenge, and the feeling of accomplishment. So, over the years, Mark had gotten in and out of the Reserves as life allowed. The navy supported this type of service, as it provided a better balance between military and civilian life. But for Mark and Alice, it had proved to be a mistake.

Mark was reeling from the news. He couldn't concentrate, so he left work and went home to tell Alice. As he walked in the door he blurted, "I have bad news."

Her heart stopped. They'd been married seventeen years. They'd seen it all. It could have been anything. "What?" She held her breath.

"I'm being mobilized by the Reserves." He'd said the words, but he still couldn't believe it was happening. He never thought it would. He took a breath and awaited her reply.

That's all Alice needed to hear. She knew right away what it meant. He was being deployed to Iraq or Afghanistan. The news hit Alice hard.

Without warning, she erupted, "I knew it. I knew it. I knew this would happen. I told you it would happen." She couldn't have known. Neither of them could have, but it didn't matter now. The tears came quickly. Her face flushed, bright red now.

Mark replied, "Honey, I always told you, if I get mobilized I'm going to go."

The news was just too much. Their beloved dog, Jackson, who was only three years old when they adopted him, had just died in August after battling cancer. Then in September, merely four weeks after Jackson had died, Jamie, their sweet old cat whom they'd found in the basement of their house when they moved in fourteen years earlier, passed away. Now this.

Alice looked at Mark and said, "We need to tell your parents." It was all she could think of.

Mark's parents had just moved to Maryland that summer to be

close to their kids in case anything happened. This wasn't what they thought they'd be dealing with.

Mark and Alice went over to his parents' house. They were all sitting around the dinner table. Mark spoke first. "I have some news."

His mother's reaction surprised him. No tears. No angry words. Just a prolonged silence. Then she dropped her head in her hands and stayed that way for a long moment. No one spoke, giving her the time she needed. Finally, she looked up and attempted a long-running "inside" joke between them, "Do you want me to write an excuse note to George W.?"

Whenever Mark had faced something unpleasant, she'd always ask about writing a note to "the teacher." They had shared that joke for more than thirty years. In this case, though, she barely got a chuckle.

When she spoke again, she asked, "Is this definite? I mean, is there any way it could be a mistake, that you might not have to go or that you'd get out of it somehow?"

As hard as he knew it would be for her to hear, he had to tell her. "I'm not gonna get out of it. I signed up. It's my duty, and I'm going."

Dad could say nothing. He was the one who encouraged the boys to get into the military. Having an abbreviated career in the navy, he'd always regretted his decision to get out. He was glad when Mark got back in.

There was not much more anyone could say.

When I saw my husband, Billy, that evening, he saw the look on my face and immediately knew that something was wrong. "What's going on?" he asked.

I tried to hold back the tears. "Mark's being deployed. He's going to Afghanistan."

A friend of Billy's had been to Afghanistan the year before. He'd spent eight months in urban warfare. While the focus was on Iraq, action was still thick in Afghanistan. We'd learned through him what combat could be like. It was ugly, and it could be deadly.

"When?"

"He leaves for training in two weeks. Eight weeks in training. A year's deployment." I could barely speak.

"Should we go see him this weekend before he leaves?" Billy asked.

I hadn't thought about it, but now that he'd said it, it was exactly what I wanted to do. It wouldn't be easy, though. My brother lives twelve hours away by car. It was a long way to go for an overnight trip, but that didn't matter to me.

"I'd love to go. As long as it doesn't interfere with him getting ready. But yeah, let's do it. I need to put my arms around him before he leaves."

For Mark and Alice, what took place over the next sixteen days was nothing short of a cyclone of activity. It was amazing from two standpoints. One was the mountain of paperwork they needed to take care of: legal documents, powers of attorney, wills, bank documents, Alice's spousal–active–duty ID card. They got the runaround from the legal office at the naval academy, which made it difficult, almost impossible, to accomplish everything required before Mark left. The other was the household responsibilities that cried out to them: prepare their boat to sell, clean and cover the pool. Their to-do list grew every day as Mark tried to think of every possible thing that would need to be done over the next fourteen months while he would be gone. He wanted to do as much as possible before he left, so his being gone would place as few extra burdens on Alice as possible.

Alice was also in school and tried to stay on track. She had exams coming up that she needed to study for. It was nearly impossible to juggle everything on her plate.

If all that weren't enough, throw into the mix all the people who had heard that Mark was being deployed and who wanted to see him before he left. Mark and Alice had settled into the town where Alice grew up and where Mark went to school. They knew tons of people, and it seemed that every one of them called, e-mailed, and visited to express their shock over his deployment and to pledge their support for him and Alice. It was a busy time. Mark and Alice were both caught in the vortex.

I knew that going to see Mark would not ease my worry over his deployment. But Billy and I felt it was important to see him off, bid him farewell, and wish him a safe return. Plus, he's my kid brother. As a close family we see one another several times a year, regardless of the fact that we are spread out over five states throughout the East and the Midwest. Despite this, I couldn't be sure Mark knew how much he meant to me. I barely let the thought into my mind and wouldn't dare let it cross my lips, but what if the worst happened to him and I hadn't let him know how I feel about him?

I knew how much he meant to me, though, and he had grown to mean more to me over the prior couple of years. Mark was never one to stay in touch on a regular basis. Calls to him sometimes took weeks or even months to be returned, if they were returned at all. It was frustrating—maddening, at times. But there wasn't a whole lot I could do about it. There were times when almost a year would go by and I hadn't spoken with him.

But over the past two years, I had gotten spoiled. Spoiled by the fact that we were working together on a family project that dictated that we speak several times a month, sometimes more. While we were working on that project, I got to know my kid brother. Not only did I come to know and love him as more than just my brother I but also come to respect him as a person and a man. And I was extremely proud.

Mark and Alice were incredibly gracious that we'd decided to visit. At any other time, I would know not to impose on their time, and they might even have tried to deter it. Alice understood, though, that this was important. Mark, I believe, was a bit taken aback that we would drive all that way to see him before he left. But how could we not? I think a military guy sees deployment as just going off to do a job. Families, on the other hand, look at it on a much grander scale. Suddenly the most important things in life are put into perspective.

So Billy and I made the twelve-hour trip to say farewell to Mark before he left. The four of us went out to dinner and then ran into some of Mark and Alice's friends. We all stayed out late, talking, laughing, and drinking a bit too much. I wanted the night to last forever. I wanted to not have to say good-bye, to not have to stop looking at him. It was just too hard to imagine him going off to war.

Relentlessly, time marched on. The very next day, I put my arms around him and couldn't let go. I never got to speak the words that clogged in my throat, but somehow I believed that Mark knew how I felt, how much I love him, and that my heart would be with him during his deployment.

Mark flew to Norfolk on October 31. He reported to the processing center the next day. There were 180 navy personnel deploying, and they all had to be readied and outfitted to go. They waited in line after line for uniforms, gear, medical exams. Friday couldn't come quickly enough. Initially, they'd been told they wouldn't have any time off before leaving for training. When Mark got to Norfolk, however, he found out that he'd have two days off before shipping out.

When he told Alice, she decided to drive to Norfolk to be with him over the weekend. Naturally, she didn't want him to go without spending as much time with him as possible. The navy had said that once the unit had gone into training they would not have leave again before they left for Afghanistan. Mark and Alice made the most of their final hours before he left.

Mark and his team finally left for Camp Atterbury, in Edinburgh, Indiana, on Sunday morning, November 6. One hundred and eighty navy reservists spent seventeen hours in three buses to get there. They would spend eight weeks being trained by the army. After his first day he gave us an idea of what it was like.

Hello All:

So far this has been nothing but typical navy stuff. A lot of standing around in line for gear issue and shots. Lots of frustration. Not much info on where we're going or what we're doing. I do know that I'll be the communications officer for our unit of 9 men (8 officers/1 chief). We're going to a city called Qalat in SE Afghanistan. Beyond that I don't know much.

We got here to Indiana last night at 10:30pm after leaving Norfolk on a Greyhound bus at 0600. Not a pleasant trip, but it's over. Those of you who have been to summer camp know what the berthing's like. At least I'm on the bottom bunk.

We go out into the field for 2 weeks on Wednesday for weapons and field training. Then we get Thanksgiving break, Thu-Sun. Well, that's all for now, but I'll try to keep everyone posted as best I can.

Please pass my thoughts along to anyone not on the list.

Thanks,
Mark

Mark's deployment was an unusual one for the navy. It was the first time the navy had received and accepted a Request for Forces (RFF) from the army. It meant that navy personnel would be in positions historically held by the army, and they would function within the army structure. Essentially, Mark's team and the others were guinea pigs in a real-life experiment, and the army was to train them.

For troops going off to war, you would think that the army would do everything possible to make their transition smooth, seamless, and as easy as could be. Apparently this was not to be for these sailors.

To start with, the army had never trained a navy group before. Plus, they had never readied a deployment group in eight weeks. The training period normally had been twelve to sixteen weeks. Most army units also deploy as a group. Army personnel spend their careers training and getting ready for combat, combat support, and army operations. They're issued weapons. They're taught how to use them. They train together, and they know one another. And they practice. A lot.

Then came the navy guys, a much different group. These navy teams were assembled from individuals who had been mobilized from all around the country, and in eight weeks they were expected to be ready to defend themselves and our country, face-to-face with the enemy on the ground. I was glad I didn't know more about his training for combat, or lack of training. But I knew enough.

My husband, Billy, is former military. Before we met he had been an airborne ranger with the Eighty-second Airborne out of Fort Bragg, North Carolina. I may have felt better, more at ease, if Billy was the one being deployed and not Mark. Billy was trained to be over there. He was trained in ground warfare and hand-to-hand combat.

My brother, on the other hand, was trained to drive ships and manage computer systems. He could navigate a submarine or an aircraft carrier. He could troubleshoot the information systems that kept those ships afloat, but could he fire a weapon in his own defense if he needed to? Could he save a buddy's life? Could his buddy save his? I wondered. Then it became all too clear one day that the fear I faced, of sending a sailor into ground combat, was well founded.

It is inherent in the training that the army receives: kill or be killed. What would a modern-day sailor know of having to make that choice? In the twelve-plus years that Billy and I have been together, we've faced our share of trials and tribulations. When dealing with particularly difficult situations, Billy compares life to combat and taught me what he has learned himself: when in combat, while being ambushed by the enemy, hiding or running away both mean certain death. Your best chance at survival, in fact, is to run toward enemy fire and fire back.

Much to my dismay, I learned Mark intended to take the opposite approach. During a phone visit after he'd been in training a few weeks, he told me what the army was teaching him.

"So," he said, "we were doing this exercise that teaches you how to react to enemy fire while you're being fired upon."

"Yeah?" I asked nervously, waiting to hear what he would do.

"Basically they are teaching us how to crawl around on the ground, fully loaded with all your gear, and that if you're being fired upon by the enemy what you're supposed to do for your best bet of survival."

I held my breath, hoping he'd learned the response I'd heard so many times from Billy. "And?"

"Supposedly," he continued, "you're supposed to run toward the gunfire and fire back while you're moving toward them."

I sighed, relieved. I was glad that the army was teaching these sailors the essentials. He was getting the combat training he had never needed in eleven years with the navy. They were teaching him how to stay alive. I smiled. I was proud of both him and my husband at the same time.

"Yeah, that's what Billy says." But my relief was premature.

He shocked me when he continued, "To hell with that," he said, "if anyone is firing at me, I'm running with all I've got . . . in the other direction."

I gasped. I hoped he was kidding. The knot in the pit of my stomach tightened.

THREE

IT WASN'T CERTAIN, but Mark had anticipated that the navy would give them Thanksgiving Day off. As it turned out, they gave them the entire weekend. Instead of Mark's flying home to see Alice, Alice flew to Indiana. Mark had met teammate Jeff while in Norfolk, and they had become close friends. They had gotten to know each other very well during training, along with Don, another team member.

Jeff and his wife, Dawn, lived in Indianapolis, an hour from Camp Atterbury, where they trained. They invited Mark and Alice and Don and his wife, Sharon, to spend Thanksgiving at Dawn's mother's home. The couples bonded quickly. They had a lot in common and plenty to talk about. Their time spent together over the holiday had been wonderful. It was bittersweet as well. Alice had already bid Mark her farewell earlier that month. She was anxious for him to be deployed. She felt that the sooner he shipped out, the sooner he'd be home. Saying good-bye again was difficult.

Finally on December 28th, Mark and the rest of the navy group departed Indiana. They traveled from Indiana through Shannon, Ireland, to Incirlik Air Base in Turkey and then on to Bishkek, Kyrgyzstan. The greeting they got at Manas Air Base in Bishkek was less than welcoming. It was a very cold place, nicknamed Man-Ass by the soldiers.

"We didn't know you were coming. There's no room for you," they'd been told when they got there.

They spent the next four days in a cramped tiny room, waiting.

Mark sent us news of his deployment so far, which gave us an idea of what he'd be doing while overseas. I was relieved that his tone sounded good.

Hi everybody! Just a quick update . . .

So far the deployment has gone fine. After completing 8 weeks of pre-deployment training (radios, weapons, first aid, defensive tactics, etc.) in Camp Atterbury, outside of Indianapolis, we were allowed to go home for Christmas on 18 Dec for 8 days. We went back the day after Christmas. It was really great to see Alice and my family, an unexpected treat. I definitely didn't want to leave home. I returned to Indy on 26 Dec and we left there at 0700 on the morning of 28 Dec, after staying up all night packing and loading the plane. We flew 22 hours from Indy to Shannon, Ireland, to Incirlik, Turkey, and finally here to an Air Base in Kyrgyzstan (former USSR).

No changes to our mission yet. Our team of 9 navy is slated to pair up with the Garrison Command staff at an Afghan army base . . . We're here as advisors/consultants to help them learn to sustain their army properly.

Currently I'm "dual hat" as the team XO [executive officer] as well as resident IT "expert." (scary thought) (Note: You techies keep your cell phones on and nearby at all times . . . ;-)) We are not in a combat role . . .

Things here in Kyrgyzstan are fine. This base is used as a stop off point. It's got a PX [post exchange, or military store], nice dining facility and small "dorm" rooms that we share 2 per room. It's 12:20 am here on Friday 31 Dec. It's 1:20pm for you on the East coast on Thursday afternoon.

Looks like we'll be on flights tomorrow or the next day to another interim destination in Afghanistan for a week or so of training. Then on to our final destination.

The base looks exactly like you'd expect for a former USSR base. Lots of barbed wire and concrete. The room they have us in is decent, but small. Nothing to do but walk around, shop at the small PX and sleep between meals. I guess that's fine for now.

. . . I still don't have a postal mailing address, but my civilian e-mails haven't changed. That's all the news I have right now. Not sure how often I can call/write, but I will when I can. . . .

All the best,
Mark

P.S. Thanks for all your support.

After Kyrgyzstan, the team went on to Kabul for several weeks. Mark spent more time training, this time for the communications and computer-networking aspects of his job.

Finally, the unit flew on to Kandahar. It was another confusing time for them. Originally, Mark's team, Juliet Six, was supposed to spend its deployment as a mentor team to the Afghan army in the city of Qalat, a city far removed from most of the coalition troops and their protective forces. It was referred to as the wild, wild west. The area was prone to rebel skirmishes. The base was small and could easily be overthrown if the rebels did any planning. Because of this, the decision was made that Juliet Six would deploy to Kandahar in the southern part of the country. There were women on the team, and Mark had heard that no one, including U.S. and Afghan commanders, wanted women deployed in Qalat. It was too risky.

Team Juliet Four would report to Qalat instead. Initially, no one wanted to make the swap. Juliet Four had just spent a week in Kandahar because their flight into Kabul had been rerouted due to of poor weather. They had started to get the lay of the land and make contacts. They weren't happy about heading to Qalat.

All in all, though, everything worked out. Ultimately, Juliet Six, Mark's team, believed they'd gotten the better end of the deal, since they would be in a regional-command location. There would be more personnel, more security, and thereby more safety for the female personnel on their team. They also enjoyed better facilities and recreational activities than they would have had in Qalat. Interestingly, Juliet Four was also happy with their eventual destination. The location of the outpost insulated them from the politics and bureaucracy of the larger base and gave them increased autonomy.

As the team was on approach into Kandahar, Mark's headphones were pumping music into his ears. He was in his own world listening to "When the Levee Breaks" by Led Zeppelin, brooding, adrenaline pumping. To this day, hearing the song brings him right back to that time and place.

Finally they landed. Mark's iPod was rigged through his body armor. He didn't have the time or the thought to take his headphones out. Everyone was moving so quickly now: rushing out, carrying gear. It was all very surreal. This was Afghanistan. This was the war zone. Boots on ground. His very own soundtrack playing in the background.

It didn't take long for Mark and his team to get the lay of the land in Kandahar. Kandahar Air Field, known as KAF, the coalition forces' base, was a city within a city. He estimated there were about five to six thousand personnel on the base. It was hard to tell, though. The coalition forces were all there: English, German, Italian, Canadian, Romanian, Mongolian, and more. Each had staked out their own corner of the base, which was basically segregated. It was a busy place. Security was tight. Bomb-sniffing dogs were a regular sight.

Although Mark and his team lived at KAF, they worked at the Afghan army camp known as Camp Shir Zai. It was located about half a mile away from the back gate at KAF. Each morning the team would leave KAF in pickup trucks commandeered from the Afghan army surplus. They made the short but harrowing drive across dunes and dirt roads wearing their Kevlar body armor. They pushed the trucks and themselves hard, driving as fast as they could, never knowing what to expect—never knowing if they were the next target for the enemy.

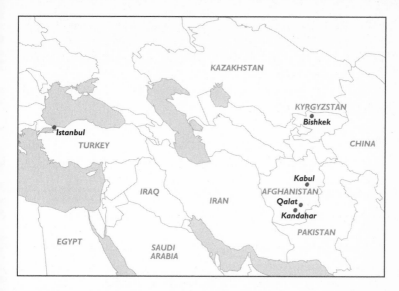

Mark's Navy Reserve Unit flew through Manas Air Base in Bishkek, Kyrgyzstan, on their way to Qalat, Afghanistan. Ultimately they were reassigned to Kandahar Air Field in Kandahar, Afghanistan.

In his first few days at Shir Zai, Mark spent his time getting to know people. It was useful for him to become acquainted with those whom he would be supporting and those who would be supporting him. It was easy business for him since Mark was a sales guy at home. It was standard operating procedure: Get to know these guys. Find out how you can make their jobs easier for them. In return, the hope was that others would make your job easier for you. Quid pro quo.

Around his third day on base, Mark walked into the American section of Shir Zai, where a small contingent of U.S. forces lived, and noticed a puppy. She had popped out from under a nearby building where she had been sleeping. It was an unusual sight. Military working dogs don't run free. They were kept in military kennels set up specifically for them. Was it a stray? Where'd she come from? He turned to a nearby soldier.

"Whose dog is that? What's her name?" Mark asked.

As Mark spoke to the soldier, he noticed the puppy romping in the sun. She was small, maybe just fifteen or twenty pounds, with a long tail and floppy ears that were too big for her head. Her coat was a rich, tawny color. He felt a slight twinge of homesickness, thinking of his own dogs at home.

"I don't think she's got a name. We call her Be-atch," he replied.

Mark thought, *Hmmm. Oh, that's nice.* But he didn't reply and continued on his way. He turned back, though, to take another look at the scrappy puppy, and as he walked away, he couldn't help but smile.

One of Mark's jobs on the base was to manage the computer network. He'd be the guy who would add and delete users, manage routers and switches—essentially manage the network. So much for being in combat. Early on, he sought out the base's network administrator, Kevin Kirkpatrick. Mark found out that Kevin lived in the area of the base where the dog was living. So he asked him about her.

"What's her name?" Mark asked.

"We call her Cinnamon," Kevin informed him.

Apparently this was just what Kevin thought her name was. It seemed that everybody called her something different.

Another soldier, an air force sergeant, told Mark, "Her name is Norma."

Mark took the liberty of deciding her name should be Cinnamon. It was much cuter for a puppy than any of the other names they'd used. Plus, the name described the color of her shiny coat. Mark spread the word and suggested this preferred name when anyone called her something else.

As soon as Mark was settled into Kandahar and had gotten the network cables up and running at Shir Zai, he set up his own office. He started e-mailing Alice on a regular basis. He had thought ahead and brought a Webcam with him, which he also set up. A few days after he had been there, Alice opened an e-mail from him:

Look what I found on base!

Mark exclaimed in the e-mail. And, as Alice opened the picture attached, she gasped. She exclaimed in her reply,

Oh my gosh! She's so beautiful.

The picture was that of a puppy staring up into the camera. Alice's heart skipped a beat. She was taken with Cinnamon from the start. From then on, whenever Alice talked to Mark, she fired away question after question about Cinnamon. She wanted to know everything about her.

What's her name? Where'd she come from? Who's taking care of her? Where does she sleep?

Mark gave Alice the answers he knew and then continued to give her updates as he learned more about the puppy. He sent her lots of pictures, a few each day, and before too long, Alice fell in love.

Dave Simpson, an investigator with the air force, arrived in Kandahar in February 2006. He met the scrappy camp dog on his first day there and took a liking to her immediately. He found out that she had come to live on Shir Zai around Christmastime. Guys from the Fourth Battalion had found Cinnamon and her mother near Forward Operating Base Price in Lashkar Gah, the capital of Helmand province in Afghanistan. It was about ten hours away from Kandahar by truck. They thought the two dogs would be a nice addition to the base and brought them along on the long trip back to Shir Zai. Cinnamon was tiny at the time, weighing no more than five or eight pounds, with a sweet face and innocent eyes. By the time Dave arrived in Kandahar, though, Cinnamon's mother was gone, and Cinnamon was already on her own.

Dave worried about Cinnamon from the start. Over time, about ten or twelve guys watched out for her. He and two other men took to feeding her every day. Dave had seen an old bag of dog food and wondered where it came from. He found out there had been another camp dog on base, but she was gone, and the food had long since spoiled. So Dave brought Cinnamon breakfast every morning. Someone had to make sure she ate every day. She was a growing puppy full of energy. He brought her bacon, sausage, and other scraps when he could.

Dave did his best to make sure that Cinnamon stayed at Shir Zai. He didn't want her to wander over to the American compound, Kandahar Proper as he called it. It was against U.S. DOD (Department of Defense) policy to have a camp mascot. He was sure if Cinnamon was found there she would be put down. He had been told that the previous camp dog had wandered over there and had been euthanized just for being in the wrong place at the wrong time.

But being at Shir Zai did not always ensure Cinnamon's safety. Many of the Afghan nationals, army and civilian alike, did not like Cinnamon or her being on base, and they often threw rocks at her or kicked her as they walked by. Dave would yell, "*Hubis nay*," Dari for "no good." Cinnamon responded by chasing them and biting at their feet and pant legs. One afternoon, Cinnamon followed Dave into the Afghan work center, where he had a meeting with an Afghan commander whom he was mentoring. The commander was not happy about Dave walking into his building with a dog. Dave just ignored the foul looks he received until he finished his business and left with Cinnamon.

Cinnamon was also exposed to environmental hazards regularly. There is no environmental agency in Afghanistan to regulate hazardous waste. Dave thought it was uncanny that Cinnamon never got into the antifreeze that was always on the ground. He worried she would walk through the battery acid that leaked from the Afghan army vehicles or the metal shards that littered the base.

Most days Cinnamon could be found curled up inside Dave's office. Temperatures in Kandahar would sometimes reach 120 degrees outside, and Cinnamon liked it inside, where it was a cool 95. Another soldier, whom Dave outranked, didn't like Cinnamon sharing their work quarters. Her diet of "people food" did not always agree with her, and the soldier, attempting to improve the air quality of the operations center, yelled, "Get that dog out of here." Jumping to Cinnamon's defense and outranking the soldier, Dave replied, "Rock, scissors, rank. Why don't you get out?"

Cinnamon seemed to return the favor by watching out for Dave and the other troops. Dave was in charge of the trucking company that handled the logistics of moving equipment and supplies around. He had been on base just three days and was overseeing preparations of a convoy that would move supplies to a forward support base north of Kandahar City. The convoy was made up of Afghan army personnel from the 205th Kandak, the equivalent of a platoon, and would be escorted by almost a dozen Americans from the air force and navy.

During these preparations, Cinnamon ran from one vehicle to another as if she were overseeing the work being done and ensuring Dave and the others had everything they needed. Or perhaps she did this to take advantage of the many tidbits of food that were handed out to her by those who had something to share. Some of the men wondered if she was waiting to be invited along but was apprehensive about actually getting in any of the vehicles. Or maybe, they considered, she knew her place was to welcome them on their return.

When the convoy departed, Dave was in the first of more than fifteen vehicles. Their destination was just a short drive from KAF. As they were crossing the bridge over a large lake that Dave called Kandahar Lake, he noticed a Toyota Corolla near where the Afghan National Police had stopped a half dozen other civilian vehicles. When the convoy reached the other side of the bridge, the Corolla pulled out and slammed into the third vehicle in the convoy. The suicide bomber noticed the explosives did not detonate, jumped out of the car, and started throwing hand grenades at the convoy. It took just moments for the Afghan police to take out the suicide bomber. Fortunately, no one else was seriously hurt, and there was minimal damage to the convoy vehicles. Next, personnel from the EOD (explosive ordnance disposal) team came, discovered 250 pounds of explosives in the insurgent's vehicle, and successfully disarmed the bombs without further incident.

On the drive back to Shir Zai, Dave and the others said little. They were deep in thought about the events of the day. As they approached the base, a short rain storm gave way to a fantastic rainbow, which arced in the sky and dropped down right in the middle of Camp Shir Zai. Someone commented that it was a sign

from above. Then their private four-legged welcoming commit-
tee ran to greet them. Cinnamon wagged her tail as they arrived
and trotted around to each vehicle, almost as if she were counting
heads to be certain all her friends had made it back safely. Dave
noticed one of his buddies had hugged Cinnamon just a bit longer
than usual. He also sensed that Cinnamon seemed to know that
something was different about her friends that day. She offered
Dave endless affection, licking his face and letting him hold her
tight. As they shared a few moments of unconditional love, Dave
felt his tension dissipate.

Since he was the intelligence officer for the battalion, the day's
experience shaped how Dave would prepare for all future missions. Dave became more diligent in preparing and analyzing all
available intelligence about where his missions took his team. He
also made sure they presented a hardness about themselves that made
the enemy think twice about attacking them and their convoys.

Being with Cinnamon took Dave away from these harrowing
realities of his time in Afghanistan. She quickly became the bright
spot in Dave's deployment, and he made time to play with her daily.
She was a welcome change to the routine and robotic life of his
long deployment. She made him feel human amidst the hardness
required of a soldier at war. It was as if Cinnamon gave Dave and
the others who cared for her the strength to do what was needed
each and every day.

After that first mission, Cinnamon was the first thing Dave
would look for when he returned from every mission. He worried
about her while he was gone, wondering if she'd get fed or wander off base. Seeing her when he got back would cheer Dave up
and make him forget the things he saw while "outside the wire,"
military speak for being off base. Cinnamon succeeded well at
this and was always surprising Dave with her antics. They would
roughhouse together, and she'd chase him endlessly. He laughed
one afternoon when she mischievously stole a pack of cigarettes
from an air force sergeant. He had chased her for over twenty
minutes before he finally gave up, not realizing how much enter-
tainment he and Cinnamon had provided for the spectators who
had gathered.

Cinnamon got her exercise, too. There was a three-mile paved perimeter around Shir Zai, called the racetrack. The army guys would run the perimeter endlessly. Cinnamon was often found making the loop with them early in the morning. Dave was glad to see her having fun. As long as she was with someone, he felt she was safe. He also knew it kept her out of the traffic at the Shir Zai main gate. Dave felt the Afghans were pretty crazy drivers and was happy when Cinnamon was safe and out of the road.

On Fridays, there were often barbecues for the troops. They loaded up on steak and chicken, and while some objected to the mascot and all the meat that she was getting, Dave gave it to Cinnamon just the same. She ate very well those afternoons.

Over time, Mark was able to piece together what life was like for Cinnamon and a little of her short history on base. Cinnamon was about three or four months old when Mark first got to Kandahar. She hadn't been the only dog at the time, though. Her mother had been there, too. Unfortunately for them both, Cinnamon's mother was rumored to have bitten an Afghan general or perhaps a colonel. No one is really sure. She was then taken away, and what really happened to her is uncertain. Some say that she was transported to another base—Qalat, maybe. Still others believe that she was shot. In any event, she was gone, and Cinnamon was on her own from the time she was just a few months old.

Kevin had told Mark that Cinnamon mostly hung around with the guys from the 4-1 Kandak. *Kandak* is the Afghan word for "platoon." The U.S. troops had started using the local language and called their own platoons kandaks as well. So she was with the First Platoon, Fourth Squad. The members of this kandak were the ones mostly feeding and taking care of her.

Mark saw evidence that there was a dog on base. He saw the remnants of stuff she had eaten in various places, a steak bone on the ground, her water bowl by the latrine. He could tell where she had been throughout the day by what was left behind.

There were lots of guys feeding Cinnamon. While there was a bag of dog food outside one of the offices she frequented, Mark never saw anybody give her this food, and he never saw her eating it. The bag never seemed to move the whole time Mark was there. He did not know whether or not she actually ate any dog food.

Mark did see her eating lots of other stuff, though. After all, there was always food around. Guys would be out driving around, running their errands, doing their jobs, and they'd give her something, maybe a taco or burrito from the chow line. Or scrambled eggs. A Slim Jim here, beef jerky there. Cookies. Cheetos. One for me. One for you.

Jeff, Mark's roommate, would come into the office in the morning, where Cinnamon liked to curl up next to the heater that they used to burn off the morning chill, and he'd dump a box of Apple Jacks on the floor for her. She never refused anything.

It seemed likely that, after grazing on whatever Mark and Jeff had given her in the morning, she'd take off to the next office, where she probably would repeat the routine with another group of guys. No one was really sure if Cinnamon got regular meals, and given what she ate, her nutrition was worth questioning.

As a puppy, eating was just one of the things Cinnamon would do to occupy her time. Naturally, playing was also part of her routine too. Mark had seen where it appeared she spent some of her nights: inside a cement bunker that was used for the troops to take cover in in case of an attack. There was an old beat-up carpet remnant and a water bowl inside for her. Mark thought Cinnamon might appreciate a little more padding for her bed, so he added a mattress. It was really just a foam bedroll. He put it in with her other things. The next morning when Mark returned, Cinnamon was not there, but evidence suggested that she had been there at some point the night before. It seemed that she must have had her puppy fun throughout the night: the bedroll he had left for her was shredded into hundreds of pieces. He smiled. After all, she was just a puppy. He wondered if Washington knew this bunker doubled as a doghouse.

There were also times when Cinnamon entertained the troops. During a weekly status meeting, Cinnamon showed up. She sauntered into the classroom, headed straight for the front of the room where Mark was seated, and climbed up on the bench next to him. She wanted to play. No work got done as she tugged on lanyards, shoelaces, or whatever else she could find. Everyone fawned over her. She stole the show.

Mark didn't want to admit it, especially to himself, but Cinnamon was climbing into his heart.

Back in Maryland, looking at the pictures that Mark sent, Alice noticed something right away. There was a familiarity in Cinnamon's eyes. Mark wasn't so sure. They debated it, but Alice insisted.

"Her eyes. It's in her eyes. She has Jackson's eyes," claimed Alice. The tears came. "He's there with Cinnamon to watch over you." Believing that someone or something was watching over Mark gave Alice some relief. It allowed her to trust that he would stay safe and make it back home.

"Honey, seriously," was the typical reply that came from my brother, the eternal skeptic, lacking in most things spiritual.

But Alice didn't give up easily. "No, I see it. I'm sure of it. He's watching over you. I knew there was something special about Cinnamon from the moment I first saw her picture. Tell me you felt it, too."

"Okay, if you say so," he relented. Alice turned away from the Webcam so he couldn't see her roll her eyes. Mark had had a connection with Jackson from the start. Wasn't it possible that Jackson still watched over Mark the way Mark had watched over Jackson?

In the summer of 2002, four years earlier, I had been to a conference in Maryland and took the opportunity to visit Mark and Alice for the weekend. Sitting at the kitchen table, I noticed a flyer about a dog that needed a home.

"What's this?" I asked my brother.

"Oh, that. Alice got the flyer when her aunt dropped it in our mailbox. I guess a local dog is in a bad situation and needs a new home." His tone was a bit matter-of-fact, so I was surprised when he continued, "Alice and I are thinking about rescuing him."

"Oh, really?" I replied. I was intrigued and hopeful. My dog Tyler, who was visiting along with me, had been a rescue, too. My husband and I had adopted him at nine years old. He was in terrible shape when we got him, suffering from allergies. No one believed he'd live another year. But he'd already had his fourteenth birthday at the time. Some say he'd hit the jackpot when he came to live with us. We believed it was the other way around.

"Yeah, apparently he's a 110-pound Golden Retriever and lives in a trailer. His family has no time for him, so he never gets out. They are trying to find him a new home. We're thinking about going to go meet him this weekend."

In a matter of hours, Mark and Alice had not only visited the dog but also brought Jackson home with them. I was thrilled when Tyler and I got to meet him. He was beautiful, and he and Tyler, who was also a Golden, became fast friends.

That afternoon, while Jackson explored his new home, Mark and Alice told me about meeting Jackson. When they had gone to see him, he was tied up on the porch of the trailer. When he saw them, he immediately wagged his tail. They learned that he rarely got walked and spent most of his days either tied up or in a crate that was much too small for him. It was no life for this big, beautiful boy.

When Alice noticed a large growth on Jackson's neck, his owners immediately reassured her and Mark that they'd had it looked at. They told Mark and Alice that it was benign and had decided that it didn't need to be removed. They even offered to provide his vet records.

By that time, though, having spent just a few minutes with Jackson, it didn't matter. Mark and Alice had fallen in love. They decided to bring him home that very day. Then, just two weeks later, Alice took Jackson to see their own vet, who reviewed his prior records.

"Do you know what this says?" the vet asked with trepidation.

Alice looked at her wide-eyed.

"Jackson has a malignant mast-cell tumor. His previous owners had been sent a letter advising them of it."

When Mark and Alice called Jackson's previous owners to discuss what the vet had told them, they just said, "Well, we can take him back if you want. We can't afford treatment. We'll have to put him down."

Euthanizing Jackson was out of the question. Mark and Alice never considered it. They just wanted Jackson's previous owners to be honest with them.

Jackson's surgery was scheduled right away. The vet removed a two-pound tumor from his neck and shoulder with clear margins. Alice spent the next three months changing Jackson's bandages three times a days because of some minor complications resulting from his surgery. It was a labor of love. And while Jackson's recovery took three months instead of the few weeks predicted by the veterinary surgeon, Jackson's wound finally healed. He was a happy, energetic boy—the perfect addition to the family, and Mark and Alice adored him.

Three years later, Mark and Alice were getting ready for a family graduation party in Chicago when Jackson started having diarrhea. Alice called the vet.

"It could just be worms or colitis," she told Alice. "Try not to worry."

When they got back from their trip, Alice took Jackson for testing. After two weeks they found nothing conclusive; Jackson threw up terribly. Alice decided he needed to see a specialist. She took Jackson to see the oncologist he had seen before. Mark was out of town when Alice got the bad news.

"Jackson has lymphoma," the vet told her.

Lymphoma was the worst kind of cancer that Jackson could have been diagnosed with because of how quickly it can spread. They started chemotherapy treatments immediately and put him on a natural diet with herbs and vitamins—all to no avail. His body was not responding to the treatment, and he had a heart condition that prevented using stronger medications. Jackson was declining quickly.

Jackson spent one of his last days as his happiest. Mark and Alice took him to the beach in Delaware. They spent the entire day and evening there. At home, Jackson could barely walk from his advancing cancer and the heart defect they had found during his chemotherapy treatments. But this day at the beach, Jackson ran and played like a puppy. He chased birds and played with his "sister," Baby, another rescued canine family member. None of them wanted the day to end.

The next day was not a good one for Jackson. Mark and Alice were with him constantly and into the night as he lay in the dark on the cool bathroom floor. He was going into cardiac arrest, and they knew he was dying. Their sweet boy, who had gotten a second chance at life, died in their arms, barely three years after they'd gotten him.

I remember Mark lamenting, "Poor Jackson just can't get a break."

I quickly rebutted, "Jackson got the biggest break of his life when he came to live with you."

"Can you bring her home? Mark, I think you should bring her home." Alice waited for his response.

"She isn't mine to bring home. She belongs to everyone here at the camp."

"But you have to. We have to get her out of there. She's just a baby. She needs a home." Alice pleaded with him.

"Honey, I can't bring her home. Besides, I already checked it out. It would cost about four thousand dollars to have an animal-transport company bring her to the U.S. That's silly." Ever the practical one.

Mark was surprised that transporting Cinnamon would cost so much, but he didn't give it more than a passing thought. Cinnamon wasn't really his to bring home, so he hadn't seriously considered adopting her when Alice first raised the possibility.

Mark focused on Cinnamon not being his when they spoke, perhaps so Alice wouldn't be disappointed if he decided not to bring Cinnamon home. In the back of his mind, however, he thought about it. It would be neat to bring her home. It would be fun to have her, and he knew she'd have a good life in the States. But he didn't want to get his own hopes up either. And still, there was the four thousand dollars. Mark was frugal, and that amount was a lot of money to spend on one dog.

Mark continued to send pictures to Alice. Subconsciously Mark knew that the pictures would make Alice want him to bring Cinnamon home. How could he refuse? Maybe it was his way of making Alice responsible for the decision.

He knew what he was doing, but at the same time he didn't want to be doing it. He didn't really know where his actions would lead. So what would be the harm of sending Cinnamon's photos to Alice? He didn't know that he would say, "Hey, I want to bring her home." He also didn't know that he would say, "No, I'm not bringing her home." Mark did not make a conscious decision at that time.

Early one morning a few weeks later, when Mark and Alice were on a Webcam call, Alice noticed movement in the background.

"What's that?" she asked.

Mark turned the camera toward the movement.

"Oh, Mark! Get her to come closer." It was Alice's first live image of Cinnamon.

"She's cute, isn't she? Look how much she's grown." His voice resounded with excitement when he talked about her.

"Watch this," he said, and with a little prompting, Cinnamon, who'd grown long and tall, walked over to the door of the office. She stood up on her hind legs and stretched up toward the door. With a long stretch across the door handle, she'd opened the door and let herself out. He laughed as he called after her, "Hey, Cinnamon. Could you shut the door behind you?"

"Oh, Mark. That is so sweet." Alice was warmed. Cinnamon grew on her more each day. While she knew that they had to get Cinnamon out of there, she also knew Mark was growing frustrated with her being after him about it constantly. She decided to let it go for a while.

Taking care of Cinnamon on the base was a joint effort. After all, she was the camp's dog. She belonged to everyone, and everyone pitched in for her care. Mark loved having her there. A lot of the other guys did, too. Cinnamon was a morale booster. A distraction. A little piece of home, fun and entertaining. She brightened everyone's day the moment she showed up. Being with her slowed down the fast tempo imposed by a 24/7 military environment. Cinnamon could make you forget where you were just by wagging her tail and playing chase or by sharing the affection you otherwise couldn't in a war zone.

As a puppy, Cinnamon was always getting into something. She was oblivious to the war going on around her. Earlier that year there had been an explosion at the Afghan storage container. There was debris all around the camp. Mark found her trotting down the street one day with an unexploded shell in her mouth. Cinnamon had found a large machine-gun round. It was about the size of the cardboard from an empty paper-towel holder. "Give me that," he said to her. He coaxed her over to him, taking the shell out of her mouth. Chewing gum had been stuck to the outside of it. It was just another plaything for the scrappy little pup.

On another afternoon, Cinnamon found yet a different way to entertain herself and the troops. The navy's construction force, or "construction battalion" SeaBees, as it was known, had a project on Shir Zai to cover and reduce the noise output of the large power generators on base. Paul Michaud, the SeaBee in charge of the project, determined that they would build walls of sandbags around the generators. Paul ordered a truckload of sand and hired local contractors to fill the bags. When the sand was delivered days ahead of schedule, Cinnamon seized her opportunity. Because the ground on base was extremely hard packed and mostly covered with gravel, Cinnamon hadn't known how much fun it is to dig. Cinnamon quickly learned, though! She played and played—for several days—whenever Paul wasn't around to stop her. She romped and dug in the sand and could be seen running in circles around the pile. She played "king of the hill" all by herself or with anyone who would take a few minutes to play with her. Most everyone had fun watching her.

Over the next two or three days, Cinnamon had dug into the pile so much that by the time the contractors came, she had reduced the pile to about half of what Paul needed! He knew who the culprit was, but being a dog lover himself, he didn't mind too much. Paul liked Cinnamon and laughed about it just as much as everyone else.

Cinnamon distracted those at home as well. In addition to sending care packages for the local children, friends and family sent boxes of toys, treats, bones, and more for Cinnamon. The flowered collar she wore had come from admirers in the U.S. She didn't really want for much. At least not for the moment.

Then, Mark started to wonder. Who would care for her when he was gone, when these troops who loved and fed her rotated out? Would the next guys care? Would she stay safe? What kind of life will she have? What kind of future? A couple of the guys talked about it. "Wouldn't it be great if someone brought her home?" Mark remembers hearing more than once. But was it realistic? Was it even possible?

About five months into his deployment, Mark was helping coordinate a vendor-outreach conference. It was the equivalent of a small-business trade show and was organized so that the local vendors and businesses could make contact with the base contracting department. The conference would be held at Shir Zai, the Afghan base, because the locals would not be able to get through security requirements to get onto KAF, the coalition base. Local nationals could get onto Shir Zai since there were no regulations prohibiting their entry. Shir Zai wasn't considered a target for the rebels.

During the preparations for the event, security brought the bomb-sniffing patrols to Shir Zai to search the perimeter. The bomb-sniffing dogs were there doing their work. Mark struck up a conversation with one of the dog handlers, asking him questions.

"Do you bring your dogs home? How do you bring your dogs home? How does that work?"

"Sure we bring our dogs home. We do it all the time." The man's name was Greg. He was a contracted dog handler working for Dog Handlers Incorporated, a U.S. company that provided working dogs to the military for security work.

Mark told Greg about Cinnamon. "There's this dog in the camp. Her name is Cinnamon. I'm thinking about sending her home to the U.S. How would I do that?"

Without pause, Greg replied, "I'll take her for you."

It couldn't be that easy. "How would you do that?"

"I'm going on leave next month. We usually fly out on the ninth of every month. I could take her with me then."

"You could do that?" Mark shot back quickly.

"Yeah, I'm a dog handler. We're probably going to ship about six or eight dogs home. One more isn't going to make a difference. We have to send a handler to accompany the dogs to our company's office in Chicago. So I'll take her."

He couldn't believe his luck. It was at that point that Mark made the decision to adopt Cinnamon and send her home. He thought, *Yeah, this is going to be easy. All I have to do is get Cinnamon to a dog handler. He would take care of the rest.* Little did Mark know.

FOUR

MARK'S TIME IN Afghanistan passed far more quickly than I ever dreamed it would. Having the ability to send e-mails, chat live on IM, and talk with him on his Webcam allowed us to connect with him in ways that families in previous wars never could. Being able to communicate with him in this way also gave us a sense of comfort that he was safe, perhaps a false sense of comfort.

We'd learned at some point during Mark's deployment that rocket-propelled grenades and mortar rounds were landing on base where he was stationed. They usually came in the middle of the night. During these raids, he and the other troops were rattled out of bed, or from wherever they happened to be at the time, and would head to the bunkers. They'd spend hours there waiting for the raid to end. Usually just one mortar would come in at a time, but surely that was enough. I'd be glad when he was back home.

Mark wondered about Cinnamon during these raids. But Cinnamon was at Shir Zai, the Afghan army base, which was not a target for the insurgents, so she was not in any danger from the grenades. Mark worried that it was more likely she would be kicked or otherwise injured by the local nationals. He had seen them kicking her and yelling and throwing rocks at her on many occasions. He knew they didn't like her and was concerned that something worse could happen to her if she bothered them enough.

Rumors started flying around our family sometime around March 2006 that Mark might be home by the summer. My mother has the habit of turning tiny bits of information into what she wants them to be, hearing what she wants and ignoring the rest. I guess we all do this at some time or another. Recently, she'd heard something that gave her reason to believe Mark would be home by June or July at the latest. She latched on to this fast. I knew how she was, so I wasn't buying in. Not this time. I needed the facts.

When I asked Mark about it, he replied, "I'll be lucky to be home by next January. The Army isn't going to spend all the time and effort to get us trained and over here, just to pull us out. My orders were for a year of service. It'll be at least Christmas before I'm home."

My spirits were deflated. I had been hoping the rumors were true. I commiserated with the others in the family. We didn't want to believe that Mark would be in harm's way for that long.

Then, a short time later, I got a real sense from him of when he might be coming home. I had sent him a few pairs of my favorite type of winter socks, guaranteed to keep his feet warm and dry in the harsh Afghan winter. He had asked for them. He told me how much he liked them when he had gotten them. I was surprised by his response when I asked him if he wanted a few more pairs.

"I'll be home before I get to wear them again," he told me.

When I asked him what he meant, he explained that his deployment would end before winter in Afghanistan set in again.

I was elated. Mark was indeed coming home. He told me that the army unit his team was attached to was rotating out of Afghanistan, and his unit would be sent home rather than stay on where they were. It all had happened so quickly. We didn't expect him home until September at the earliest, January at the latest. We had been told not to get our hopes up, but now he'd be home by the summer.

To top it all off, apparently Mark and Alice had decided to adopt Cinnamon. How did *that* happen? *When* did that happen? Last I knew, Mark had said she wasn't his to bring home and that it was going to cost him four thousand dollars if he were to do it. I'd have to remember to ask him what could cost so much to bring a puppy home. How much could her plane ticket possibly be? I wondered if she'd be flying first class. I'd assumed dogs rode in the belly of the plane, but for four thousand dollars, you'd think she'd get first-class service.

Ultimately, how Mark made his decision wasn't important. What mattered most was that Mark was coming home, and he was bringing Cinnamon with him.

When Mark decided to take Cinnamon home with him, he asked around in case anyone else had the same idea. Everyone he spoke to thought it was a great idea. Although she was the "unofficial" mascot for the camp, Mark still felt he should ask the colonel in charge of their camp for his permission. Mark didn't know what to expect. He thought the colonel didn't like Cinnamon. The colonel had left word that she was not to be let into their office spaces. Mark had been pleasantly surprised with the colonel's reaction, though. "I don't like dogs," he started to say in his thick Kentucky accent, "but I like that dog. I'm glad she's going to a good home. Let me know if there's anything I can do to help."

Once he had the colonel's consent to take Cinnamon home, Mark started to work out the details. He wanted to surprise Alice. She had been after him for so long to rescue Cinnamon. She had fallen hard for Cinnamon, and with good reason. She was worried for Cinnamon's safety and future. Afghanistan was not a warm and fuzzy place for a puppy to grow up, and losing Jackson had been hard on both of them. It would be good to save this puppy and have a new addition to the family.

Mark called Alice to give her the news. "I wasn't gonna tell you this, but I may have found a way to bring Cinnamon home after all."

"Oh my gosh, Mark! That's fantastic!"

"Yeah, I thought you'd be happy. I'm gonna need help on your end making travel arrangements for her in the States."

"Of course. Whatever we have to do. I'll take care of it all." She was thrilled. In fact, she was so excited she couldn't sleep.

Over the next few days, Alice daydreamed about what Cinnamon's life with them would be like. She was comforted knowing that Cinnamon would be safe and secure once she got to Maryland.

Mark did not always have such a soft spot for rescuing animals. It was a gradual softening that occurred over time after he married Alice. Alice had a Golden Retriever named Gretchen when they met. Gretchen had been a gift for Alice's eighteenth birthday from a friend. Alice's parents had taken care of Gretchen while Alice was away at college, and when Alice moved back home, Gretchen, aging with arthritis, moved back in with her.

Less than a year into their marriage, Mark was on deployment with the navy. They were living in Virginia Beach. Learning the life of a military wife, Alice did her best to keep things running smoothly while Mark was gone. Alice took Gretchen for a walk one day, as she often did. While on their walk, Alice noticed Gretchen was panting in an unusual way. Before Alice could get her back home, Gretchen collapsed. At eighty-five pounds, Gretchen was too big for Alice to lift. Fortunately, two kind men stopped to help. They took Alice and Gretchen to the local vet for an emergency visit. Alice got the bad news that Gretchen's heart was failing. And though her mom was there beside her, she couldn't reach her husband. Struggling with what to do, she kept Gretchen on life support for four days. Finally, Alice made the heart-wrenching decision to let Gretchen go. She was just ten years old. It was the first in a long series of tragic good-byes that Alice would say to her beloved pets.

Later came Molly, Elsa, and Baby—each with their own stories, each with their own heartwarming lives and sad endings.

Molly was Alice's first rescue. Alice was driving home from work when she saw the little brown Corgi mix running along the road, dodging traffic. Stopping in the median, Alice got out of the car in her nylons and high heels. Fortunately, the dog jumped right into her car.

Mark was out when she brought the dog home that night. Frightened by the storm that had rolled in, the dog that Alice named Molly paced and pooped all night. When Mark finally got home, the first words he uttered when he saw Molly were "That's the ugliest dog I have ever seen." But even as Mark wondered if they should keep her, the little Corgi mix touched his heart.

Over the next few days, Alice tried to find Molly's owners. She visited the local shelters and put up flyers, but when no one claimed her, Mark and Alice kept poor Molly. And as homely as he thought she was, Molly became Mark's best friend. She had grown on him, and he had gotten very attached. It seemed that Mark's heart was softening, and he found that, like Alice, he had a soft spot for rescuing a dog in need.

About two months after they took Molly in, Mark and Alice adopted Elsa. She was the first dog that they adopted together. It had taken some time, but they felt that they had healed from losing Gretchen. It was time for another Golden.

Elsa Belle was one of twelve puppies. They adored her from the start. When they brought her home, Molly mothered her like she was her own. She played with Elsa, protected her, and taught her all the puppy things she needed to know. Alice walked every morning with a neighbor who had a new baby. And while Molly trotted alongside, Elsa rode in the baby carriage with her friend's little girl.

When Mark and Alice moved to Maryland, they took Elsa to a new vet there. Alice had noticed that Elsa couldn't manage the stairs very well. One of her back legs didn't seem to be working quite right. The vet x-rayed Elsa's leg, and Alice learned nothing significant. Then, Elsa started having terrible seizures every day. Mark and Alice consulted a specialist, who didn't take long to make a diagnosis. Elsa, who was just seven years old, had a brain tumor. There was nothing they could do for her.

It was a difficult time for Alice. She had a tremendous workload, which kept her from spending the time with Elsa she would have liked. Elsa's last days were not quite what Alice wanted for her sweet, gentle girl. And neither was their final good-bye.

When Mark and Alice had finally decided it was time to say good-bye to Elsa Belle, they took her to their vet's office, where she would be put to sleep. Their regular doctor was not in that day. While Mark and Alice were ready to let Elsa go, sadly the doctor who attempted to euthanize Elsa was unsuccessful in his first attempts. When Elsa finally slipped into her last slumber and Mark and Alice said good-bye, it was two hours after they first arrived. It was one of the hardest things that they had to go through.

Baby was another dog that Mark and Alice rescued. Alice had some friends over for the day when she met Baby, a little gray

Terrier mix. "Where'd you get the dog?" Alice asked her friend, who had brought Baby with her.

"Someone left her tied to my front doorknob with a note that read, 'Please take care of Baby.'" Her friend filled her in. "I can't keep her. It's against the rules at the apartment where I live. I'm trying to find her a home."

Alice fell in love with Baby and asked her friend to leave Baby with her. When Mark arrived home that night, Alice said, "Let's keep her."

Alice saddened when he quickly replied, "Absolutely not."

Baby bounced around for several days. She went from Alice, back to her friend, and then to the pound. Then, she went back to her friend and to the pound again. When Alice heard that Baby was scheduled to be put down that afternoon, she couldn't allow it. Urgently, she called her friend and cried, "Go get her now before they euthanize her. I'll deal with Mark." She wasn't quite sure what she would say to him, but she pressed on, "I won't take 'no' from him."

Alice hadn't realized that Mark was just trying to be practical by not taking in a third dog. He actually liked the little dog, and after giving it some thought, Mark decided that having three dogs couldn't be much more work than having two. Although she wasn't aware of it at the time, Alice's love of animals had grown on Mark. His heart softened more and more with each one they rescued. He realized how much love and happiness they added to his life and how rewarding it was to give an animal a second chance.

Shortly afterward, Baby found her place in their family. Her nickname became Chibi, which is a loose translation of "little one" in Japanese. And their little one ruled the roost. It wasn't long before Chibi, like Molly before her, grew to hold a special place in Mark's heart.

I was thrilled that Mark had decided to bring Cinnamon home. I had watched her antics and seen her grow through the pictures Mark had sent. She was adorable, and she needed a real home. Mark and Alice loved her so much that they'd be perfect parents for her. Even though Alice hadn't even met her yet, she had grown attached to her quickly. I wasn't surprised by this decision, though, knowing how much Alice loves animals and how hard losing Jackson had been.

I phoned Alice. She picked up. A victory. Before Mark went off to war, it was unusual to call Mark and Alice and find them home or that they would pick up the phone when they were. With Mark gone, the family was united in a bond of worry and support. We craved and shared news of his whereabouts, activities, and safety. Such communication wouldn't change whether or not he was safe, but somehow, it made us feel better.

Cinnamon was flying with the dog handler to the States ahead of Mark. Mark was scheduled to be on a military charter sometime in June, after all the teams had traveled back to Kabul to be "processed out" of the war zone. There was no way Mark could care for Cinnamon while he was in transit. When their unit was scheduled to fly to Kabul, Mark's roommate, Jeff, had to stay behind at KAF for a few extra days. Mark offered to stay with him. It worked out for both of them. They could help each other pack up and get ready to move out. Mark's "official" story was that he didn't want to leave a team member alone. They had been taught by the army to always pair up, to use the "buddy" system.

Jeff knew Mark's real reason for staying, though, but he didn't mind. He knew how attached Mark had become to Cinnamon. Jeff knew that in reality, Mark jumped at the opportunity to stay behind so he could make sure that Cinnamon was safely on the next transport with the dog handler who would accompany her to the U.S. Mark still wasn't sure who that would be. He'd also be more comfortable getting her ready and seeing her off himself than leaving it to someone else.

Cinnamon was originally supposed to fly out of Afghanistan on Tuesday, May 9. Mark headed over to the dog handlers' office looking for Greg, the dog handler he had met the previous month, who'd agreed to fly Cinnamon home. It was Monday, May 8. He walked into the office and inquired about the flight out.

The country manager for Dog Handlers Incorporated and

liaison to the military for the dog-handler program, Henry Carson, informed him, "The flight is tonight."

Mark was caught off guard. "What do you mean the flight is tonight? Greg said it was on the ninth."

Henry explained to Mark that the flight on the ninth was out of Bishkek, not out of KAF. They'd have to leave a day or more in advance of that flight to get to Manas in Bishkek with enough time to prepare for the flight out. And, unfortunately, Greg was already gone. Having no say in his assignment and without any notice, Greg had been transferred to another base. He hadn't had time to even let Mark know.

Mark had been hoping that Cinnamon's trip with the dog handler would be delayed anyway. She wasn't ready. He hadn't arranged for her veterinary exam, shots, and health certificate yet. He'd have to wait another month before she could fly out. It would be cutting it close. It would be June, and he was scheduled to fly out soon after her, but there wasn't much he could do. He'd have to find someone else to take her.

Now what? Mark wondered.

"Who else could do it?" Mark pressed Henry. He didn't know what his options were.

"Don't worry about it. We'll find somebody else."

Easy for Henry to say. To Mark it wasn't that simple. Cinnamon had to go before him. He didn't want to leave her behind. He didn't want to leave her fate in someone else's hands with him already gone, but there wasn't much he could do.

As it turned out, the delay gave Mark the opportunity to research what health examinations, vaccinations, and documentation Cinnamon would need in order to travel. These were just a part of the preparations he needed to make to get her home. He hadn't realized before that so much was required. He considered what needed to be done and who would do it. There was a lot more to it, and it was all going to take significant planning.

Back in Maryland, Alice got detailed updates from Mark about the arrangements for Cinnamon. She was amazed at what he had to go through—so many particulars, so many obstacles. She was excited that Cinnamon was coming home, but she felt bad for her husband. He had to take care of all the arrangements himself and still tend to his official duties. There was little Alice could do to help him. Mostly, she just waited to hear how it was going and what he needed her to do.

Through it all, though, Alice had faith in Mark. He would call with his frustrations, but she had confidence in him. She knew Mark's approach was: if there's a will, there's a way. She never doubted for a minute that if there was an obstacle in his way, he'd find a way to get through it.

Mark stopped by the dog handlers' office at Shir Zai every week or so. He wanted to check in to see when the next group of handlers and dogs was going out. At the same time, Mark made contact with the American army veterinarian who he hoped would conduct Cinnamon's exam and administer her shots. The vet told Mark that army regulations prohibited him from treating local animals, but he knew a woman in Kabul who could arrange for an Afghan vet to come examine Cinnamon and give her the shots. Mark had his interpreter call the Afghan vet and make the appointment. He thought it should be a piece of cake.

The morning that Cinnamon would get her shots, Mark had to get to the office early to find her. If he didn't see her first thing in the morning, sometimes he wouldn't see her at all that day. If he got there at 5:30 or 6:00 A.M., she would be there to greet him. Since he'd be one of the first ones there, she'd be looking for her breakfast.

When Mark got to Shir Zai that day, he went straight over to the American section. Cinnamon was there wagging her tail and wanting to romp and play.

"Sorry, Cinnamon," he said to her, "we can't play right now."

He went to Cinnamon to put her on a leash. He couldn't risk her wandering off and then not seeing her the rest of the day. Although the soldiers had put a collar on her with ID tags in case she wandered over to KAF, this was the first time in her life that she had been on a leash. Cinnamon didn't mind, though. In fact, Mark disliked it more than she did. When he hooked the lead to her collar, Cinnamon barely noticed and slowly wandered to the end. Mark let the slack out and gently guided Cinnamon toward his office. Cinnamon's gentle, carefree manner was one of the traits that fostered the bond between her and Mark.

Together, Mark and Cinnamon strolled along the base as if they'd been walking like that for years. The plans had been made for Cinnamon to have her health exam that day. Mark would feel better once it was done. It would be one less thing to worry about in getting her ready to fly home.

Next, Mark brought Cinnamon to his office at Shir Zai. He asked one of the men to watch her while he went back to KAF to get the army veterinarian. He would bring the rabies vaccine, since the Afghan vet wouldn't have any. Also, while the army vet couldn't administer the shot to Cinnamon, he wanted to supervise the Afghan vet to ensure it was given properly. He'd then countersign Cinnamon's health certificates.

Previously, Mark had asked his interpreter, Daniel, if he would go to Kandahar City to pick up the Afghan vet before work that day. Mark was not completely comfortable with this, since interpreters who worked for the Americans had been targeted by insurgents in the past. But Mark couldn't see any other way. Daniel knew this, too, and he liked Cinnamon. He had gone to Kandahar City many times to buy supplies for the Americans. He agreed to help Cinnamon without hesitation.

After picking up the army vet, Mark returned to Shir Zai at 8:30 A.M. to meet Daniel and the Afghan vet, who should have been there by then, but they weren't. Mark called Daniel on his cell phone.

"Daniel, what's going on? Why aren't you here?"

"The vet is not here." Daniel had gone to Kandahar City, where he and the vet were supposed to meet, but he didn't find the vet there. He knew Mark wasn't happy. It had already taken some effort to coordinate.

"Okay, Daniel. Just come back to Shir Zai," Mark told him. He was devastated. All his plans were falling apart, while Cinnamon's future hung in the balance. If she didn't get her shot that day, there wouldn't be enough time for the shot to incubate before her flight home.

When Mark hung up and told the army vet what happened, the vet replied, "If you can find the vet and get him here, I don't mind waiting."

Mark secretly wished that the man would offer to give Cinnamon the shot and sign her papers, but he wouldn't ask him to break regulations. He knew the vet was already doing all he could do to help.

Once Daniel arrived at camp from Kandahar City, he tried calling the Afghan vet. It took a while, but they finally reached the Afghan vet by cell phone. After much discussion and a promise that he would be reimbursed, Daniel convinced the Afghan vet to take a cab to KAF. Mark would have to go pick him up and drive him back to Shir Zai. Mark took Daniel with him to the gate. Often, there were many Afghan civilians hanging around near the gate, many looking for work and some just watching the activity. For many reasons, Mark had to be sure that he picked up the right man. The army vet stayed behind at Shir Zai with Cinnamon.

When they finally got back to Shir Zai, Cinnamon was splayed out asleep on the floor. She barely moved. The Afghan vet, who was supposed to do her physical examination and approve that she was fit to travel the long distance to the United States, entered the office with Mark. Without so much as bending down to examine her, he took one look at Cinnamon and said something to Daniel. Mark looked at Daniel expectantly.

"He says she's fine," Daniel said.

"What else do you need me to do?" the Afghan vet asked through Daniel.

Mark couldn't believe it. The vet hadn't even touched her. Is this what he needed to go through all this trouble, all his investigating, planning, and coordinating for? He took a deep breath and tried to relax. He had been on edge when the vet hadn't shown up. Cinnamon still needed her rabies vaccine, and if the vet didn't finish the exam and give Cinnamon her shot, he couldn't issue Cinnamon's health certificate. It could jeopardize Cinnamon's clearance for travel.

Mark reminded the vet about giving Cinnamon the rabies shot. The army vet then supervised as the Afghan vet administered the shot to Cinnamon. Cinnamon never even flinched. In fact, she barely lifted her head.

As it turned out, the vet was delayed that morning because he had to visit an Afghan government office to purchase the health certificate that he would issue for Cinnamon. This had taken longer than he had expected, and he had no way to contact Daniel to tell him he'd been delayed. As the vets finished, Mark filled out Cinnamon's health certificate, and the Afghan vet signed his name. It was over in mere minutes.

Mark was ecstatic. He couldn't believe that they'd pulled this off. He offered the Afghan vet some money. The man refused. He was proud, but Mark knew that the vet had to buy the health certificate from the government. Plus, he'd paid for his cab ride to the base. Mark insisted. He gave the man much more than the vet had expected, possibly as much as a few days' wages. Mark would have paid much more than that.

Finally, this part was all done. Cinnamon was ready to go. The vet thanked Mark, while Cinnamon continued napping on the floor of the office. Feeling triumphant, Mark left with the veterinarians.

June 9 was coming up fast. Mark headed over to Shir Zai to talk to Henry around June 2. He still needed to find out if Henry had found someone to take Cinnamon home.

"Matt said he would take her," Henry told Mark. Matthew Roberts, like the first dog handler who was supposed to travel with Cinnamon, worked for Dog Handlers Incorporated.

Mark asked Henry, "Can I meet Matt? Can we find a time for Matt to meet Cinnamon?" To want to meet the guy with whom he would entrust Cinnamon was not an unusual request. Mark wanted to know what Matt was like. Knowing he was a dog handler, Mark figured he must like dogs, but Mark still wanted to meet him.

"I think he's on his way back here now." So Mark waited, and he waited.

When Matt finally showed up, he and Mark met. It was several days before Matt was supposed to fly out. His plans had already been made. Matt was due for leave so he already had his tickets. Mark asked to see his itinerary, which was back at his bunk.

Matt took Mark back to his bunk to look at his itinerary. During this time, Mark took the opportunity to get to know Matt as best he could. The few minutes that it took to get from Shir Zai to KAF allowed for little but small talk. Matt seemed all right to Mark. According to his flight itinerary, he was, indeed, scheduled to fly to the U.S. on June 9.

On June 4, Mark stopped over to see Henry again. He wanted to know everything that needed to be done, everything that needed to happen to ensure that Cinnamon was ready to fly. He wanted to be ready. He wanted to make sure she was ready.

He approached Henry, "What's happening?"

"They're leaving tomorrow night," Henry replied, a little matter of factly.

"What?" Again, Mark was caught off guard.

"Yeah, they're flying to Kyrgyzstan. The flight on the ninth is out of the Bishkek airport."

This can't be happening, Mark thought to himself. He tried to stay calm, but inside he was fuming at Henry. Mark had checked in with Henry every few days, knowing he probably wouldn't get much notice. So how could Henry not have called to let him know? Mark thought Henry understood how much this meant to Mark and Cinnamon. This was exactly what Mark had wanted to avoid—a last-minute rush that might result in something going wrong.

On the outside, Mark kept his cool because he knew he needed Henry's help, and he reminded himself that Henry had more important things on his mind than Cinnamon's transportation. He quickly decided to roll with it and that he'd just have to drop everything else. There was no other way. He had to be sure everything got done and that Cinnamon was ready to fly out the next day. He couldn't miss another chance. If he did, it was likely that he would fly out before she would. Mark couldn't risk that. If that was to happen, who would make the arrangements to fly her out? Mark knew that if he was going to get Cinnamon out of Afghanistan, it had to be now.

Mark hadn't had time to get a crate for Cinnamon, so he got

one from Henry. He had plenty that were used for the military working dogs. Mark took the crate and put it near where Cinnamon slept at night. She wasn't around, but he left it open, hoping she'd explore it. Either way, he'd have to use it to get her over to Henry the next day.

The next morning, Mark came to Shir Zai early and got Cinnamon on her leash. She hadn't been leashed since her visit with the vet a month earlier. Cinnamon once again had no problem being tied. Mark thought that Cinnamon's easygoing nature was part of her survival skills and was the reason that she was still around for him to take home.

Mark took Cinnamon to his office so some of his team members could bid her farewell. Next, he got her into the crate. Mark coaxed Cinnamon inside, which was easy to do, but it left him with a lump in his throat. As she climbed inside, she sat down as if to say, "Now what?" She looked out at Mark with her sweet and innocent eyes, taking it in stride as she did everything else. It was hard on Mark, but he knew it was necessary. The crate would be her den for the long flight to the U.S. She'd be in it for her long, long journey.

One of the men who also took care of Cinnamon helped Mark lift her crate onto the truck. The next stop was the dog handlers' office. When they got there they took Cinnamon along with her crate, and put them into the kennel area, where she waited to make her final trip home.

Mark then met up with Matt. Matt seemed surprised by how big Cinnamon was.

"I thought she was a puppy," Matt said when he saw her.

Perhaps he had envisioned an eight- or ten-week-old little bundle of fur. Cinnamon had grown quite tall in the past few months. She was anything but little. She was still a puppy, yes, but she wasn't small.

Mark eyed him warily, wondering what Matt had meant. Was he having second thoughts? Mark gave Matt all Cinnamon's papers, including three copies of her Afghan health certificate, her U.S. health certificate, the record of her rabies vaccination, and all of Mark's contact information. He had printed identification labels for the crate, and even included a roll of tape.

Matt assured Mark that he would affix all the necessary information to Cinnamon's crate when they boarded the plane. He was armed with Mark's local and U.S. cell-phone numbers and Alice's home and cell-phone numbers. Mark gave Matt some money for incidentals and a prepaid phone card in case Matt needed to contact him for anything. Mark was still a bit uneasy but figured it was just nerves. Cinnamon had a long journey ahead of her, and Mark wouldn't rest easy until he knew she was safe and sound in the U.S.

"Don't hesitate to contact me if anything comes up—anything at all," Mark told Matt as they parted.

"Sure, no problem. But what do you want me to do if I have a problem with her?" Matt asked Mark.

Mark quickly looked up at Matt. "What do you mean, what do I want you to do? You're making me a bit nervous here. Why would you ask me that?"

Matt replied, "I'm not expecting any problems, but she's not my dog, so I wanted to ask you what you'd want me to do if there's a problem."

Mark was stunned by the question but answered, "Whatever you do, don't leave her anywhere."

"No, I wouldn't do that. It's just that you have no idea what this leave means to me. I really need to get home."

Mark wasn't comforted. In fact, his instincts were on high alert. Another dog handler who was traveling to the States with Matt sensed Mark's apprehension. He offered, "Don't worry about it. No one is gonna leave her anywhere. She'll be fine. We'll get her to Chicago."

Mark felt a little better. This other guy seemed to understand Mark's concerns and allayed them in a way Matt hadn't been able or willing to do. Mark worried anyway.

With nothing more for him to do, Mark bid farewell to Cinnamon and sent her on her way. As he left, he looked back one last time. Cinnamon was sitting in her crate, which was inside the kennel. It was an image that burned itself into Mark's mind.

"She's finally on her way home." And as far as he knew, she was.

FIVE

DAVE SIMPSON WAS upset when he heard that Mark was taking Cinnamon home. He had no idea who Mark was or that Mark had been helping care for Cinnamon. Besides, Dave dreamed of having Cinnamon as his own. He had been a dog lover since having his first dog as a young boy. His family hadn't allowed him to have pets after that first one. But he had a dog back home now, and being with Cinnamon made Dave miss him. As he considered the life that Cinnamon led, Dave wondered why dogs were less fortunate because of where they were born. It wasn't fair.

When Mark learned that Dave didn't like the idea of his taking Cinnamon home, he went to talk with Dave about it.

"I heard that you are upset that I'm taking Cinnamon. If you want to take her home, that's great." Mark knew Cinnamon belonged to everyone, not necessarily to him. "Do you want to take her?" He held his breath while he waited for Dave's reply.

Dave wanted to make it right for Cinnamon, to give her the forever home he envisioned for her, but he just couldn't. He was active-duty military and was away from home too much to burden his family with another dog. "I can't care for her right now." It broke his heart.

Dave remembers well the moment he knew Cinnamon was gone. He had been on the firing range teaching the Afghans how to shoot. He heard a loud noise and looked up overhead at the C17 cargo plane that had just taken off. "There goes Cinnamon," he said out loud to no one. His heart ached as he silently bid farewell to the camp puppy he'd grown to love.

A few days later Dave noticed how lonely he felt. The base was just not the same without Cinnamon. Upon returning from his first mission since she'd left, he automatically looked for her. He stopped short when he realized that she was gone. Over the next few weeks, Dave couldn't ignore the hole that Cinnamon's leaving had left in his heart.

Chief Master Sergeant Michael Blake had been a reservist in the air force when he was deployed to Afghanistan in February 2006. He was in law enforcement back home and was now part of the security team at Manas Air Base. His responsibilities included investigating security issues and running intelligence operations at the base. This entailed looking into suspected fraudulent activity that affected base personnel and operations.

Chief Blake was kept busy by the security activity at Manas. He was surprised by how demanding the job was. At times he felt that he'd conducted more hours of investigation since he had been in Kyrgyzstan than he ever had back home. Whatever suspected security and intelligence issues that came up were looked into by Chief Blake and the other Security Forces personnel. The investigations seemed endless. He was thus not surprised when yet a new security concern was brought up at meeting one afternoon.

"There's a dog in the kennels that no one recognizes," someone briefed them. "We aren't sure if she belongs here or not."

"Where'd she come from?" another inquired.

"She was brought in by a Department of Defense [DOD] dog handler. We assumed she was DOD, but apparently she's not."

This presented another problem for Blake and his team to look into. Military working dogs were part of the security team. They were used throughout the war zone for bomb sniffing at the bases where Americans were stationed. The kennels where the dogs were kept at Manas fell under Chief Blake's area of responsibility. It was against regulations for nonmilitary dogs to be at the kennels and mixed in with the working dogs. It put the working dogs at risk for sickness and disease. He and his partner, Technical Sergeant James Kamrad, initiated an investigation.

Initially, Chief Blake thought it was just another airlift issue. It was common for personnel coming through to use military airlifts for personal gain. They would often attempt to transport goods and equipment on military flights without paying the appropriate transportation fees. This was fraudulent activity and was not allowed. Perhaps the dog that showed up at the kennels was a civilian dog that someone was trying to fly home for free.

Blake started digging. He needed to find out where the dog had come from and why she was in his kennels. Finally, he found the dog's paperwork, which included the owner's contact information. The paper trail led to Mark.

The next day, as Mark went about his business, he got a message from Henry. He noticed that uneasy feeling had returned. He went over to the office to see what Henry wanted.

Henry clued him in. "A guy named Jim Kamrad called. He's security from Manas."

Mark was filled with a sense of foreboding as he recalled the troops' nickname for the wintry base, Man-Ass. He wondered why the base had such a negative impact on people. He guessed that he was about to find out.

Henry continued. "Apparently, Security Forces is looking for you."

Mark returned the call. Kamrad was unavailable, so he wound up speaking with Chief Michael Blake. Blake was cordial but pressed him. "There's a dog here at the military kennels. She's not a military dog. The paperwork says she's yours."

Mark was confused but cooperated. "Chief, the dog was supposed to be accompanied by a dog handler, Matthew Roberts."

"Well, we can't find him. He's nowhere to be found."

As Mark thought about it, he realized he'd never considered what would happen to Cinnamon between the fifth and the ninth. They'd been so rushed getting her ready, and Henry and Matt assured him he didn't need to worry, that it never really crossed his mind. He chided himself.

Chief Blake continued. "What was she doing on that flight anyway?"

Mark thought about it. Technically, she should have been turned away at the Kandahar airport when they first boarded her. The flight Cinnamon had been on was a military flight, and she was not a military dog. She shouldn't have been on the flight in the first place. He wondered how, indeed, they got her on board. The dog handler hadn't seemed concerned about it, so Mark wasn't either.

Mark respectfully, but realistically reasoned with the chief as they tried to find a solution. "Chief, the sin has been committed. You're not gonna commit another sin and send her back here on another military flight, are you?"

His answer did not comfort Mark. "I don't know," the chief started slowly. "I'm gonna have to talk to the commander about that. It makes sense. She's here now. Why would I send her back to you?"

Mark hesitated. The chief was in a tight spot, but Mark needed him. Cinnamon wasn't due to fly out for another couple of days. If he didn't play his cards right, they just might send her back to KAF. Then where would he be? Not at square one—more like square zero.

With Roberts's disappearance, Mark considered how he would get Cinnamon to the U.S. He volleyed back to the chief. "I understand I can't put her on another military flight. But if I can get her on a commercial flight out of Kyrgyzstan, are you guys okay with that?"

"I don't see why not. I've got approval to keep her in the military kennels for a few more days."

Mark was relieved. The chief didn't have to, but he was doing what he could for Cinnamon and for Mark.

Mark pieced the story together over the next few hours. He had gone to see the air force captain in charge of KAF's air operations to find out how Cinnamon had gotten on the flight to Kyrgyzstan. It took several trips to catch up with him. Communications on base were slow, voice mail didn't exist, and very few people had phones.

"She shouldn't have been on the flight to begin with," he admitted when Mark finally found him. "That's my guys' fault. They didn't check the paperwork. I'll take the hit on that one." The captain was a stand-up man.

It was a start. Mark pressed for more. "Would you be willing to contact the colonel over in Kyrgyzstan? We can all fall on our swords. That way everything will be all right. I don't want them to think I was trying to falsify anything or to put anything over on anyone."

The captain agreed and told Mark to come back in a couple of hours. He expected to have received a response by then.

In the meantime, Blake gave Mark more details about the findings of his investigation. Apparently, Cinnamon wound up at the working-dog kennels when Matthew Roberts was passing through on his way home on leave. He'd approached the canine officer at Manas when he arrived in Bishkek.

"Is it okay if I leave her here with you?" asked Roberts. Dog handlers were always passing through. It was common that their dogs were left at the kennels while they waited for their flight home. Roberts had led personnel there to believe that Cinnamon was a working dog so he could leave her with them. He didn't exactly tell them she was a military dog, but he didn't tell them she wasn't either. With a couple of days to kill before his flight, Roberts wanted to head into downtown Bishkek in Kyrgyzstan. He was on leave. It would be impossible for him to go with the dog.

It didn't take Chief Blake long to connect Cinnamon to Roberts. But when the chief went looking for him, he couldn't find Roberts anywhere. Blake was now on alert. It was against base policy for military personnel to sleep off base. Although Roberts was a civilian, as a military contractor he was subject to military regulations. He'd broken the rules. He'd gone downtown and didn't come back for days.

Chief Blake left a message with Roberts's roommate: Roberts was to come see Chief Blake when he got back. The chief had some questions that needed answers, and he was determined to get them. To prevent Roberts from taking his leave without seeing Blake, the chief put a hold on his flight. He'd have to see Blake one way or another, since he wouldn't be able to get the escort required to get off base and board his flight home.

Blake needed more details, and he needed to talk to Roberts to get them. He still wasn't sure what was going on, and Roberts still was nowhere to be found.

Alice had been busy for days, getting ready for Cinnamon to come home. There were many details she needed to take care of. Mark would be coming home after Cinnamon, so Alice had time later to prepare for Mark.

Paul Michaud was deployed to Afghanistan with Mark. When his wife, Lola, learned about Cinnamon, she had lovingly sent her care packages filled with treats, bones, and toys—as were countless other care packages Cinnamon had received while on base. Like Alice, Lola had begged her husband to adopt Cinnamon, but they, too, had recently had a treasured dog pass away, and Paul wasn't ready for another.

Paul and Lola lived in the Chicago area. When Paul heard that Cinnamon was flying into O'Hare International Airport, he had offered to have his wife help with Cinnamon's travel. Alice appreciated their offer to help and called Lola to introduce herself. The two had never spoken before, but there was an instant connection. Lola was more than happy to lend a hand. From that moment on, she moved like a whirlwind.

Lola coordinated with the airlines. She researched flights, made Cinnamon's reservation from Chicago to Baltimore, and, ultimately, even reserved the flight with her own credit card. While making the flight arrangements, though, Lola ran into a snag with restrictions on Cinnamon's crate. Apparently, the crate Cinnamon would be arriving in was too big for the domestic airline to accept. Unless they had a crate for Cinnamon that met airline regulations, Cinnamon would not be allowed on her flight from Chicago to Baltimore. Alice considered driving to Chicago to pick her up.

After spending five hours on the phone with the airlines and coordinating with Lola, Alice had finally worked out the logistics. She and Lola determined who would meet Cinnamon's plane in Chicago, how they would get a new crate, and how Cinnamon would be transferred to her flight to Maryland.

Lola was unable to meet Cinnamon's flight, so she had arranged with a close family friend, Bob Gielarowski, to pick up Cinnamon at O'Hare. While he didn't talk about it much, Bob was also motivated to help by his love for dogs. He was a veteran of the Vietnam War and had a working dog while he was there. The dog's death had been difficult for Bob, so he knew a little of what Mark and Alice were going through.

Bob had been generous in his offer to help. He had not only gone to the local pet store to purchase the right size crate for Cinnamon's domestic flight but also agreed to take Cinnamon to his daughter's house when he picked her up. Cinnamon was scheduled to arrive at O'Hare on Friday and had a layover of several hours before her flight to Baltimore. Bob thought she would do well to get out of the crate, stretch her legs, and rest a bit. He would then bring Cinnamon back to the airport and board her on the next leg of her trip. Mark and Alice, as well as Cinnamon, would have been stuck, once again, without the help of such a volunteer.

In the meantime, Alice had another concern to deal with. The cargo-receiving area at Baltimore-Washington International Airport closed at 11:00 P.M. Cinnamon's flight was scheduled to arrive from Chicago at 10:50 P.M. Alice worried. It was a disaster waiting to happen. Alice wanted to ward it off, so she called the airline.

She explained the situation, then asked, "What happens if the flight is delayed? How am I going to pick up my dog? Where would my dog be if the cargo employees locked up and went home for the night?" The airline representative offered few answers and little reassurance. There was not a whole lot more that Alice could do. She hung up, frustrated but hoping for the best. Her hope quickly turned to prayer.

———————

A few days after Cinnamon was discovered in the military kennels, Roberts finally showed up and went to see Chief Blake. He told him that Cinnamon belonged to a navy officer who was about to fly out of Kandahar. "No, sir. She's not a DOD dog," Roberts told Blake.

Since Roberts and Cinnamon were due to fly out of Bishkek in just a few hours, Chief Blake's problem was just about solved. To alleviate the issue of Cinnamon being with the working dogs, Roberts took Cinnamon to his room. It wouldn't be long before they'd be gone, and the case would soon be closed. To complete his investigation, Chief Blake needed to find out how Cinnamon had gotten on a military flight to begin with. It just wasn't allowed. He called air operations at KAF.

As far as Mark knew, the security investigation continued. So did Mark's anxiety. What would he do if Roberts didn't come back for her? Who would take Cinnamon home? He got an e-mail from Chief Blake that gave him some hope that he didn't need to figure it out.

> Just wanted to send you a quick note and let you know that everything seems to be straightened out on this end. I have contacted Mr. Roberts and everything is set for them to fly out. . . . Cinnamon is fine and I will be getting with Mr. Roberts this afternoon. Cinnamon is with him here on base and I was going to send you a picture so you know she is all right.

Blake's investigation continued. Air operations in Kandahar admitted that they made a mistake when Cinnamon had slipped on board the military flight. They assured Chief Blake that there had been no illegal intent.

Chief Blake also found out through the canine officer at Manas that Mark had done everything according to the rules. He learned that there was a program through the Afghan government for military personnel to adopt dogs out of the country. He wished that Mark had known about it. He also confirmed that Mark had gone through the proper channels. Cinnamon had been seen by the vet, had gotten her shots, and all her papers were in order. The only thing that went wrong was that the dog handlers had convinced Mark that getting her on their regular military flight was not a problem.

Blake was convinced it was an honest mistake. He'd learned what he needed to know. Cinnamon's case was nearing its end so the chief briefed the commander. They were both relieved she would soon be on her way home.

After receiving the chief's e-mail, Mark felt a bit more at ease, but no one was too happy with Roberts. The investigation had determined that Roberts had misled personnel at the military kennels at Manas for his own purposes. He left Cinnamon where she shouldn't have been and without approval. He didn't let Mark know any of what he'd done, and he had broken military regulations by going downtown and staying off base. He hadn't created any goodwill for himself with personnel at Manas.

By June 9, Cinnamon was due to fly out, and Mark was ready to get her home. He'd be glad once she was Stateside with Alice. Maybe then he could relax and enjoy the fact that he was heading home as well. He picked up the phone to call the chief to make one last check on Cinnamon.

"Chief, what's happening? Have you seen Roberts today?"

"I assume everything is fine. Roberts checked out of his room, and Cinnamon is not in her kennel. I'm guessing they're on their way." The chief tried to reassure him.

It was out of Mark's hands.

Another avenue he checked made him feel a little better as well. Mark had gotten a reply from Henry after e-mailing him to ask if he'd let Mark know if he heard from Roberts.

Mark I sure will . . .

When I spoke to Larry [the Dog Handlers Incorporated manager in Kyrgyzstan] last night he said that . . . Matt/Cinnamon will not be held up. . . . I assume that they all made it out safely.

But if I hear anything I'll let you know.

Henry Carson
Country Manager/Afghanistan
Dog Handlers Incorporated

Next, Mark waited for word that Cinnamon had made it to the U.S., to Alice in Maryland. He went to bed comforted in knowing Alice would be picking Cinnamon up around 11:00 P.M. EDT.

SIX

CINNAMON WAS DUE to arrive in the States on Friday afternoon, June 9, 2006. I was so excited. With Mark looking after her and all the care packages she had gotten, her once difficult life was getting better and better. Gone were the days of scrounging for leftover scraps just to fill her hollow belly. Gone were the days of hiding from anyone who might be ordered to shoot her or who would kick her and throw rocks at her. The land of Milk-Bone biscuits and honey was only days away. The streets would be paved with doggie gold. Cinnamon was Maryland bound. She couldn't have been luckier, and her arrival could not have been more anticipated.

I called Alice for the details. The flight Cinnamon was booked on from Bishkek would come in to Chicago. I asked Alice what would happen next. How would Cinnamon get from Chicago to Maryland? She wasn't sure. When I talked with her, she had yet to confirm those arrangements.

"I may wind up driving out there to get her. This way she won't have to endure another flight," she told me.

I couldn't stand the idea of Alice making that drive alone, and I love a road trip.

"Why don't I go with you? We could meet in Pennsylvania and drive out together." I was excited.

Alice's response was lukewarm. "Oh, I don't know. Let's just wait and see."

I was frustrated. I wanted to help. I am a doer, and I love being spontaneous. I am ready to launch into action at any given moment. Now that Cinnamon was on her way home, I'd welcome something fun and adventurous to take my mind off my boredom. My face was hot. How could she refuse? It would be so much fun. Why didn't she jump at the chance as I did? I tempered my response.

"Okay, well let me know what you decide."

We chatted a few more minutes about the anticipated arrival and what it would be like once Cinnamon was Stateside. The excitement of her homecoming was overwhelming. I wanted to be in Chicago. I wanted to be in Maryland. I wanted to be wherever Cinnamon was coming in. I wanted to be there to welcome her into the family.

But I expressed none of this. I was ecstatic for my brother, and more so for Cinnamon. She was, after all, going to be their new baby, not mine. I had to be happy with being her aunt.

The anticipation of Cinnamon finally being home was still thrilling. By the next day she would be in the U.S. with her new family. I could hardly contain myself. You'd think she was going to be mine.

So I went to sleep the night of her arrival like a child on Christmas Eve, knowing that when I woke the next morning Cinnamon would already be Stateside. Our sweet little girl, with bright eyes and a wagging tail, would be home. But I couldn't have been more wrong.

At 8:00 A.M. on Saturday morning, I couldn't wait any longer. I knew Alice would have been up very late the night before meeting Cinnamon's flight in Baltimore, getting her settled in at home, and letting Mark know that she was home safe and sound.

I was sure it would have been an exciting night for all of them. I wanted to be part of it. I wanted to hear how she was doing.

On any other day, I would be pushing it if I dialed my brother's house before 9:30 A.M. Even then, Mark or Alice often answered in precaffeine morning voices. I would always start the conversation with an apology.

"Hi, did I wake you?" I would sheepishly begin, knowing full well it was possible.

Usually the response was something like, "Oh, no, we were just getting breakfast." I could never really be sure if that was true or if they were just being polite.

It was hard waiting to call. I was usually up by 7:00 or 7:30, even on the weekends. Waiting hours to phone the family, I'm like a Thoroughbred waiting for the starting gates at the Preakness to fly open. It was torture. I chomped at the bit. I was raring to go.

Finally, I couldn't wait any longer. I dialed Alice's number, my heart pounding in my chest. It was a familiar feeling, like having gone to bed before the World Series was over because it was on too late to stay up. I still do it to this day, waking up wanting to know if my team won, with anticipation driving me crazy.

The number rang on the other end. And it rang. My heart pounded harder. The ringing finally stopped. Alice picked up. The morning haze was there, but something was different. Maybe it was just the late hour she went to bed. I couldn't be sure.

As usual, "I am so sorry to be calling so early. I know you had a late night. But how is she? Is she home? How excited could you possibly be?"

Her words sliced through me. "It's a nightmare."

Huh? That wasn't right. No, it was a dream come true.

"We don't know where she is."

"What?" I couldn't have heard her right.

"The dog handler abandoned her. We think somewhere in Turkey." Her voice was monotone. Her words were flat. What she'd said didn't register. I needed to know more.

"I have been on the phone since yesterday afternoon trying to find out where she is. I'm not having any luck. The dog handler never contacted us. And I couldn't reach Mark for the longest time."

I heard her words, but they still didn't sink in. My head spun. The floor below me felt like it would give way. I couldn't catch my breath. My gut wrenched. My heart went out to her. Mark was still in Afghanistan, and she was dealing with this all by herself.

I was stunned, but I let her continue.

"Mark finally called last night. He's gonna try to find some-

thing out and get back to me. I didn't get to bed until four A.M."
Alice's voice trailed off as she strained to tell me what had happened.

Her sorrow and disbelief resounded in the hollowness I'd heard in her voice. I yearned to know more, but I knew she was sleep deprived. It would have been selfish of me to keep her on the phone.

Alice filled me in on the details she had, though. She told me she was thinking about getting a flight to Istanbul, where, she was told, the dog handler had abandoned Cinnamon. Alice said she wanted to go to Turkey to try to find Cinnamon herself.

I expressed my shock and sorrow. Sadly, there was not much I could say to comfort Alice. I knew in that moment she needed sleep more than anything. So I made my apologies again for waking her and told her I would call her later. As I hung up the phone, the disbelief took hold. How could this have happened? The arrangements for Cinnamon had all been carefully made. She was on her way home after having been cared for by countless people for seven months. She'd already had her shots and her health certificate. Her transportation had been arranged. An experienced dog handler was to accompany her home. People we hardly knew had been in Chicago to meet her and send her on her way home to Maryland.

But from what Alice had just told me, none of it happened that way. Not even close. The sweet, innocent puppy that Mark helped raise and lovingly agreed to give a new life to had not been on the plane when it landed in the U.S. And now no one knew where she was. How did it go so terribly wrong?

Alice had heard the shocking news from Bob. He had been at the airport to pick up Cinnamon just as they had planned. But when Matthew Roberts had arrived, he didn't have Cinnamon with him. Bob was taken aback. Roberts mumbled something about losing the dog on the way.

Bob couldn't be sure he'd heard Roberts right. He thought he'd told him he'd left Cinnamon in Turkey at the airport in Istanbul. Before he could ask anything more about it, though, Roberts was gone.

Bob and Alice had arranged ahead of time that he would call Alice from Chicago after he'd gotten Cinnamon. When her phone rang around 3:00 P.M. EDT on Friday, she expected good news.

"Hello?" It was the moment she'd waited for.

"Alice, she's not here," was all Bob said.

"What do you mean, 'she's not here'?" Alice cried.

"He doesn't have her. He doesn't have the dog."

Alice was shocked. She fired questions at Bob, barely giving him a chance to answer. "What do you mean he doesn't have her? Why doesn't he have her? Where is Roberts? What happened to Cinnamon?"

Bob seemed just as stunned as Alice had been. He had no answers for her. He merely replied, "I don't know. Roberts is gone." And then, because there was nothing else to say, he'd added, "Alice, I'm so sorry it didn't work out."

Alice couldn't believe what was happening. She needed to do something—and fast. She convinced Bob, who was still at the airport, to hurry and have Roberts paged. Maybe he was still in the airport. Bob agreed and said he would call her back.

Alice tried to stay calm while she waited for Bob to call her back. It seemed like an eternity. In reality, he phoned her just twenty minutes later.

"Alice, he's not answering the page."

Of course he's not, Alice thought to herself. *He probably booked out of there as fast as he could.*

"I'm sorry. I don't know what else to do," was all Bob could say. He felt terrible.

Alice knew what happened wasn't Bob's fault. She thanked him for trying and hung up the phone in a panic. Immediately, she called Lola.

When Lola answered, the words spilled out of Alice, "Lola, Cinnamon wasn't on her flight. She didn't make it to Chicago. Bob said she's somewhere in Turkey, in Istanbul."

Lola was stunned. *How could Cinnamon be in Istanbul?* Lola did her best to calm Alice down and reassure her. She said she'd call Bob and find out what happened. She'd help her find Cinnamon and get her home. She felt awful about it and wanted to help. She promised to call Alice back when she knew more.

Alice didn't know what to do. What was happening was a nightmare. She had to call Mark to let him know what happened, but it was the middle of the night in Kandahar. She hadn't ever needed to reach him at that hour of the night before. It would be eight hours or more before he'd be in his office again. Even then, he'd be hard to reach. Typically during his deployment, if she wanted to reach him, she'd ring him on the Webcam, which he'd kept set up for that reason. If he was within earshot of it, they'd speak, but now, since he was getting ready to come home, the Webcam had been disconnected. She sent him an e-mail. It was a long shot that he'd be up or in front of the computer, but Alice felt she had to try.

Mark,

Call me ASAP. It's about Cinnamon. That guy left her in Turkey! I need info on this guy. He gave no info to Bob in Chicago. Neither Bob or Lola have any info on this Roberts guy . . . Bob is paging the guy at the airport to see if he has any info . . . This is a nightmare!

Next, Alice remembered a number Mark had given her. It was an emergency number she could call that would connect her to him in Afghanistan. She dialed the number. Over and over. She kept getting a busy signal.

Frustrated, she called the international operator for help and explained the problem to her. Alice was put on hold while the operator tried the number herself. Finally she came back on the line.

"I'm sorry, ma'am. You can't call into Afghanistan."

"What? But my husband gave me this number. He's in the military serving over there. It's a number we were told to use in case of an emergency. What do you mean I can't call Afghanistan?"

"I'm sorry, ma'am. I'm going to have to transfer you into a recording."

This can't be real, Alice thought to herself. The recording she heard on the other end of the line stated that the U.S. government had put restrictions on calls from the U.S. into Afghanistan. No such calls would be allowed through.

Alice was furious. Her own government had blocked her from

reaching her husband. The emergency number Mark had given her didn't work. Alice racked her brain. How else could she get to him? "I know, the Red Cross," she said out loud to herself.

But they couldn't help either. When she explained her emergency to the staff person that answered the phone, he merely replied, "We can't do it. Not for that."

Alice felt helpless.

Alice remembered that there was an office within the navy that was supposed to help with family situations such as these, but Alice had experience with them. When Mark was deployed during his previous years of service, she had tried to get in touch with him. They had policies, too. She'd never had any luck reaching him through that office either.

Alice kept moving, her mind racing. She thought of Cinnamon. Where was she? Was she okay? Was she stuck on a plane somewhere with no food or water? Was she hurt? Was she even still alive? The thoughts and images fueled her activity and her rage.

Next, Alice called Dawn, the wife of Mark's roommate, Jeff. Alice had met her in Indiana at Thanksgiving. Alice and Dawn had stayed in close contact while their husbands were overseas.

When Dawn picked up the phone at work and heard Alice's voice, she panicked.

"Oh, God. Are they okay?" Dawn feared the worst. Alice hadn't called Dawn at work before.

Immediately, Alice replied, "Yes, they're okay. I'm so sorry to scare you."

She told Dawn what had happened. Alice remembered that Jeff had a satellite phone. She thought she could reach Mark that way. She asked Dawn about it.

"Alice, I'm sorry. Jeff doesn't have the phone with him." Dawn felt helpless for Alice. Her heart went out to her.

Next, Alice called Sharon, the third in the trio of wives who had met in Indiana while their husbands trained for deployment. Sharon suggested that Alice call the navy and get in touch with Mark that way.

Alice told her she'd already thought of that. "Thanks anyway, Sharon." Out of options, Alice hung up the phone.

It's not over yet, Alice thought. But she didn't know what to do next to find Cinnamon, so she poured herself a glass of wine. Then Alice picked up the phone and called her parents. She spoke with her mother and told her what happened. Her mother listened intently. "We'll pray for her," she offered.

Alice began to pace. And as she paced, she went back over what happened and what she knew. None of what she'd been told made sense. What else could she do that she hadn't thought of yet? Alice paced some more as the hours ticked by ever so slowly.

Mark awoke on Saturday morning and couldn't wait to call Alice. He was anxious to hear the good news that Cinnamon had made it home. She'd be in Maryland by now. He wanted to see how she did on her long journey and how she was doing now that she was finally home.

Mark and Alice had arranged to talk around 9:30 A.M. his time. It was after midnight in Maryland. By then Alice was supposed to have picked up Cinnamon at the Baltimore airport and returned home. She'd be getting Cinnamon settled in. Mark went to a friend's office at KAF, picked up the phone, and dialed home.

"Hello?" Her voice didn't seem quite right. Mark just figured it was because Alice had been up late.

But then she uttered words he would never forget. "Mark, something terrible has happened."

Mark felt the blood drain from his face as he held his breath.

She went on, frantic. "I have been trying to reach you all night. Cinnamon didn't make it to Chicago."

He shot back, "What do you mean, she didn't make it to Chicago? Where is she?"

"She's been left in Istanbul. She's in Turkey. I tried calling you all night. The number you gave me to reach you doesn't work." Alice was fragile. The tears came quickly.

Mark wanted more than anything to be with his wife in that moment. "Why is she in Turkey? What did Roberts say?"

"I haven't talked to Roberts. He never called. Bob told me."

Mark fired questions at her. "What do you mean he didn't call? Why not? He had all our numbers. He had all our contact information. You never heard from him?"

"No, I never got a call from him. Bob called me after he met Roberts in Chicago. Roberts didn't have Cinnamon with him."

They spent about half an hour on the phone. Alice told him what she knew and what she had done in the hours since she spoke with Bob.

Mark was furious about the news that his wife shared with him. He thought he was going to be sick. How in the world did this happen? How could Roberts have done this to Cinnamon? What had gone wrong? And why hadn't Roberts called anybody?

"Mark, I'm going to fly to Turkey to try and find her. I was waiting to talk to you, but I'm going to look into flights." Alice had to do something.

"Hold off on booking anything," he said. "Let me go make some phone calls and see what I can do. Maybe I can make contact with Turkish Airlines from here and find out where she is." They hung up as he assured her that he would call as soon as he had anything to tell her.

SEVEN

THE FIRST THING that Mark did when he hung up with Alice was head straight to the dog handlers' office, to see Henry from Dog Handlers Incorporated.

"Henry," he started gruffly, "what the hell is going on?" Mark told Henry he wanted answers, and he wanted them now. Mark explained what he knew and what Roberts had done. He told him that Cinnamon had been abandoned in Turkey.

Henry listened intently to the details Mark shared, then without further comment offered, "Let me make some calls."

Henry tried to reach Roberts any way he could. He tried him on his cell phone. No answer. He tried Roberts at his home of record. No answer. He called his parents' house, where he said he'd be while on leave, in case anyone needed to reach him. Henry spoke to Matt's mother who said that Matt had not yet arrived and that it would likely be several more days before he did.

Mark was plagued with questions. Why didn't anybody have any idea what Roberts's plans were? Generally, contractors on leave are supposed to be reachable, in case their assignment changes while they are home. Why did he put his parents' home down as his leave address if they didn't know when he'd be arriving? But as Mark was finding out the hard way, Roberts didn't seem to follow through on much of what he said he would do.

As Henry kept trying to reach Roberts, Mark's unanswered questions kept coming. How could this guy have done what he did? What problems had he encountered that caused him to abandon Cinnamon? Why didn't he make any phone calls to try to reach Mark or Alice? Why didn't he use the money Mark had given him to do something other than abandoning Cinnamon?

Mark's fear was now as high as his anxiety. Where was Cinnamon? Who was taking care of her? Was she stuck in her crate somewhere without food, water, or relief? Mark was going crazy not knowing. Even worse, he felt ultimately responsible. It had been his decision to send her home—and to send her with Roberts. Mark felt he should have been more thorough. He should have been more specific with Roberts about what to do if he ran into problems.

But the guy was a dog handler. Didn't he have his own dogs? Surely he wouldn't have abandoned them if he'd run into a problem, and he'd reassured Mark that everything would be okay.

Mark needed to find out something. And soon.

After Alice gave me the details about Cinnamon's disappearance she and I hung up the phone. She tried to go back to sleep, but it was pointless. Reality was creeping back in. The nightmare was still happening. At 8:30 A.M., the phone was ringing again. It was my father. I had called him to explain what happened.

Alice picked up, "Hello?"

"Alice, I heard what happened to Cinnamon. I'm so sorry." He didn't know what else to say. He tried, but there wasn't much he could say that would comfort her.

Alice tried to face the day. There was a family party for our nephew who had just graduated from high school. Alice was expected to be there. It was the last thing she wanted to do. All she could think about was Cinnamon.

Throughout the morning, Alice's worry mounted. But then her thoughts cleared, and she had an idea. Cinnamon had been booked on Turkish Airlines. If she had gone missing in Turkey, then Alice's next step would be to call Turkish Airlines in Istanbul and find someone who could help her. Surely they would know something about what had happened.

Alice went to the Internet to look up the phone number for the airline in Istanbul. She placed the call. The agent who answered seemed to understand English, but when Alice tried to explain that

Cinnamon was missing there, he said he couldn't help. He transferred her to someone he thought could.

Alice went through the story again. Again, the person on the other end of the phone said he couldn't help. Alice went through this over and over. She couldn't get anyone to help her. She couldn't make them understand the urgency of Cinnamon's situation. To her growing frustration, they wouldn't even let her speak. She was desperate and needed their help, but they offered little. Alice was furious.

Alice learned through her phone calls, though, that there was another airport in Antalya, Turkey. She tried calling there as well. She got the same rude service on the phone that she had gotten from the employees in Istanbul. It was no use. Angry but not deterred, Alice went back online. She thought she might have better luck contacting Turkish Airlines through e-mail. Surely there'd be a customer-service e-mail contact. She found what she was looking for and typed an e-mail.

Saturday, June 10th, 11:00 A.M. eastern time

To Turkish Airlines,

I called the Ataturk airport in Istanbul to try to speak to someone in assisting me. I was first connected to Customer Service, then to Lost and Found, and then to Immigration. I was told by all that they could not help me. The last gentleman in Immigration put me on hold and never returned. Can someone please help me?

She continued with the details of Cinnamon's flight and her being left behind. She didn't have much hope that they would help her after the way she was treated, but she felt she had to try. Alice never did hear back from them.

Frustrated with getting no help from Turkish Airlines, Alice decided to look into flights to Turkey. It was the only way. If Cinnamon was in Turkey, Alice would have to go and find her. The airfare wasn't cheap, but she didn't care. In fact, she decided that she would fly to Istanbul, rent a car, then drive to Antalya. That way, she could search for Cinnamon at both airports. She thought that she would ask me to go with her. Alice spent hours trying to find a flight. By the time she was done, she was exhausted.

While Alice tried to make headway, she had been bargaining with God. "Please, God," she prayed. "Please let me know if Cinnamon is okay." She didn't know if her prayers would be answered, but she had to try. "Please. Just give me a sign. I didn't mean to be selfish. I don't have to have this dog if you don't want me to. I just need to know that she's okay."

Alice collapsed in her chair and sobbed.

Finally, Henry received an e-mail from Roberts. He relayed to Mark that Roberts indicated he'd had a problem with his flight and was too tired to deal with the situation at that time. Roberts had said that he'd be going to bed and would contact Henry in another eight hours.

Mark was seething. Was this guy for real? Was that all Roberts had to say? Couldn't he take five minutes to tell him more about what had happened? Mark wanted to blast the guy. He wanted to give him a piece of his mind—a big piece. But Mark had to keep his cool. He still needed Roberts. He needed the information that only Roberts could provide about what happened to Cinnamon, about where she was now, and about whether she was even all right.

As expected, Mark's anxiety and frustration only grew. He couldn't stop thinking about Cinnamon and if she was okay. He was desperate to know if she was being well taken care of. He e-mailed Roberts for any information he could offer.

> We're gonna try to find Cinnamon. I want to get her back. Who'd you give her to?

Mark pressed Roberts for whatever he could remember, but he just didn't answer the e-mails.

In the meantime, Henry called one of his men in Kyrgyzstan, Larry, who also worked for Dog Handlers Incorporated. He headed up their dog-handler operations in Kyrgyzstan. He would have gone to the airport with Roberts. He'd know something.

Henry told Mark, "Larry's a good guy. He'll get back to me. He'll know something. I'm sure he went to the airport with Roberts."

But Larry never got back to anyone.

Information about what had happened and why Roberts left Cinnamon in Turkey was hard to come by. Mark couldn't find out anything. He felt like there was a conspiracy against him. He had just been trying to get his dog home, and now he wasn't even sure where she was.

Mark pressed Henry, "Well, why don't I talk to Roberts? What's his parents' number? What's his home address?"

Henry wouldn't allow that. He wouldn't give Mark any information with which to contact Roberts directly.

Mark pleaded with him. "Henry, I just want to know what's going on."

"Let me deal with it. We'll get a hold of him. We'll get to the bottom of this. Don't worry about it. We'll find her."

Easy for him to say. Why should Mark believe him? It was his employee that abandoned Cinnamon to begin with. These guys were dog handlers. They all had assured him it would be okay, that Cinnamon would make it home just fine. Why should he trust him at this point?

Mark was still in Kandahar. He sent Alice an e-mail with the update.

> . . . I am flying through Bishkek/Manas in 6 days. I can't get there any sooner, but I will be there for at least 24 hours. I'm going to see if I can make contact with . . . a guy in Manas [Chief Blake] to see if he'll go make some inquiries for me, and perhaps get her and bring her back to the military airport. He's a guy I spoke to last week when she flew from Kandahar to Manas.

Mark called Chief Blake to see if he could help. He explained to Chief Blake what had happened, that Cinnamon never made it to Chicago, and that he believed that she had been abandoned by Roberts somewhere in Turkey.

"Do you think you can make some calls and try to find out what happened in Turkey? Maybe our guys up there can tell you something," Mark pleaded with the chief.

"Sure," the chief replied. "Let me see what I can do." Chief Blake thought that he had sent Cinnamon on her way, that his case involving her had been closed, but apparently it wasn't over. He would make some calls to see what he could find out.

Although it felt like an eternity, it was just over a day later, on Sunday morning, when Mark spoke with Henry and got the first bit of information about what had happened to Cinnamon. Henry had gotten another e-mail from Roberts. This time, with some useful information. As it turned out, Roberts hadn't left Cinnamon in Istanbul. He had left her in Bishkek. She'd never gotten on the flight to Turkey to begin with. Roberts told Henry that there had been a problem getting Cinnamon on the flight, and he left her behind with a female airline employee.

Chief Blake found out from Mark that Cinnamon never made her flight out of Kyrgyzstan. He briefed his superiors on base about this latest development, and then went back to work looking for Cinnamon.

Basically, chief was told, "Do what you can to find her and get that dog out of the country." While it was an unofficial investigation and mission, the chief took it seriously.

Chief Blake and his security squadron had access to his commanding officer's interpreter, Maria Onisenko. Without Maria, it would have been almost impossible for Chief Blake to do his job. She spoke the local language, and she helped him make his way around the city. She was a tremendous asset in his investigation into Cinnamon's disappearance. Unfortunately, Maria wasn't always available to help Blake. She was tied up during the day with her official duties. He had to work around Maria's schedule.

When they finally found some time to work together, Chief Blake and Maria first went to the airport to try to find the woman who took Cinnamon from Roberts. Most military personnel had to get special permission to leave the military base to go to the civilian side of the airport. It was a matter of security and accountability that military personnel could not leave the base at will, but the chief was able to go at any time because of his position in security. Chief Blake and Maria had to make several trips to make any headway. They had started at the Turkish Airlines ticket counter, where they were directed to the freight employees. The freight employees remembered the incident with Cinnamon but told the chief and Maria that it was the counter people who had taken care of her. Back and forth they went.

Finally, they found out who the woman was who had been working that night. She, however, wasn't scheduled to work again for another day or two. She regularly worked the flight that Cinnamon had been scheduled to be on, which departed every other day at 3:00 A.M. To complicate matters, getting to the airport at that hour of the morning was nearly impossible, even for the chief.

Under normal circumstances personnel had to report back to base by 5:00 P.M. and by 9:00 P.M. for special outings, such as the ones Chief Blake made in his capacity as head of security on base. The chief wouldn't be able to get to the airport at that late hour to talk with the woman. He'd have to find another way.

Over the next few days, Mark was packing and getting ready to leave Afghanistan. He'd fly from Kandahar to Kabul, then on to Bishkek. From there, he'd head for home.

Before he could leave Kandahar, Mark had to transition his responsibilities over to the next XO. But he had a hard time concentrating on his official duties. He was in a constant state of anxiety, which seemed to intensify with every moment. He couldn't relax. He couldn't breathe. He waited for a call from Henry. He hoped for word. Something. Anything. He checked in with Henry twice a day, sometimes more.

Now that they'd finally heard from Roberts, Mark queried him directly for details.

Roberts replied to Mark that Cinnamon had been turned away from the flight because animals over six kilos (approximately thirteen pounds) cannot travel in the passenger cabin. He continued, saying that Cinnamon was also not permitted to travel in the luggage compartment since the heat there had not been working and Cinnamon would have frozen. He stated that he had arrived five hours before his departure and spent four and one-half hours trying to make other arrangements for Cinnamon, including trying to change his ticket, but the next flight to the U.S. had been full. He also reported that "the lady that took Cinnamon works at the boarding counter for Turkish Airlines at the Bishkek Airport."

What Roberts told him didn't make sense, though. Mark was still plagued with questions. Why hadn't Roberts called Mark to let him know? Why hadn't he just taken Cinnamon back to the kennels, where she would have been safe? It was only a five-minute cab ride back to the base. Mark could have gotten her on another flight. The questions kept coming, but there were very few answers.

Finally, Mark left Kandahar on June 13. He flew to Kabul, where the rest of the unit had gone, for out-processing. All the members of his team were there when he arrived, hanging out, just waiting to head home. They were watching movies, relaxing, having a good time. Mark, on the other hand, didn't do any of that. There was no relaxing for him. He couldn't decompress from his time serving in Afghanistan, as the rest of the unit was doing. He couldn't eat. He couldn't sleep. All he could do was worry.

Some of the guys asked him about Cinnamon. They were shocked and outraged by what Mark told them.

"Is there anything we can do?" they asked.

"No," he told them. "We're already doing everything we can." Mark appreciated everyone's offers to help.

Mark spent six days in Kabul. The debriefing process was tedious and boring. He just wanted news of Cinnamon. He was on the phone to the security office every chance he got, two or three times a day.

"Nothing new, sir," they'd told him more than once.

Dejected, he'd reply, "Okay, thanks. Guess I'll try you again same time tomorrow."

It was hard. Mark didn't want to impose. These guys had jobs to do. They were being nice, trying to help him out when they really didn't have to.

When I first learned of Cinnamon's disappearance on her way home, I was furious. Why would a dog handler just abandon a dog in a foreign country? I worried incessantly about Cinnamon: where she was, if she was being cared for, and if she was even alive. I couldn't imagine what Mark and Alice were feeling.

I wanted to help Mark find her. I wanted to fix what had happened and make it right.

I began to brainstorm. What could I do? Who did I know that could help? One name popped into my mind. It was the name of the most active animal-rescue person that I knew. Or, I should say, knew of. I didn't really know her. I had only met her. Even that was a stretch, and she certainly didn't know me.

I was thinking of Terri Crisp, the founder and then the executive director of Noah's Wish, the animal-rescue organization that I had volunteered for in Louisiana after Hurricane Katrina. I first encountered Terri when I went to New Orleans during the Hurricane Katrina rescue and relief operations. The staff and volunteers with Noah's Wish had been rescuing and sheltering animals in disasters for several years. They had set up operations in Slidell, Louisiana, teaming with Slidell animal control.

After volunteering in Louisiana for more than a week, a friend I had made there insisted he introduce me to Terri. I wasn't so sure it was such a good idea. Terri lived and worked just outside the shelter in an RV, which doubled as the Incident Command Center—the hub of everything that took place behind the scenes to keep Noah's Wish and its operations in Slidell running smoothly. Except in extreme circumstances, few were allowed inside the RV. Katrina was one of the worst disasters that Terri and Noah's Wish had responded to. They were busy and overwhelmed, and Terri rarely interacted with the volunteers. All of this added to the mystery surrounding Terri and the uneasiness I felt about meeting her.

As I continued to object, my friend pressed on with his

plan for Terri and me to meet. He marched me into the RV, made our introduction, and, as expected, I felt awkward and silly. Terri had a lot of work to do. I just wanted to take care of the animals. It was over that quickly, and I was happy to get back to the shelter.

It was much later on that I found out that Terri Crisp had a long and successful career in animal rescue, which I didn't know about at the time of this brief encounter. I had no idea about the far-reaching impact she'd already had as an animal rescuer, and little did I know that Terri would have the single most important effect on a rescue operation of my own in the not-too-distant future.

So while I wasn't convinced that Terri would recall who I was, I still wanted to call her and spill out our story. I thought she could save the day and find Cinnamon, but still, I hesitated. I am a gutsy person. There isn't a lot that I am afraid of. In this situation, though, I was afraid of two things. First, I was afraid that Terri would say she couldn't help. I wasn't ready to face that. Second, I was afraid that she would agree to help but that I didn't really know what she could do for me. After all, Mark was in the region where Cinnamon had disappeared. He had the help of the Security Forces in the area and an interpreter who was a local and knew her way around the city. They were right there where Cinnamon's flight had originated. They were likely her best bet at being found. If they couldn't find her, how in the world would anyone seven thousand miles away find her? I didn't want to waste asking Terri for a favor before I really knew what it was that I needed.

I also couldn't stand by and do nothing and let this puppy vanish without a trace. I couldn't stand by and let my brother continue to hurt the way he was without trying to do something.

So, instead of calling Terri, I did what I thought was the next-best thing. I called Debbye Prock. Debbye was a woman I had met in Louisiana as well. She is my kind of woman: a pistol, a spitfire full of spunk and attitude. We had spent just a few days together at the Noah's Wish shelter in Louisiana. Then we'd stayed in touch afterward.

Debbye was also a neighbor and close personal friend of Terri's.

I thought she could tell me if Terri could help find Cinnamon. If she *would* help find Cinnamon. She could also give me Terri's number. Debbye was in California, so I had to wait until late morning to call. A few hours later, I dialed her number.

"Oh, Chris! Hi! What a great surprise!" With her energy and exuberant greeting, Debbye always made you glad you had dialed her number.

"Hi, Deb. I'm calling with kind of an unusual request." I explained what had happened to Cinnamon, that she had been left somewhere in Turkey. I had yet to learn that Mark found out Cinnamon was in Bishkek, not Istanbul. Then I continued, "I'm thinking of calling Terri to see if she can help. Do you think she has any international contacts that could do something to help us find Cinnamon? Do you think she might be willing to help us?"

Without hesitation, Debbye shot back, "Absolutely. She does have international contacts, and I know she'd be willing to help. What do you need from her?"

That was just it. I didn't know. I explained my predicament to Debbye. She encouraged me to give Terri a call anyway. In fact, she offered to contact Terri herself first. I wasn't sure, though, that it was the right thing to do just yet.

I thanked Debbye for her support and encouragement and told her I'd let her know what I decided to do. Other than that, I wasn't really sure what more either of us could do, and so I waited. It killed me to sit by and just do nothing, but, at the same time, Mark believed that the investigation they were conducting in Bishkek was the best chance they had of finding Cinnamon. I had to respect that. It was still frustrating, though. I felt that my help wasn't needed, so I did all that I could do. I waited.

On his second day in Kabul, Mark approached the navy senior officer there and told him what had happened to Cinnamon. The commander had met her when he had visited Kandahar earlier in the deployment. Mark asked his permission to remain in Bishkek when the team flew on to the States. He wanted more time to search for Cinnamon himself.

"Sir, I can take leave," Mark suggested. "I know this isn't official business, but there must be some way."

"No way," the commander told him. "I can't leave you there alone. You're on orders. You're part of Team Juliet, and when Juliet leaves Kyrgyzstan, you're leaving too."

Always looking for alternatives, Mark continued, "How about this? If I can find her before we leave, and I get permission from the air force and the charter company, will you authorize me to take Cinnamon on the plane with us?"

"If the air force and the charter company say it's okay, I see no problem with that," the commander said.

Mark spent the rest of that day on the phone. He knew that he was imposing on the Kabul administrative staff by sitting in their office and using their phone, but he had important work to do. He had to find a way to get Cinnamon home. First, Mark called the air force to see what flight his team would be on. Once he found the flight, he had to find out the name of the charter company. Then he had to contact them and find out their policy on animals.

It was tedious work. Call after call, piecing together the information. Finally, he got to the charter company. After explaining the situation, Mark was told, "No problem. We fly animals all the time. If she's part of your group, she's coming with us." To his surprise, they even told him, "In a lot of cases, we'll put them up in the passenger compartment with you. It's up to the pilot and the crew." The image of Cinnamon sitting in the seat next to him on the way home made him smile. That would be kind of cool.

Mark called Chief Blake with the good news. But the chief wasn't hopeful, "Sir, I don't know if air ops here in Manas will allow it. It's against policy."

"Chief, I'll get her on that plane somehow. I'll go to the base commander at Manas if I have to." Mark was determined to get Cinnamon home, but he knew the reality of the situation. "For now, though, let's concentrate on finding her. There's no point in me trying to get authorization for her to fly with us if I don't even know where she is."

Mark had heard that Special Forces units were allowed to bring their animals with them, including their mascots. So he knew exceptions could be made. He knew he wouldn't get the same consideration that the Special Forces guys got, but he was confident that once Cinnamon was by his side, he'd work it out. Once he found her, he wasn't going to leave Bishkek without her. One way or another, he'd get her out of there, even if he had to disobey orders to do it.

In the meantime, though, all he could do was hope the chief could find her before he arrived at Manas.

To Mark, the pace of the chief's investigation seemed excruciatingly slow. While it had only been a few days since Cinnamon was abandoned, it seemed like an eternity. Mark appreciated what he was doing, but the waiting was hard. He knew that the chief had other responsibilities, but he had to do something to try to move things along faster. He thought of another strategy and called Chief Blake to tell him what it was.

"Hey, Chief. Why don't we put together a flyer? We can circulate it at the airport."

Mark sent Chief Blake a copy of a flyer he had made. Hoping it would get noticed, Mark included a clear photo of Cinnamon and big bold letters.

It was a possibility, but the chief thought twice about it.

"I don't think we can go around hanging up flyers at the airport in English. I'd have to get approval from the airport security guys and their management."

"Well," Mark asked, "couldn't Maria translate it?"

Chief Blake wasn't so sure it was the best idea and didn't really know what to do. He just knew that he had to find the woman at the airport who had taken Cinnamon. The chief said, "Let me get out to the airport. Let me see what I can do." He tried to reassure Mark, but allaying Mark's anxiety wasn't that easy to do.

While the chief kept looking for Cinnamon, Mark had finished his out-processing in Kabul and flew to Manas Air Base in Bishkek, Kyrgyzstan. When he first got there, Mark walked all around

REWARD!

For information leading to the return of this dog!

She was left in her dog crate with a female baggage clerk
at the Turkish Airlines counter on the moring of 9 June
after being turned away from a Turkish Air flight.
We are seeking to make contact with the baggage clerk
to arrange for the return of the dog to its owner.
Please contact _____ at _____ if you have
any information.

Mark offered a reward for Cinnamon and made a flyer, hoping that by hanging it at the Bishkek airport it would help him find Cinnamon.

the base looking for the security office and Chief Blake, but didn't know where they were. He came upon a bunch of air force guys gathered outside the chow hall and asked, "Do you guys know where the security office is?"

Seeing the navy uniform and recognizing the voice, one of them turned and said, "Hey, sir. Are you Mister Feffer?" Chief Blake and Mark, having been on different bases up until then, had only spoken on the phone. They had never met face-to-face.

"Chief Blake? Is that you?" It was. Of all the air force personnel on base, Mark had stumbled upon Chief Blake quite by accident.

"Hey, we were just gonna go get some chow," Chief Blake said to Mark. "Why don't you join us?"

Mark accompanied Chief Blake to breakfast. It was good to spend some time to get to know the man with whom he had spoken so many times and who was going out of his way to help him and Cinnamon. He was impressed by the chief's diligence.

"I have a dog at home. I have an idea what you must be going through," the chief told him.

Since he no longer had access to a phone, Mark told the chief that he'd stop in to see him periodically for updates. They were still looking for Cinnamon, and assuming they would find her, Mark started to work on new plans to fly her home.

While Mark, Alice, and Chief Blake were doing all they could think of to find Cinnamon, my brain kept coming up with ideas as well. I didn't know how useful they might be; nor did I know how receptive Mark would be to them. But, if even for my own sanity, I had to do something. I had to feel like I was helping.

I remembered that my husband had a friend who was from the former Soviet Union. I wasn't sure how long he had been in the U.S., but he still spoke his native language and had retained his thick accent. Perhaps he could help.

I tracked down his e-mail address and boldly sent him my request.

Hi Vitaly,

Chris Sullivan here . . . Jolene gave me your e-mail today.

Do you know anyone in Kyrgyzstan near the Bishkek airport?

I know this is a crazy question . . . but . . .

My brother is coming home from Afghanistan, made arrangements to bring an abandoned dog home, and the dog is lost . . .

having been left at the airport in Kyrgyzstan, with an employee
from the Turkish airline . . . I just have been racking my brain trying to think of who might be able to help.

Let me know if you have any contacts there . . . whatever small
bit might help is appreciated.

I was naïve and hopeful at the same time. I desperately needed
to find this dog.

Through their persistent efforts, Chief Blake and Maria ultimately
found out that a woman named Anna was the Turkish Airlines'
employee who had dealt with Roberts at the ticket counter. After
that, it took them several days to get to the airport when Anna was
there.

Chief Blake and Maria approached Anna and asked her what
she knew. Anna remembered the incident they were asking about.
It was hard for her to forget. She told them about the angry traveler, and how he had frightened everyone working that night.
He'd had problems getting his dog on the flight because the dog's
ticket and paperwork were not in order. He had tried to get them
to let her on the plane. When he was unsuccessful, he said that, if
he couldn't take the dog with him, he'd have no choice but to
bring her outside and kill her and then he'd return for his flight.
Anna had been frightened by his behavior, and she felt bad for the
dog. She had agreed to take Cinnamon from him so that he
wouldn't kill her.

Chief Blake and Maria were shocked. Roberts's story had been
that the airline had denied Cinnamon's flight because of a faulty
heater in the cargo hold and that the Turkish Airlines' employee
felt bad, so she had agreed to take Cinnamon. He'd said nothing
about her ticket or her paperwork not being in order or about the
part where he had threatened Cinnamon's life.

Through Maria, Chief Blake asked Anna where the dog was
now. Anna gave what details she could. This information wasn't
what the chief was hoping for. He'd have to go and give Mark the
news.

Mark hadn't been in Kyrgyzstan long. He checked in with the chief frequently. It had been a while since they last spoke, so early Sunday morning he went over to the security office to find out the latest. He saw the chief's partner, Sergeant Kamrad. Kamrad had been working side by side with Chief Blake on Cinnamon's investigation. The two were a team, but Mark had dealt mostly with the chief.

Mark went into the office. "Where's the chief?" he asked.

Kamrad was quick. "He should be here shortly. I think he has some news for you."

"Well? What?" Mark's jumpiness was evident.

"You probably just want to talk to him."

Mark's heart sank. Kamrad didn't linger. When the chief arrived, Mark held his breath.

Chief Blake began, "Sir, we finally got to the airport last night. We found the person who took Cinnamon. She said that she gave Cinnamon to some guy in the airport. He had just gotten off a flight. He had overheard what was happening with Cinnamon and offered to take her in. She doesn't know if he lives in the area or if he is from somewhere else." The chief continued with what few details he had. It wasn't much. "She said that, if she saw him again, she'd let him know you are looking for Cinnamon. I'm sorry, Mark," the chief offered, "this looks like the end of the line."

Mark was stunned. He couldn't believe it—didn't want to believe it. Based on what Chief Blake had just told him, Cinnamon was gone, and Mark would never see her again.

The reality of what the chief said sank in slowly. It was a harsh reality, one Mark hadn't really prepared for, but he did his best to face it full on. He had to let Alice know. Since he was in Bishkek now, he didn't have access to phones as he'd had in Kandahar. It was also the middle of the night at home. He didn't want to wake his wife, so he decided to tell her in an e-mail. Mark walked slowly to the Internet café at Manas while he tried to get his emotions under control. He sat down and typed an e-mail to Alice.

Just a note to let you know that we are basically at a dead end in trying to find Cinnamon. We found out this morning that the dog handler told the Turkish Airlines people that if they didn't take her, that he would have to put her to sleep. So, they took her, and gave her to a man in the airport who said he would take her. They have no contact information on this man. They do not know if he's a passenger or was dropping someone off or picking them up. They don't know where he lives or who he is.

They said that they'd keep an eye out for him and let the security guys know at the base if they see him again, but that's such a long shot that I don't have hope of that happening. If by some miracle it does, they have our contact info.

I'll be in the States Tuesday night.

Love,
Mark

The rest of that day was a blur. While everyone else was full of excitement and anxious to go home, Mark slept. He tried to read, then he slept some more. He kept to himself. He didn't want to dampen everyone else's good cheer. Their words of comfort and righteous anger, while well intended, didn't make him feel better. After dinner, he headed over to the Internet café again. There were so many people pulling for him and Cinnamon. He had to let them know what had happened. He typed slowly.

Friends and Family,

I just wanted to send a note regarding Cinnamon, the camp dog that Alice and I were bringing home from Afghanistan. As most of you know, she was left in Bishkek, Kyrgyzstan by the dog handler (Matthew Roberts) who was escorting her home for us. Turkish Airlines would not let her on the flight because their cargo space was not heated.

After 10 days of investigation, we have determined the following:

The dog handler created an atmosphere of deceit & distrust when he arrived at the USAF base in Bishkek (MANAS) on June 5th because he basically dropped off Cinnamon in the military kennels and headed to downtown Bishkek without authorization. The security personnel said that he misled them and tried to pass her off as a military working dog. I worked through that from Kandahar and got authorization for her to stay with the military dogs at the base. This is significant because we believe this is why he didn't opt to bring her back to MANAS AB when Turkish Airlines denied her flight to Istanbul.

When he checked in for his flight to Istanbul on June 9th, he was told that he could not take Cinnamon with him due to a faulty heater in the cargo hold of the plane. He later told us that he was 5 hours early for his flight. But, he didn't call us. He didn't take her back to MANAS. He simply told Turkish Airlines that if they didn't take her, that he would have to have her put down. One of the Turkish Airlines employees stated that she'd take her.

We've been told that later that night the Turkish Airlines employee gave Cinnamon to a man at the airport. We don't know if this man was an arriving passenger, or was dropping someone off or picking them up. We don't know if he lives nearby or not. We have no contact information or any way to track this man down. The airline employees have said that if they see him again that they will contact us via the USAF personnel at the MANAS AB, but we aren't confident of that happening.

The bottom line is that the dog handler, Matthew Roberts, gave her away, in spite of having the option of taking her back to MANAS. Then he avoided telling us for 2 days what he had done, and where Cinnamon was. He didn't tell anyone that she was left behind until he arrived in Chicago, some 20+ hours later. Then he caught his flight [home], and went to bed. Again, without contacting us or anyone, in spite of the fact that I had given him $300 for expenses and a 250 minute phone card.

We wonder why a person who handles dogs would be so cruel and irresponsible . . . He showed no compassion for us or for Cinnamon. I'm quite certain that he wouldn't have left his own dog with strangers at the airport without making further arrangements for her travel. I feel very guilty for trusting a person like this with Cinnamon.

At this point, all we'd want is some assurance that Cinnamon is OK and living a life that is better than the one she was living in Afghanistan. The peace of mind that information would bring us is immeasurable, but we aren't confident that we will ever hear more about her.

That is all I have for now. Please pray and hope that Cinnamon is doing well and is happy. That is what we will do. That is what we wanted.

Mark

Mark swallowed hard and sent the e-mail. It was about 10:00 P.M. in Bishkek, Sunday, June 18. Cinnamon had been missing for ten days.

Alice was devastated by the news in Mark's e-mail. *He may be giving up, but I'm not*, she thought to herself. She considered trying to find Cinnamon by flying to Bishkek. She was furious with the dog handler for what he had done. She couldn't believe that they had gone through so much to care for Cinnamon and get her home and that it had come to this.

To keep from falling apart completely, Alice prayed, "Dear God, if this is what is meant to be, please just give me a sign." She merely wanted to know that Cinnamon was in a loving home. Praying was the only thing that kept her sane.

Following the news of Cinnamon's being gone for good, Mark was in Bishkek a few more days. During that time his sorrow intensified. Mark's grief was crushing. He felt as if a loved one had died.

I wouldn't have done this if I had known this was a remote possibility, he thought to himself. *She would have been better off staying where she was in Kandahar. I can't believe this has turned out this way.*

All Mark and Alice wanted was some news that Cinnamon had been given to a good person, that she'd be taken care of. But as Mark had said in his e-mail, he didn't think they'd ever know even that much.

Mark didn't know how he'd reconcile what had happened. He felt responsible for Cinnamon's disappearance. He thought that he could have prevented it—that he *should* have prevented it. The grief and sorrow he felt were insurmountable. The guilt, devastating. Mark tried to brace himself to feel this way for the rest of his life. He then prepared for his final journey home.

EIGHT

WITH THE SEARCH for Cinnamon reaching a dead end, Mark's homecoming had an incredibly dark cloud over it—a cloud that cast a far-reaching shadow of sorrow. It wasn't fair. He had served his country. He had stayed safe. He had done his job and was now returning home to those who loved him. Cinnamon was supposed to come home with him. She had been a puppy whose future would have been uncertain without him, whose existence in Afghanistan would have been just a step above that of a stray. She was supposed to start a new life.

Many people had grown to love Cinnamon. They had followed her story of life on base, sent care packages for her, and e-mailed to find out how she was and what she was doing. They craved pictures that showed how Cinnamon loved to play and how she had grown. For an orphaned puppy, she was loved near and far.

As Mark prepared to head home, he carried heavy burdens with him. Would Cinnamon have been better off if Mark had never decided to adopt her and had left her back on base? At least then he would know where she was. Maybe she would have been safe there. Maybe the next troops coming in would have taken care of her. Such a life wouldn't be the American dream for her, but it might have been better than where she was now.

Mark's e-mail with the news of Cinnamon arrived Sunday morning. It took me hours to recover from what I read. I cried and cried.

I was sick to my stomach. My heart broke for him and for Cinnamon.

Our family had gotten through Mark's time serving in Afghanistan. It just didn't seem right that Mark was coming home with this burden bearing down on him. He deserved better. Cinnamon deserved better. The person who caused this horrible mess had to be confronted. He had to give us some answers. He had to tell us why.

Once I got my wits about me, my wheels started turning. I love Mark dearly and couldn't stand that he was hurting. I also couldn't bear the thought of what might have happened to Cinnamon. I didn't just want to help. I *needed* to help. I needed to do something to change the outcome of this situation, and I was ready to do whatever I could think of.

Despite a great education, a good life, and a fairly decent career, my life up until that point felt pretty meaningless. I had spent years in corporate America, which had left me empty and uninspired. So I had quit my job and spent almost a year traveling, looking for my next opportunity. I'd then started numerous business ventures, trying to find my niche, but nothing seemed to work out quite right. Given all that, I wasn't sure what made me think that I could find a lost dog seven thousand miles away, when I couldn't even find myself.

None of that mattered now, though. My past wasn't important. What mattered was that I was motivated and ready to act. The first thing I did was pick up the phone and call Alice.

"Hello?" Her voice was as lifeless as ever, lately.

"Hey, Alice. It's Chris." I tempered my enthusiasm to match her mood. While I was ready for action, she was grieving and in despair. I expressed my incredible shock and sorrow at what happened. Then I proceeded with caution with my next thought. "I'm thinking about calling Terri Crisp, the woman that I told you about from Noah's Wish, to see if there's anything she can do. Maybe she has contacts overseas that can look for Cinnamon. What do you think?"

Her response was heart wrenching. "Chris, if you want to do that, that's fine, go ahead, but Mark and I are just depleted. It's over. I just don't see what else can be done. We are so physically and emotionally exhausted from all this."

Her pain and heartache were unmistakable. She was unable to do any more and was ready to accept that Cinnamon would never be found. Still, I wanted her okay to do some digging on my own.

"That's fine," she surrendered, "if that's what you want to do, but I just can't do any more."

That was just the opening I needed. I sprang into action. Remembering Debbye Prock's words of encouragement, I forwarded Mark's e-mail to her, which explained what had happened to Cinnamon. I thought she might send it to Terri, and I'd have a better chance that Terri would respond. I had no idea what would come of it.

> Hi Deb,
>
> Here is the update on Cinnamon . . . my brother's dog that I spoke with you about.
>
> I did not contact Terri as my brother was investigating what happened and I didn't want to call her until I had a sense of what we would want to ask her help with.
>
> At this point, I don't know if there is anything she could do. Maybe you could forward this to her and see what her thoughts are.
>
> I am heartbroken for my brother and for Cinnamon.
>
> How does this stuff go on?

Debbye was an inspiration. Nothing was impossible in her mind. And she took this on like she took on life—head on. She forwarded my e-mail to Terri.

> Hi Terri, Chris Sullivan was one of the girls I became friends with in Slidell, she had called the other morning to get the office

phone numbers about this dog dilemma so I am forwarding the
e-mail at her request in the event you should have any ideas of
how to unstrand a dog in Turkey! Thanks, Deb

Debbye hadn't realized that we'd learned Cinnamon was in
Bishkek, but she had broken the ice with Terri. Now that she had,
I thought it was time to give Terri a call myself. Up until then, I
didn't think there was much she could do to help. But now Mark
had reached a dead end. He had given up trying or even hoping
to find Cinnamon. Deb had given me Terri's contact numbers
and suggested I speak with her assistant to start.

I dialed Terri's number. My heart raced. Unfortunately, all I
got was an answering machine on the other end. I left as brief
a message as I could while providing the details of Cinnamon's
story and a sense of urgency. I hung up the phone and slumped in
my chair.

A short time later, my phone rang. Caller ID told me the call was
from the same area code as the number I dialed to reach Terri.

"Hello?" I would have jumped through the phone if I could have.
I didn't really expect a call back, and certainly not so quickly.

"Chris, hi, this is Thea Martin. I'm Terri's assistant at Noah's
Wish."

It couldn't be good news. Terri didn't call herself, so I figured
she was probably too busy to help. Chances were, she might even
be out of the country.

"I spoke with Terri, and she wanted me to pass along her suggestions to you." Thea was kind and to the point. I knew they
were busy, and locating lost dogs was not really their mission.

"Okay." I waited for her to continue.

"Terri just came from a conference with the WSPA in London.
It's the World Society for the Protection of Animals. She suggested that you contact them to see if they have a member-welfare
society in the country where the dog is lost. Maybe they can help
you find her."

"Oh?" I had heard of the WSPA before but really had no idea
what they did.

"And then she also suggested that you contact CNN or FOX
News, and maybe they could help."

"Oh, that's a good idea," was all I could come up with. I wasn't really sure if it was or not.

"Well, let us know how you make out. Good luck."

I thanked Thea and asked her to pass along my gratitude to Terri. I had hoped that Terri would be able to do more, that perhaps she had personal friends or contacts in the area that could help us search for Cinnamon. Learning that she didn't left me feeling anxious, but I continued to act on Cinnamon's behalf, not knowing if doing so would make a difference. Besides, Terri had been rescuing animals long before I had. Maybe she knew something I didn't. And maybe, somehow, my love and compassion for animals, which had set the stage for me to meet Terri the year before, now would lead me to find out just what that was.

Following the wrath of Hurricane Katrina, I sat glued to the TV. The images of the destruction in Louisiana and Mississippi were difficult to watch: the lives torn apart, the homes in ruins. The stories ran day after day, night after night for weeks. I knew early on there was another story looming behind those pictures that wasn't being told. What about the animals? Surely there had to be hundreds, if not thousands, of animals that were victims of the hurricane as well. What was happening to them? Who was saving them? What were their stories? Surely they needed help, too.

Finally, the images of the animals showed up on the news, and their stories unfolded. They were horrifying and gut-wrenching. Dogs, cats, horses, and more were surrounded by floodwaters, clinging to rooftops, abandoned on porches, swimming in the toxic waters. How would these poor animals survive? Who would rescue and take care of them? I felt helpless as I watched the news. There were estimates of hundreds of thousands of animal victims from Katrina. It haunted me day and night. I sobbed as I sat glued to the TV for hours watching their stories. Who was helping them?

Driven by my need to help, I looked into which animal-rescue organizations were responding to the disaster. Surely they needed money. The least I could do was make a donation to the rescue effort. There were so many organizations asking for money, though, that it was overwhelming. I couldn't decide where to contribute, so I waited. Then, after several weeks, I decided to donate locally to a group of veterinary technicians who were going to New Orleans to volunteer. I wrote out my check, dropped it off, and was on my way. It felt good. I thought I had done my part, but it just didn't seem to be enough.

I decided I needed to do more. Watching wasn't good enough. Sending a check wasn't good enough. I had to go. I had to go to New Orleans to help take care of those animals myself. I was ready, willing, and able. The groups that were in the South to rescue the injured, stranded, and orphaned animals were not as receptive to my coming as I had expected. Their Web sites said that if I didn't have animal-handling experience, I should stay home. If I didn't have their formal training or if I wasn't a veterinarian, vet assistant, animal-control officer, or something like that, I should just make a monetary donation and stay home.

I couldn't believe it. There were reports that volunteers were desperately needed, but while I was willing to help, the rescue organizations were turning me away. In truth, I had to restrain myself from getting in my car and just driving down there. It was a tough reality to face. Some Web sites went so far as to suggest that if inexperienced people like me were to show up, we would actually be a hindrance instead of a help.

I was frustrated, but I kept after it. I e-mailed several animal-rescue groups, volunteering to help. It took several weeks, but I finally got a call from Noah's Wish. I agreed to go and made my plans before I really thought about what I was agreeing to. I didn't care what I found when I got there. I just knew I had to go. Thankfully, my husband supported my decision. I felt bad leaving him and our own two dogs, but it would only be for a week or so. The animals in Louisiana clearly needed me far more than my own family did at the time.

I'm not really sure where my intense desire to help animals came from, but at some point in my life I became "a dog person." My parents might tell you it was when I was about ten years old and we got Samantha, or Sam as I called her, a cocker spaniel puppy who would be all mine. She wasn't our first dog. We had others—Snoopy, Pluto, Misty—but Sam was *my* first dog.

Well, during her first night home, Sam did what most any puppy would do: she cried, and she cried, and she cried—not just the first night, but night after night after night. My parents couldn't take it anymore.

"She's just a baby," I said. How advanced I was for my years. I had no idea, though, how to make her stop.

So my dad did what dads do. He made Sam sleep in the basement. *The outside basement.* At night. In the dark. On a concrete floor all by herself, as far away from his earshot as she could get. So not to be outdone, Sam cried some more, only louder.

It was hard to handle. I couldn't sleep. The crying kept me awake. More important to me, though, Sam was just a baby. She was *my* baby, and she was all alone. I was her mother. She needed me. So what did I do? I grabbed my pillow and blanket and went outside into the cold, dark night, to the creepy, dirty basement. I curled up on the floor and snuggled next to her. My being there didn't stop her crying, but it did stop my sleeping. Apparently it still stopped my dad's sleeping, too. And before too long he came out as well. Night after night he came out to make sure we were okay. He didn't like the idea of my sleeping out there with her, but he wouldn't let her come in. So I wasn't coming in either.

This went on for weeks. The crying didn't stop. I didn't know what to do. She may have been my baby, but I was a kid. What did I know? Her housebreaking didn't go any better. I tried. I really did. I did my best and hoped it would get better.

A few weeks later, I went to a sleepover at my nana's house. I was thrilled when my grandfather gave me some steak scraps from dinner to bring home to my new puppy.

"Thanks, Pop. Sam will love them. I can't wait to get home to give them to her." My grandmother eyed me steadily.

The next morning, my mom picked me up to bring me home. I hopped in the car. I couldn't wait to get back to Sam. "Look, Mom. Look what I brought home for Samantha." I held up the baggie with the special morsels. "It's steak. Pop gave it to me. Sam's gonna love it."

Mom didn't say a word. We pulled into the driveway, and I raced into the house.

"Sam? Sam, I'm home," I called. "Samantha, come, girl. Look what I have for you."

No Sam.

"Sam?" I tried again. "Sam?" It wasn't like her. She always came to me when I got home.

My mother came in through the door. "Mom, have you seen Sam?" No reply from either of them.

I started running through the house looking for her. Room to room. Calling and calling. "Sam? Sam? Sam?"

Up the stairs, then back down. "Sam, where are you?"

I panicked. "Sam?" I started running faster.

"Mom, where is she? Where's Sam?" I was frantic. "Sam," I screamed even louder.

The tears started. Where was she? The tears came harder and harder until I was sobbing.

"Mom, Mom, Mom, where's Sam? Where *is* she?" More tears.

And then I looked up into my mother's face, and I knew. And through my tears I pleaded with my mother. "No, no, no. Where is she? Mom, where's Sam? What did you do with her? What did you do with her? She was mine. She was mine. How could you?"

Just like that, Sam was gone. My world was shattered. It couldn't be true. I couldn't believe it. Sam had gone to the make-believe farm in upstate New York, where all the pets from the city go when they don't work out for their families. Pluto and Friskie had gone there. Misty would, too, a few years later. And now Sam. There was nothing I could do. Not a single thing. And as the tears continued running down my face; the baggie filled with steak still dangling from my small hand fell to the floor.

As difficult as it was, I came to accept over time that my parents had their reasons for sending Samantha away. I'd also learned that she didn't actually go to a "farm" to live. In reality, she had gone to live with the family of one of my dad's coworkers. My dad had a soft spot for animals, and while it hadn't worked out well with Samantha, he wanted her to have a good life. I also know that my parents love me and that they did what they thought was best, as any good parents would do. And while I thought about Sam a lot over the years, it wasn't until more than fifteen years later, when I had a dog of my own, that I realized how much responsibility came with him. It was, I believe, the cumulative experiences of having and loving these dogs that led me to want to find Cinnamon so badly.

Reggie had arrived as a gift for my twenty-fifth birthday—a surprise that I was not prepared for. I had found out several weeks beforehand that he was coming, and trying to be a responsible, practical adult, I solicited the help of friends and family to put a stop to it. I wasn't ready for the responsibility of raising and training a puppy. Besides, I worked full time almost an hour from home and lived in a third-floor walk-up apartment with wall-to-wall carpeting. I just couldn't see providing all that was necessary for a puppy under those circumstances. As much as I protested, I just couldn't get through to anyone.

So this little eight-week-old, five-pound ball of white fluff arrived, red ribbon around his neck and all. He fit perfectly into the palms of my hands. He was so cute, but still I thought about the life that I wanted to give him, which my work schedule just wouldn't allow. How in the world would I have the time to take care of him? Housebreak him? Give him the love that he deserved? I just didn't want to fail him.

I felt my protests were reasonable, but apparently no one was listening. And there he was, all furry and cute, his red ribbon tied just so.

The first night in his new home, what do you think Reggie did? Yup. He cried. But his crying was different than Samantha's. Reggie cried, and when he did, he put his little furry paws up on the side of my bed and cried some more. As it turned out, he had to do his business and didn't know where to go. Once I showed him, he rewarded me and in turn showed me how smart he was. He promptly relieved himself on his paper, and in two days he was paper trained. He hit his mark on the paper night and day, missing only once or twice. No. Reggie wasn't going to the "farm" in upstate New York. He was staying right here with me.

That was it. Within three days, I was in love. It took me those three days, but once I fell, I fell hard. He became my baby. My boy. My firstborn. And so began my journey with Reg and a bond of love, loyalty, and friendship that lasted more than fifteen years.

Reggie went with me wherever I went. We did everything together: hiking, running, Rollerblading, boating, sailing, canoeing, skiing, tubing, sledding, snowshoeing—even flying. We were best friends. And, as best friends do, when I went through the deepest, darkest days of my life, Reg was right there beside me through it all. Through thick and thin. He snuggled with me for hours and days on end, lathered my face with kisses when I needed them most, and even licked away my tears when they wouldn't stop rolling down my face.

When Reggie had to be put to sleep, tragically, one winter day, it was one of the toughest days of my life. But with the passing of time, as I was able to look back on the life, love, and memories we shared, I knew that having Reggie in my life had made everything richer, fuller, and more rewarding. My love of and compassion for all animals continued to deepen and extend to a wider network of furry friends, creating the circumstances that led me to volunteer in Louisiana with Noah's Wish and to be able to help Cinnamon when she needed it the most.

It was a hot, dusty Monday afternoon late in October 2005 when I arrived at the makeshift animal shelter run by Noah's Wish and the Slidell animal control office. By the time I had gotten there, two thousand dogs, cats, ducks, bunnies, horses, and the like had already been rescued, sheltered, and cared for in Slidell alone since Katrina had devastated the South. I was taken aback by the greeting I received. Two very tired but exuberant volunteer coordinators greeted me, grabbed my bags, and threw their arms around me.

"I can't tell you how happy we are to see you!" exclaimed one of them. I was taken off guard and didn't quite understand. Then I found out that since it had been almost two months since the hurricane, the number of volunteers at the shelter had dwindled. They were short on help, and those who were still there had been there since the beginning or had returned over and over again. Everyone was tired and burned out. The coordinators who had greeted me were ecstatic to have another pair of helping hands, which explained the greeting I had just received.

Having been briefed about my role as a volunteer, I was excited to be there and anxious to get to work. Since I had arrived at lunchtime, the staff and volunteers were taking a much-needed break. There wasn't a whole lot for me to do. Even the animals, all 950 of them, were taking naps.

To satisfy my need to get down to work, one of the volunteers said I could do some snuggle time. I sure lucked out having arrived during lunch. Snuggling was my specialty. While all the animals in the shelter were sleeping, the animals in the infirmary, those requiring special attention for medical or stress-related reasons, were given some extra TLC. It was a perfect way for me to start my volunteer work. I couldn't have been happier.

Over the next few days, I got to understand the routine at the shelter and found where I fit in. The animals needed the basics: food, water, shelter, and potty breaks. Our activities centered on those needs. The routine was that simple—walk the dogs, feed the dogs, clean the kennels, change the water, then start all over again.

We arrived at the shelter between 6:00 and 7:00 A.M. each day, putting in twelve-hour days of walking dogs and taking care of their needs. At night, there was just enough time and energy to take a shower, have dinner, and perhaps make a quick call home before falling into bed. Then we'd start all over the next day. It was an exhausting but simple and satisfying existence.

I made fast friends with a man named Dick Dahl from Durango, Colorado. He showed me around the shelter and clued me in to the inner workings. When I got there, Dick had been at the shelter for four weeks. He was a hard worker and well regarded by the paid staff and director of Noah's Wish.

Dick and I fell into a routine. We got along famously. Together, we took care of the dogs in the infirmary and helped the vets and vet techs with their exams and treatments. Mostly, though, Dick and I laughed. We traded stories and perspectives on life. He told jokes from one end of the day to the next. It made the awful plight of the animals more bearable and let the stress fade into the background, sometimes when we needed it the most.

Being a relief worker for animals after Katrina was about the most satisfying thing I had ever done up to that point. The work was simple, hard but simple. It entailed long, hot days of strenuous, dirty work. We were served catered food that was often cold by the time we got to it. We slept in a flooded-out, mold-infested hotel. Sometimes forty adults at a time slept in a hotel ballroom and shared just two bathrooms and, at times, one shower, but hardly anyone complained. When my time there was coming to an end, I didn't want to leave. So I didn't. I extended my stay another week. I was thrilled at the chance to continue the work that had become so rewarding. And without realizing it, I had set up the "chance" circumstances that led to meeting Terri Crisp.

NINE

SINCE MARK'S MISSION to find Cinnamon had ended, it was time for him to focus on getting home. He had to put his energy into something other than Cinnamon. It was the only way he could function at that time.

Fortunately, Mark was very busy getting home. He and his team were hustling from place to place preparing for their journey back to the U.S. They had to turn in uniforms and clean and turn in weapons. The process was the reverse of getting ready to deploy, only at a much faster pace because it needed to be completed in just a matter of days.

At this point, Mark kept busy and did his best to keep his emotions over losing Cinnamon at bay. The pain and guilt were too much. He thought about her, but not to the extent that he had during his search. He had to get home. He had to get on with life. He knew he would get through this, but he just didn't know how.

Mark boarded his flight home on Tuesday, June 20. He flew with his team members from Bishkek through Shannon, Ireland, as they had on their way over. He walked through the terminal with the rest of the navy guys. The hallway where their flight arrived was separated from the departing passengers by a glass wall. As he walked through, the terminal erupted with applause.

There must be a group of army guys coming through, Mark thought to himself. As he looked around, he realized that, no, there were no army guys arriving. The applause was for him and his team.

The crowd was welcoming them home. They were welcoming Mark and the whole team of navy men and women. The experience was very surreal for him, yet the black cloud still hung over his head.

Mark was Stateside on the night of the twentieth. Once he was on the ground in Indiana, the anticipation of getting home was building. He needed to get there. He needed to rest and recover from everything he had been through. It would be a few more days, though, before he'd be in Maryland. After I hung up the phone with Thea, I had to put my disappointment behind me. I was desperate. I had hoped that Terri and Noah's Wish could help find Cinnamon, that Terri herself would get involved and make it all happen for me. But finding animals was not their mission, so I had to work with what I had.

Once I got some perspective and resolved to do something about this awful injustice that I felt had been committed against Cinnamon, Mark, and decency in general, I functioned as if I was on autopilot. I was like a glider plane slicing through the air, wind beneath my wings, not really knowing where I was going—or caring, for that matter. I simply acted without hesitation, without thought of impact, results, or consequences. I just knew that if Cinnamon was going to be found, I had to keep moving, had to keep doing whatever I could. Besides, there was no one else who would do it. There was only me. I had the energy, the belief, and the simpleminded naïveté that a dog abandoned in a foreign country seven thousand miles away could be found. Why not? I never considered that there could be any other outcome.

Next, I went to my computer to find a way to contact the WSPA. A quick search on Google yielded what I was looking for, the society's Web site and an e-mail address. Then I considered what to say and how I could get their attention. Terri thought they could help, so I gave it a whirl.

Subject: Soldier and Dog need your help

I thought that was a good attention grabber. They must get a lot of mail. Mine would surely stand out. I continued.

Stephanie,

At the suggestion of the wonderful folks at Noah's Wish, I am contacting you to see if you can help.

Do you have any members in the Kyrgyzstan area?

My brother has been serving in Afghanistan for the last 6 months and made arrangements to bring a local dog home to the U.S. She was a stray living on the military base. Without his permission the dog was given away at the Bishkek airport by the man entrusted to help bring her home.

My brother and his wife have spent the last 10 days trying to find her but have now run into a dead end.

I am extremely hopeful you can help and provide guidance and assistance in finding her.

My brother and his wife are beside themselves with worry about her welfare. Their first priority is to make sure she is okay, then of course they would love for her to find her way home to them.

Please let me know if you can help. I can provide whatever other details you may need.

I ended the e-mail with the standard,

Please feel free to contact me . . .

And then, one last thing. Before I sent the e-mail, I added to the top,

Could you please forward this message to Stephanie Dawes? I do not have her direct e-mail address.

Since I had only found a general e-mail address on the WSPA Web site, I wasn't all that hopeful that I would get a response. What were the chances? But maybe, just maybe, a lost puppy was an urgent international matter and I would hear back from them in no time.

It was 12:48 P.M., Monday, June 19. Cinnamon had been missing for eleven days. Mark's shattering e-mail had arrived the day before. Not having all that much to do at that time, I found purpose in trying to find Cinnamon. So I checked my e-mail constantly, as if that would make Stephanie get back to me sooner. It didn't, but it helped to pass the time.

Imagine my surprise when, not a day later, I received a reply from Stephanie.

Dear Chris,

Thank you for your email. Yes, we do have a Member society in Kyrgyzstan and they are based in Bishkek. Their contact details are as follows . . .

[Yulia] does speak very good English. I would recommend writing to her to see if she can assist you in any way. I realise that this must be a very distressing situation for your brother, however I do need to let you know that there is no legislation for the protection of stray dogs in Kyrgyzstan and they do not currently have a system for registering and identifying dogs, so it will prove very difficult to track her down.

I am sorry not to be able to be more positive but please do contact Yulia. I am sure she will assist in any way she can.

Please send my regards to Terri at Noah's Wish and please feel free to contact me if there is anything else I can help with. I do hope they are able to track her down.

With best wishes
Stephanie

I was astounded by what I read. Not only did the WSPA have an affiliate organization in Kyrgyzstan, but their office was in Bishkek, the very city where Cinnamon had been abandoned. As an added bonus, the contact person spoke English. I hadn't considered a language barrier before, but thinking about it now, I was encouraged. Maybe our luck was starting to change.

I skimmed over that last part of Stephanie's e-mail, about the difficulty of tracking down animals in Kyrgyzstan. I didn't let it register. I didn't want it to. If I was going to find Cinnamon, I couldn't let anything deter me. I never considered for a minute that what I was doing was in fact a long shot. How in the world did I think that I could find a puppy that had disappeared seven thousand miles away, when several people in the exact same city couldn't find her? I didn't think about it. I couldn't. I just wasn't willing to consider that I couldn't find her.

I didn't know how I would find Cinnamon, but I just knew I had to try. I knew some of the things I did during that time were ridiculous, but it didn't matter to me. All I thought about was that Cinnamon needed me. And whether or not my brother admitted it, he needed me, too.

I was hesitant to tell Mark and Alice what I was up to. They knew on the surface that I was doing something, but they didn't really believe it mattered anymore. Mark and Alice were grieving. It seemed to me that they were moving into the acceptance phase of Cinnamon's disappearance, having skipped over the anger phase. I wasn't sure, and I could have been wrong. I, on the other hand, was furious that an "animal professional" had done what he had. I was going to do something about it. It wasn't going to end this way.

Later that day, I typed the next e-mail to go out. It was to Yulia Ten, the contact given to me by Stephanie at the WSPA. Yulia is the head of the Animal Welfare Society of Kyrgyzstan. I sat down at my computer and wrote to her.

Dear Yulia,

Stephanie Dawes of WSPA gave me your email address and thought you could help.

In a nutshell, my brother is traveling home (U.S.) from Afghanistan after serving in the military there. He befriended a stray dog on base in Kandahar and then made arrangements for a military civilian employee to assist in getting her home. Basically, as a result of some travel problems and without my brother's permission he gave her away at the Bishkek airport. This was completely unnecessary as my brother had given him contingency options in case of any problems. My brother and his wife (Stateside) have spent the better part of the last 2 weeks trying to find her or find any information about her. They have now reached a dead end. They are completely distraught about this turn of events and gravely concerned about her welfare. If at all possible they still want to find her and bring her home. Unfortunately, my brother had to board a flight from Kabul and is landing Stateside today.

I am hoping you can help find her. Please contact me at your very earliest convenience and tell me what more information I can provide for you.

I can fill you in on additional details, but to start with know that they have posted signs, pictures and a reward notice at the airport . . . with no luck.

You may reach me via email or anytime in the U.S.

I am praying and hoping for a miracle.

Most sincerely,
Christine Sullivan

USA

Attached was a simple picture of Cinnamon that was the calling card of my cause. It showed a sad, lonely puppy with forlorn eyes looking up into the camera. Since Yulia worked for an animal-welfare organization, I figured she had a soft heart. I hoped the image would grab her.

I held my breath, hit the SEND button, and off it went into cyber-space. I looked toward the heavens and said a silent prayer.

It was Tuesday, June 20, at 3:27 P.M. Cinnamon had been miss-ing for twelve days.

My time was now consumed with finding Cinnamon, and I checked my e-mail constantly. With each passing hour, I grew frustrated that I hadn't heard back from Yulia. What could be tak-ing so long? Of course, I failed to consider that it was in the middle of the night in Kyrgyzstan. What did I know? I tried to focus on faith instead of doubt.

Next, I thought I would try Terri Crisp's suggestion to contact the media. I had no idea how to do that, so I just let my mind brainstorm. I'm definitely not what you call a news junkie. Or-dinarily, I watch my fair share of cable news and tune in once in a while to the morning network news. With Mark overseas, though, I watched more news than usual. I needed to stay on top of any incidents that occurred near his location.

Inspired by the idea, I started another e-mail.

Subject: PLEASE HELP—Soldier without PUPPY—Broken
Hearted Homecoming

What can I say? I have a knack for the melodramatic. It was completely true, however, and I wanted their attention.

I am writing to desperately request your help.

My brother is a sailor and has been serving on the ground in Afghanistan for the past 6 months. While on base he befriended a
stray dog that made the base home.

When he learned he was coming home he decided to adopt Cinnamon and made arrangements for her to be flown home.

In a nutshell, through a series of very frustrating events, Cinnamon was given away at the Bishkek airport in Kyrgyzstan by the

man entrusted to get her home. Because of a problem with the plane, the airline could not board Cinnamon on her flight. The airline was then told by this man that unless they took her he would have to put her to sleep. A kind airline employee did take her but then gave her to someone else. My brother and his wife (Stateside) have spent the better part of the last 2 weeks trying to find out what happened to her and to get her back, but no one has been able to find her since.

There have been pictures of Cinnamon posted at the airport along with a reward, but all to no avail.

My brother arrived Stateside on Tuesday of this week but instead of bringing a stray puppy to a new home, he came home with a broken heart.

Please, please, please tell me if you can help.

I am hoping that we can celebrate his homecoming with a completely joyful heart and we can do that by getting Cinnamon back.

You may contact me via email or by phone anytime.

Most sincerely,
Christine Sullivan

After I was done typing, I researched the e-mail addresses of all the cable anchors I could think of. I'd send an e-mail to all of them. They each had their own staff, and I figured somebody among them had to be an animal lover. Somebody had to be looking for a different angle to report about the military. This could be it, I fantasized. It would be just the exposure that Cinnamon's story needed and, maybe, our way to find her and bring her home.

Before I finished, I attached the sad picture of Cinnamon that I now included in all my e-mails about her. Then, I added all the e-mail addresses I'd found to the top of my e-mail. Before I sent it off, I needed to get Mark's okay. There had been a few military rules broken along the way in transporting and kenneling Cinnamon, and I didn't want to get anybody in trouble. Plus, if any of the major stations picked up the story, Mark's and Alice's lives would be catapulted into a media frenzy. It was what I hoped for, but perhaps they'd feel differently. I saved the e-mail in my draft folder; then I e-mailed Mark, asking for his consent, and waited for his reply.

To pass the time and to help stay positive, I started using the visualization techniques that I had learned and read about in the piles of success books and magazines I had read over the years. I did my best to never let a moment of doubt enter my mind that Cinnamon would be found. I thought about her constantly. I pictured her being found. I pictured her being reunited with Mark. I pictured her playing in her new backyard, at home in Maryland. I held this image in my mind day and night. I knew she would love her new home. Then there was nothing else I could do, and so I waited.

Yulia Ten founded the Animal Welfare Society of Kyrgyzstan in 2000, after making friends with an American who thought it would be a worthwhile cause. The welfare society's mission is to reduce animal suffering through social education, public awareness, and practical application.

Circumstances for stray animals in Kyrgyzstan are not very good. Yulia did what she could to help animals in need. She had always had cats and dogs in her family. She was constantly busy helping puppies and kittens obtain medical care or finding a permanent home for them. Yulia couldn't remember a time when her family cared for fewer than three at a time. Now she worked to better the lives of animals in Kyrgyzstan.

Naturally, Yulia was drawn to the e-mail the moment she saw the subject line.

URGENT—WSPA REFERRAL—PLEASE HELP—Soldier and
Dog need your help

The message had been delivered to her bulk folder, having been labeled as spam. Just by chance, it had not been automatically deleted.

Yulia was stunned by the e-mail about a dog abandoned in Bishkek. She wanted to help. She sensed the urgency, but while her heart went out to Mark and me, Yulia knew the realities of abandoned dogs in Kyrgyzstan. It was going to be very difficult to find this lost dog. She believed it was a hopeless situation.

Having been involved in animal welfare for many years, Yulia also knew that she should not let her emotions drive her actions. Not sure what to do, she talked with some friends about the e-mail. They were not very supportive or encouraging. They, too, believed the circumstances to be hopeless.

But Yulia realized she did not have a clear understanding of what had happened. She had images in her mind of a puppy having been starved, tortured, or killed. With those images, she felt she had to do something. She just couldn't give up. She was moved that someone from so far away would care so much for one dog. She thought how lucky the dog was. Yulia decided she would find out what happened, even though she believed she'd find out the worst. Yulia sat down to type her response to my e-mail about Cinnamon.

Waiting for e-mails consumed me. They were my primary means of making connections and investigating what had happened. Finally, the one I was waiting for had come. It was Thursday, June 22, 8:24 A.M. Forty hours and fifty-seven minutes after I had sent my e-mail to Yulia.

Dear Christine!

I liked the exclamation point. It gave me hope and a general good feeling.

Sorry for the delay—somehow your message was sent to the bulk.

Imagine! I had been waiting a whole forty-one hours. What could be more important across the world—sleep, maybe?

I don't want to give you any hope, because I do know how miserable is a stray dog's life here for our officials [sic], but I will do everything I can to try to investigate the situation.

I need:

Name of the person, who gave away the dog here in Bishkek.

Where is this person now? Is it possible to get any details of what has happened?

When was it happen [sic]? What was the flight number? What airport?

Have they had any documents for the dog? Any other details you think would be helpful.

Thank you for all your attempts to save this dog.

Sincerely yours,
Yulia

Another stroke of luck. Thankfully Yulia dug through her bulk e-mail. Sometimes I don't check mine for weeks.

Yulia hadn't been hopeful, but she was willing to help. What more could I ask for? And then she was thanking me. *No, Yulia,* I thought, *Thank YOU. You have no idea.*

I couldn't believe it. Maybe things really had started to turn our way. Did I dare tell Mark and Alice? I thought twice about it. Mark had just gotten home. He had been through enough with this awful ordeal and the long, somber journey home. I didn't want to add to his burdens. I didn't want to give Mark and Alice any false hope. I didn't want to tell them anything unless I found Cinnamon. I hadn't done that yet, but I felt I was just a tiny bit closer.

TEN

TWO DAYS AFTER Mark's arrival in the U.S., I phoned him. He was still in Indiana. Although he didn't feel much like talking, he picked up the phone anyway.

"Hello?"

"Hey." He recognized my greeting. "What's going on?"

"Not much." He was tired and couldn't muster much enthusiasm.

"Well, I have something to tell you." I tried to sound casual.

What now? he thought, but only said, "Oh? What?" He tried to sound interested.

"Well, remember I asked you if you wanted me to contact Noah's Wish to see if they could help us find Cinnamon?"

"Yeah." Sure he remembered, but he didn't think there was anything they could do that he couldn't. After all, he had been in Afghanistan, then Kyrgyzstan. Noah's Wish was in California.

I took a deep breath, then continued. "Well, I finally called Terri." I had thought better of telling him. I didn't want to give him false hope, but I thought he had a right to know. "I got a message from her through her assistant. She gave me some direction on trying to find Cinnamon. I just wanted to let you know that I've found an animal-welfare society in Kyrgyzstan, and they've agreed to help."

He heard what I was saying, but it didn't really sink in.

"Isn't that great news?" I tempered my excitement. After all, it could turn out to be nothing.

"I guess so." What else could he say? Mark was afraid of hoping. Too much had happened. He didn't dare allow hope to seep in. Besides, even if these people were willing to help, how were they going to find Cinnamon? She had been given away to an unknown traveler. The people at the airline had no contact information for him. They didn't even know if he lived in Kyrgyzstan or was just passing through. The odds couldn't have been stacked higher against finding Cinnamon.

Mark appreciated my efforts. I was sure that he did. He just didn't think it mattered anymore. He was trying to get on with his life, trying to deal with what had happened to Cinnamon. He wasn't even home yet.

It just so happened that when I got Yulia's e-mail, I was online. I jumped at the chance to get back to her right away. I furiously typed a reply.

Hi Yulia,

I am soooooooooooooooooo glad to hear back from you.

Here is a summary email from my brother (below).

She was not really a stray, as she was given from person to person.

I will get you the missing details asap . . . names, flights, etc. . . . that are not included.

Unfortunately, this whole thing happened because the man entrusted to get her home (Matthew Roberts) proved to be untrustworthy, deceitful and evasive with my brother, which is so infuriating because he is a dog handler (bomb sniffing) for the army.

You will find details below in the copy of the email my brother sent out to us all. He (the guy that was supposed to get her home) is presently on a 20-day military leave.

My brother's name is Mark Feffer and Cinnamon had been in a crate that supposedly had his and his wife's contact info on it. But given how the handler behaved it is uncertain whether or not this is true.

If you'd find it helpful, I would be glad to call you directly . . . just send me your contact info.

Otherwise we can communicate via email . . . or perhaps you have Instant Messenger . . . I use AOL IM.

We are doing our best to find her . . . it just can't be that it would end this way.

Did you get the picture of Cinnamon that I sent?

Thank you so much,
Chris

I attached the e-mail that Mark had sent explaining that he'd reached a dead end in his investigation. It gave many of the details that Yulia had been asking for and also provided background to the story that I felt was important for Yulia to understand.

After I had offered to phone her, it dawned on me that I really had no idea how to do that. She was in Kyrgyzstan. I'd never called that part of the world before. I didn't care, though. She had replied back to me, willing to help. I would do anything to make it as easy on her as possible.

After rereading what I had written and feeling that I'd covered the necessities, I hit SEND. It was Thursday, June 22, at 8:39 A.M. Yulia's e-mail had reached me at 8:24. Could she still be at her computer? Cinnamon had been missing fourteen days.

Sitting there, thinking of what to do next, I was inspired with a notion. I was always getting requests to help and pray for people in need. Surely, I could send my own plea for help. Why not? Perhaps friends and family might be sympathetic to Cinnamon's plight. It certainly couldn't hurt. So I drafted an e-mail to ask for support, well wishes, and prayers for Cinnamon to be found.

I started with a catchy subject line. I hoped few would hit the DELETE button before they'd opened the e-mail.

URGENT—Puppy and Soldier need your help

To my animal lover friends and family,

Please take just a moment to read this story.

We need your help.

My baby brother is a navy man and has served on the ground in Afghanistan for the past 6 months. While there he befriended a stray dog who lived on the base . . . her name is Cinnamon. When my brother found out he was coming home, he made the decision to adopt Cinnamon and made arrangements to have her flown home.

Through a series of very frustrating events, she was given away at the Bishkek airport in Kyrgyzstan and no one has been able to find her since. My brother spent 10 days trying to find her and has now returned home under the shadow of this sad ending.

All I am asking, is that you PLEASE, PLEASE, PLEASE say a prayer for Cinnamon. We do not know if she is safe and being taken care of. We are praying for a miracle that at least she is well taken care of and hopefully can be found and brought to the U.S. to be with her adoptive family.

I sincerely believe that the more people who pray for Cinnamon's return the more likely that we will indeed be blessed by her homecoming.

Please pass this along to as many animal lovers as you know.

There won't be any money in the mail if you do and there won't be a lightning strike if you don't.

It will only take a moment to change the life of this puppy and the family that came to love her.

Blessings and many thanks,
Chris Sullivan

I surprised myself. I really wasn't all that religious, but I truly believed what I had written. I wasn't sure how anyone's prayers could change Cinnamon's and Mark's lives, but I just knew that they would. I believed others thought the same as well.

I attached Cinnamon's picture and sent the e-mail to all my closest animal-loving friends and family members, perhaps seventy or eighty people. Little did I know how many times over that e-mail would be forwarded.

Later that afternoon, one in a long string of amazing events took place as I mounted my search for Cinnamon. I had been taking a break from my online activities—which sounds pointless, however, since my phone and Internet connection shared one line, I often missed incoming calls while on the Internet.

I was sitting at my kitchen table around 2:30 that Thursday afternoon, and since the line was free, a call rang through. I quickly glanced at caller ID and saw "unknown caller." I hesitated, since I almost never pick up an unknown caller, but I answered anyway.

"Hello?"

I noticed a delay and then heard, "Hello? Hello, Chris?"

"Hello? Yes, this is Chris." I found myself shouting, not really sure why. Perhaps because the caller had been.

"Chris, hello. It's Yulia, from Bishkek. From Kyrgyzstan."

"Yulia! Oh my gosh! Hello!" My surprise spilled over into the phone. I didn't know what to say next. How are you? What a surprise! The choices were limited and sounded, well, stupid. I was shocked and giddy, so I didn't say anything. I let her speak.

"Chris, I am calling because I wanted to get more information from you. I need more information in order to help me find the dog."

I was listening and doing my best to hear what she was saying, but at the same time, I was still trying to get my wits about me. I was talking to a woman in Kyrgyzstan, in the former Soviet Union. I was having trouble concentrating. I had led a sheltered life, so I was thrown by the thought. I snapped myself back to reality. Cinnamon's life was in the balance.

"Sure, Yulia. Anything. Just tell me what you need."

"Chris." She elongated my name as she pronounced it. "I need the flight number that the dog was supposed to be on. The flight number for Matthew [Roberts] and for Cinnamon."

"Okay." I raced to find a pen that worked and paper. I scribbled notes, hoping I could read them later.

"And the name of the flight attendant that the guy gave the dog to. And did the dog have a ticket?"

"I don't know. But what else do you need? I can talk to my brother and get you all the information you need." My heart raced. What luck. We were inching closer to Cinnamon.

"And did the dog have her documents?"

She was asking details that I didn't have. "I don't know, but Mark can tell me."

"Also, what is the name of your contact at Manas Air Base? The name of the chief that helped your brother look for her?" And then, more hope: "This guy can't just throw the dog away like that. I'll see what I can do to find out what happened and see if I can find her."

I couldn't contain myself anymore. I bubbled over.

"Yulia, this is so great that we found you, and that you called. I will get you all the information that I can. I'll send you an e-mail as soon as I get the information from Mark."

We spoke for about fifteen or twenty minutes. I didn't want to hang up. Yulia was quite businesslike and friendly. I'm an American; I'm chatty, and I was thrilled that she called. I acted like I had a new friend, but there was work to be done. I finished with Yulia and promised to e-mail as soon as I had her answers.

My next task at hand was a bit sticky. I had to call Mark to get the information that Yulia had asked for. I hadn't wanted to get his hopes up about finding Cinnamon. I was purposely brief when I had told him I was researching international contacts to help find Cinnamon. I hadn't told him much about what I was doing. At the time, he was grieving and didn't have much interest anyway. I hadn't even included Mark or Alice when I sent the e-mail to friends and family asking for their prayers for Cinnamon.

Apparently, my mother mentioned the e-mail to Alice. I imagined their conversation. Mom, "Oh, wasn't it so nice? The e-mail that Christine sent out for Cinnamon?" My mother is very religious, her prayers never-ending. She's always forwarding e-mails blessing you for some occasion, or none at all. You know the kind of e-mails that I mean. The ones that close by saying, "Send this to twenty friends that you want to have blessed in the next five minutes, and you will receive a miracle by tomorrow morning." I have often wondered how many blessings and miracles I have missed out on by hitting the DELETE button instead of the FORWARD button. Maybe I don't really want to know.

"What e-mail?" Alice must have replied. "I didn't get an e-mail like that from Christine."

And later that day, Mom wrote to me,

Oh, Alice said she didn't get the e-mail you sent to everyone, so I told her all about it.

Oh, great, I thought.

"Hope you don't mind."

Well, that was that. I sort of did mind. Mom meant well, and I knew that. But I had intentionally omitted Alice from the e-mail distribution. I hadn't wanted to upset her. Upset her any *more* than she already was, that is.

I had spoken with Alice a day or two before I sent that first "friends and family" e-mail. I am not sure what possessed me, but we had been talking about Cinnamon. One thing led to another. Before I knew it, I found myself saying, "I know we're gonna find her. I have been picturing her in my mind playing in your backyard with you and Mark at her new home, romping."

Silence on the other end of the phone.

I continued, not to be cruel but because I thought I was being inspirational, that I was giving Alice hope. "That's what I have been doing, and that's what you have to do, too. We're gonna find her."

The silence broke, and there was sobbing—no response to what

I had said. Just Alice whimpering on the other end, barely able to speak.

"I have to go," was all she'd said.

I could hear how shaky her voice was. Then, click. The line went dead. She had hung up. Just like that. What had I done?

And so, no, I hadn't sent her the e-mail. She was too fragile. I hadn't realized it before, but I did after that. It hit me how raw her emotions were. I wasn't going to make that mistake again.

Now I had to take the chance of upsetting Mark, but with good reason. We had a contact in Kyrgyzstan who was willing to look for Cinnamon. She was right in Bishkek of all places, the city where Cinnamon had been abandoned. I was elated that she was willing to help but hadn't considered the dead end Mark had already reached. His experience was the reason my well-intentioned efforts had gotten such a lukewarm reception from Mark in the first place.

Now Yulia was asking for details that only Mark could provide, so I had to do it. I had to call him and pick at his wounds.

I dialed his number. "Hey, it's me," I said.

"Hey." He was Stateside, and he was safe. I was thrilled at that, but I had to restrain myself from sounding as excited as I was over finding Yulia to help me. It was hard for Mark to be jovial these days.

"You aren't going to believe who I just hung up the phone with."

He wasn't in the mood for guessing games. "Okay, who?"

"Yulia Ten, the woman from the Animal Welfare Society of Kyrgyzstan. She called me just a couple of minutes ago."

"Really?"

I forged on. "Yeah. I was here when she called, and I actually picked up the phone. I mean the number came in "unknown caller" on the caller ID. I never pick up those calls. What are the chances?" I still couldn't get over the luck.

"Wow." He didn't seem that impressed.

"Anyway, she's asking for details about some stuff that I didn't know. So I needed to ask you."

"Okay, like what?" His voice was flat. I couldn't blame him.

He'd been through hell. I could be lighting the flames again if this didn't go anywhere.

I fired away with Yulia's questions. Mark had most of the answers, and what he didn't know for sure, he said he would find out and get back to me.

We hung up quickly. I wanted to get the information out to Yulia as soon as possible.

I typed another e-mail to her.

Dear Yulia,

I spoke with my brother today (Mark Feffer) and below is most of the additional information that you requested.

Any information that is missing, we will get you asap by putting you in touch with my brother's contact at MANAS Air Base. That is the air force security investigator, Chief Master Sergeant Blake and his interpreter, Maria. Maria will be able to give you additional extensive information. They have the names of the Turkish Airlines employee that initially took Cinnamon and other airport personnel that remember the events as they happened. My brother will email you directly with the contact information for them.

Cinnamon did not have a ticket with the airline or a passport. The handler believed he could board her as his "excess baggage."

She did have a health certificate, rabies vaccination and the okay from the American and Afghan vets and the Kandahar kennels.

She was wearing a blue collar with yellow flowers and tags that read "Cinnamon, U.S. Army, Zhir Zai" (misspelled on the tag, should have been Shir Zai) when she was last with my brother. Mark was told that her crate was labeled with his contact info along with his wife's in the U.S.

We doubt this is true since no one at the airport contacted either of them.

We don't know the flight number that she was supposed to be on, but it was the only Turkish flight from Bishkek to Istanbul departing at 3 A.M. They only fly every other day, so it was either 3 A.M. on the 9th or 10th.

I forgot to ask Mark about contacting the dog handler, Matthew Roberts again, but I will email and ask him to send you his contact info. He was largely unhelpful and evasive after he left Cinnamon behind . . . despite the fact that my brother gave him money for his travels and a phone card to contact them if anything were to happen. He did not contact them at any time . . . so I am not sure he will be that helpful.

Lastly, Terri Crisp at Noah's Wish suggested I contact the American media . . . Fox News or CNN perhaps. I have no idea if they would pick up the story, but I am ready to give it a try unless you think it would hinder your efforts there. Please let me know your thoughts.

Do please let me know what else you need. And again call me at any time . . .

If you need to try to reach my brother his U.S. cell phone number is . . .

And I have your number as. . . . Is this correct?

Most sincerely,
Chris Sullivan

I gave her as much detail as Mark was able to provide. I sent the e-mail. It was Thursday, June 22, at 4:01 P.M. I felt like we were getting somewhere, that we were heading in the right direction. But by no means was Cinnamon any closer to home.

ELEVEN

THE INFORMATION I sent to Yulia was incomplete. Mark gave me as much as he could remember when I had called him, but I needed to provide Yulia with everything she had asked for. I intended to make her job as simple as possible. So I also sent Mark an e-mail.

Mark,

Please send the contact info for Chief Blake and Maria to Yulia directly. cc me so I can stay in the loop.

Also, Yulia has asked for contact info for the dog handler, Matthew Roberts.

How much longer is he in the U.S.? Is he going back to Afghanistan after his leave is up?

I gave Yulia your cell # in case she needs to reach you . . . it comes up "unknown number" on caller ID.

Talk to you later,
Chris

Next, through her assistant, I had to e-mail Terri Crisp to let her know that her suggestion had paid off. I was grateful for her advice and wanted her to know that I'd found a contact that would help. I banged away at the keyboard.

Hi Thea,

Just wanted to update you and let you know the WSPA does have a member group in Kyrgyzstan. I have been in touch with them and they have already begun to re-initiate the search for Cinnamon. The head of the group is right in Bishkek which is rather fortuitous. She is not too hopeful, but she is taking up the cause nonetheless.

Please thank Terri for me and have everyone say their prayers for Cinnamon. I'll let you know how it turns out.

Regards,
Chris Sullivan

These e-mails continued to make me feel like I was doing something productive to find Cinnamon. Whether or not that was true, I wasn't really sure, but it kept my nerves at bay.

Another angle I worked involved my husband, Billy. He had been in the military and is currently in law enforcement. Billy is the kind of guy who can talk to anyone he meets and immediately establish a bond. He is friendly and easygoing. Because of these attributes, Billy has a far-reaching network of friends and professional associates who would do just about anything for him. He reached out to them and asked for their help.

As it turned out, one of his coworkers had taken a leave of absence to work as a contractor in Afghanistan. He agreed to make some contacts to see if he could find out anything new about where Cinnamon was. It was another long shot, but I followed every lead that came my way.

Later that night, Billy forwarded me the results of their investigation to find Cinnamon.

The contact wrote:

Okay, just got an update. Our guys have been working this too. This dog handler was a DOD contractor.

Nothing new there. He continued:

He dropped the dog off here at Manas International because the Kyrgyz wouldn't let him take it on board because the heater element in the animal cargo hold was inop [inoperable]. He couldn't put the dog in the AF [Air Force] kennels here because of AF Reg's [regulations] (not a certified SF [Security Forces] K-9, it can't be boarded with or around SF K-9's). So the guy left it with a lady at the Manas Air Base who in turn gave it to a local national–who is unknown at this time.

So, Cinnamon is in Kyrgyzstan somewhere, we just don't know where. The guys are doing what they can for Mark.

It was exactly the same information that Chief Blake's investigation had yielded. I suspected that they may have gotten this information by speaking to the security guys at Manas. This is what Chief Blake's report would have said. It was nice of these guys to do some checking, but they had hit the same dead end.

While everyone was doing what they could, it still felt like no one was getting anywhere. The roller coaster continued. During the moments between sending e-mails and making phone calls, I started to get a sense of how far-reaching awareness of Cinnamon's plight had become. E-mail replies began to come back from friends who had read my e-mail asking for prayers and encouragement for finding Cinnamon. They had forwarded me messages from their friends who had sent prayers and messages of hope. The messages came from across the country, and they came all day long.

Later that night, I forwarded some of them to Mark.

Just to let you know a lot of people are praying for Cinnamon and her safe return to you.

I did say a prayer for Cinnamon. Best wishes. Kristina

I will keep her in my prayers. Denise

Will keep praying! Count on it. Can't wait for the follow up with a happy reunion, that little face really got me. Janet

I will post this on our intranet and send to everyone I know. With a prayer for Cinnamon, Alissa

It will be an honor to include my prayers for this puppy and his soldier! Paul

Prayers have been sent. . . . It's in God's hands now . . . Warm regards, Billy

Cinnamon will be in my prayers, along with your brother, you can be assured of that. Peggy

She's in my prayers.

Prayers are there, it is being done. Rene

I will be praying for her and your brother. I really hope they'll find her. Sheyda

I was moved by the compassion and support I received from so many people. It sounds like a cliché, but until you experience receiving kind, loving thoughts and prayers of hope and encouragement from perfect strangers, you can never truly understand what it feels like. It was incredibly uplifting—and humbling, to say the least. Words do not do justice to how it made me feel.

I hoped that the sentiments did for Mark and Alice what they had done for me: given me hope. I wasn't quite sure. And with nothing left to do but hope, I went to bed.

TWELVE

AFTER GETTING THE details from me about what happened with Cinnamon, Yulia determined what she'd do next. She called Turkish Airlines and explained who she was and why she was calling. The office manager recognized the situation instantly. By then, most of the employees had heard what happened with the American and the dog. The manager gave Yulia the name of the employee who had been personally involved with Cinnamon at the airport: Anna Soloviova.

Yulia thought about how to approach Anna. Because of Anna's work schedule, it would be difficult to reach her. Yulia would only be able to contact her during check-in of the same Turkish Airlines flight that Cinnamon had been on. It departed Bishkek at 3:00 A.M., four times a week. Yulia would have to call Anna in the middle of the night. She quickly realized this wasn't her typical animal-welfare case.

After two nights of phone calls, Yulia finally reached Anna. Yulia told her what she'd learned about Cinnamon and that she was looking to find the dog that had been abandoned at the airport. Yulia asked Anna more about what had happened.

Anna relayed the incident to Yulia. "The American was boiling with anger when we refused to take the dog on board. He did not have a ticket for the dog. And since she was not so small like a kitten, which could be transported on his knees, she would need a special heated space in the cargo area. It was too late to arrange this specific condition right before the flight."

Yulia could hear the tension in Anna's voice as she continued the story. "He shouted at the personnel and kicked the cage with the dog inside. He shouted he would rather kill the dog than change his own plans. I was afraid he would kill the dog outside the building. He was kicking the cage toward the exit. I rushed to the telephone, thinking I could find someone who will take the dog."

Yulia listened intently.

"It was a stranger at the airport who finally took the dog. I'm not sure I would see him again, but if I do I will contact you and let you know."

Yulia thanked Anna and hung up. She wasn't quite sure she believed everything that Anna had told her. Something wasn't right about the story. Yulia couldn't quite put her finger on what it was. Perhaps Anna wanted the reward that Mark had offered for Cinnamon's return. Surely Anna would have heard about it at the airport. It was a nagging feeling that Yulia had, that Anna was leaving something out.

Yulia thought that perhaps she would have better luck if she met Anna face-to-face. As Yulia continued her investigation, she learned by pure chance that Anna worked a regular schedule at the Turkish Airlines office in the city. Yulia decided she would go there instead of to the airport. She prepared for her meeting with Anna. She dressed professionally, hoping that would make a difference with Anna. Yulia was anxious about approaching Anna. Her clothing and the intense heat that day increased her discomfort.

When she arrived at the Turkish Airlines office in the city, Yulia spotted Anna right away. She was quite young, perhaps in her mid-twenties. In front of her was a pile of tickets that she was working on. Yulia waited, not far from Anna. Another customer sat nearby who shook his legs while he sat, which made Yulia's chair vibrate, along with his. She was already nervous waiting to talk with Anna, and this just added to her anxiety. It was just an hour before the office was to close, and to make things worse, Anna looked angry and worn-out.

Since it was near closing time, Yulia decided to wait outside for Anna. As Anna came out, Yulia approached her, catching her off guard. Yulia explained in more detail about Cinnamon: "The man at the airport was just someone who was hired to take Cinnamon to the U.S. Her real owner did not know the terrible thing that this man did. The real owner is an American who loves her very much and wants her back. Please, you must help me."

Getting Anna to tell what really happened took some persuading. Yulia had to go over the story several times and reassure Anna repeatedly. Ultimately, Anna was quite moved by what Yulia told her. Then, at last, Anna told Yulia the whole story, the real story. She confessed that she knew where Cinnamon was.

Yulia couldn't believe what she was hearing. She was overjoyed at finally getting to the truth. The story was remarkable. Now that she had found out what had really happened to Cinnamon, she couldn't wait to tell us. Yulia went straight home and typed an e-mail to me.

Friday morning began like all the others since Mark had gone to war and Cinnamon had gone missing. I fired up my computer, logged on to the Internet, and checked my e-mail. I scrambled to open the one I saw first. It was from Yulia.

Hi Chris!

Good news—I have found the lady from the Turkish Airlines who was involved in the situation.

My heart raced. I tried to take it all in at once.

Her name is Anna. She said that Matthew did not book the reservation for the dog for this flight in advance. This is why TA [Turkish Airlines] couldn't take the dog aboard (the place for the animal was not prepared). Matthew wanted to take the dog into the salon [terminal] and pay for the ticket, but it is prohibited. Then he said that he had only one solution and that was to kill the dog and he showed that intention absolutely clearly.

We had heard this from Chief Blake's investigation, but it still horrified me. I kept reading.

They were frightened by his behavior and Anna took the dog and later she gave the dog to one of her relatives who is a hunter. I asked to give me contacts of that person but she doesn't want to do that before speaking to him. She said that both her relative and his family love the dog very much and actually thought that Matthew was the owner and they fill [sic] that they've saved the dog from him. We have agreed that I will call her tomorrow night when she will be on duty and I will get more information.

Also, she asked me to ask you if you want to take the dog anyway or, if she feel good [sic], they can have it?

By the way the name of the dog was written on the cage was Chappy, not Cinnamon. But by the description it is your dog and she said that it was the only one accident on the TA that day.

So let me know of your decision.

Sincerely yours,
Yulia

I couldn't believe what I was reading. Yulia had found Cinnamon. This was incredible! Less than a week ago, we thought that Cinnamon was gone for good, that we'd never know where she was or if she was okay. Now not only did we find her, but she was with a family who seemed to be taking good care of her.

My one concern was the single line that read, "she asked me to ask you if you want to take the dog anyway or, if she feel good, they can have it?" I tried not to think about what Yulia was asking. We'd deal with that later.

I had to call Mark to tell him the news.

I dialed his number. It was early, but this time it didn't stop me.

It was early when the phone rang. Mark remembers it well. He was in the States but not home yet. He was in the lobby of the

BOQ [bachelor officers' quarters] in Norfolk. Seeing the number on the caller ID, he answered on the first ring.

"Hello?" he answered.

"We found her!" I blurted the words out, but he wasn't sure he had heard right.

"What? Who found her?"

I could hear his disbelief as my words spilled out quickly, "I just got an e-mail from Yulia. She found the lady at the airport who took Cinnamon. She didn't give Cinnamon to a stranger passing through the airport. She gave her to a relative."

Mark was stunned. It had been less than a week since his own investigation to find Cinnamon had reached a dead end. It had been torture dealing with the news, and now this. While he asked for more details, he knew they didn't matter now. What he really wanted to do was just go tell everybody.

I raced to fill him in on the details, and then hesitated before I delivered the bombshell.

"They asked if you want her back or if it is okay for them to keep her. I sort of figured what you would say, but I told Yulia I would check with you to be sure."

After what he had been through, how could anyone think he'd give up Cinnamon now?

"Of course we want her back," he snapped. His tone was harsher than he meant it to be. I knew that. I wasn't the one asking the question. I was just the messenger.

I wasn't deterred. "Well, that's what I figured, but I just wanted to be sure. I had to ask."

Mark hung up the phone and immediately called Alice. He barely waited for her to say hello. "Christine found Cinnamon."

"What? You have to be kidding. How? Where is she?"

He gave her the details, just as I had given them to him. Alice couldn't believe it, just as Mark couldn't when I had told him. Her mind raced.

"Okay, so what's the plan? When can Yulia go get her? What about the woman at the airport? Are you gonna give them the re- ward? What else did you find out?"

Mark tried to calm her down. He downplayed the whole thing. He had been burned so badly before that he didn't want to be burned again. Cinnamon was with a family that had taken her in when her life had been threatened. Who knew if they'd be willing to give her back to them?

Alice understood Mark's reaction, but she was just so excited. Her prayers for Cinnamon had been answered.

After speaking with Mark, I had to let Yulia know what he decided about Cinnamon. I knew before I had asked what he would want to do, but to be official about it, I asked anyway. I hadn't wanted to give Yulia the impression that I was speaking for him.

I considered the response I would send to Yulia. I didn't want it to seem like Mark was being hasty or selfish or that he didn't appreciate everything Anna's relative had done. He'd had a relationship with this puppy, and so had Alice. I wasn't certain that had come through in my initial e-mail to Yulia. I had to be sure that Yulia understood that now and that she knew how they felt.

> Yulia,
>
> I spoke with Mark and they definitely want Cinnamon returned to them. Mark spent 5 or 6 months on base with her from the time she was a puppy. So it isn't as if he just got her before he left for home. He has taken many pictures of her and sent them home to his wife. So they both have fallen in love with her.

Yulia had asked about a picture to identify Cinnamon with her collar, and so I continued with,

> I will send you a more current picture of Cinnamon and one that shows her collar and tag.
>
> Let me know what you find out from Anna about the family's willingness to return her.
>
> I don't know if it will make a difference but there had been a

reward offered for her return. I am certain my brother would honor that offer.

Kind regards,
Chris

I sent the e-mail and held my breath. We were at the mercy of the family who had Cinnamon. We had no idea if they would give her back. After all, they had asked if they could keep her, and they were the ones who had her. They wouldn't even let Yulia contact them directly. She could only reach them through Anna at the airline. It seemed like another long shot, but my hopes remained high. I couldn't be certain, but I hoped the reward would be just the nudge they would need. And off the e-mail went—another prayer sent into cyberspace.

It was Friday, June 23, 8:22 A.M. Cinnamon had been found after fifteen days, but she was still just beyond our grasp.

I sat back and took a deep breath. I needed a moment to just reflect on all that had happened, and as it sunk in, again, I couldn't believe what had taken place. Mark's investigation had ended unsuccessfully after ten days. It had been just five days since I started looking for Cinnamon myself, and less than a day since I had asked friends and family for their prayers that we would find her. That e-mail had been forwarded over and over, and had potentially gone out to hundreds of people. I was convinced that this support is what led us to find Cinnamon. There was no other way. She had been lost to us for good, and now we had found her. Although I had witnessed the whole thing, it was still hard to believe. Finding Cinnamon was truly a miracle. I was astounded. And I was so happy, I sat down and cried.

THIRTEEN

EVERYONE WAS TRULY amazed that we had found Cinnamon, but the ordeal was far from over. We now faced a new set of issues. Would the man who took her give her back? How would we get her back to base? Who would take care of her when she got there? How were we going to get her home? We needed a few more miracles. I kept believing we'd get them.

After getting my e-mail, Yulia let Anna know that Mark definitely wanted Cinnamon back. Anna agreed to talk with her relative, Katib Ridvanov, to see if he was willing to return Cinnamon. Yulia and Anna arranged to meet on Saturday night, when Anna would be working again. Anna would let Yulia know then what Katib had decided. It would be an uphill battle.

Yulia knew a bit about Katib from what Anna had told her. He, too, was a Turkish Airlines employee who worked in the baggage department. He had been working during "Cinnamon's day," as the airline employees referred to the incident with Cinnamon. Anna was hysterical when she had called him, trying to explain that a passenger was going to kill a dog. Katib responded immediately. He ran to the departure area and took the dog from Roberts, who seemed satisfied with this solution. Katib took the dog home to care for her.

While Yulia negotiated through Anna to get Cinnamon back from Katib, I looked into transportation options. If we could find Cinnamon, surely we could get her home. I brainstormed ideas.

Someone suggested calling the American embassy. They had told me that diplomatic courier flights come and go all over the world at any given time. We just needed to find one flight to get Cinnamon home. We believed if Cinnamon flew with a diplomat, she would not be subjected to the same health, vaccine, and certification requirements that she'd need on a commercial flight.

With this thought, I remembered that my neighbor's son and daughter-in-law worked at an embassy. I tried to remember which one. Was it Yugoslavia? Or Romania? My brain hurt trying to recall the tidbit of information. I thought they were stationed in Washington, D.C., at the time. I talked to my friend Serena, who knew the family.

"Hey, Serena. You know Shirley's kids, who worked for the embassy overseas? Where was it? Romania?" Serena is a good friend. She had been through this whole ordeal with me, meeting Cinnamon through pictures, finding out she'd gone missing, and cheering me on when I contacted Yulia. She had called and e-mailed me, day and night.

"Any word from Yulia?" she would ask me first thing in the morning.

I would always reply with the latest news, if there was any.

She answered, "Yeah, sure. It's her son Kevin who worked at an embassy. I think it was Romania. But they're back now. I think they're in D.C."

"Oh, well, they're diplomats, right? Do you think they could find out if someone could get Cinnamon on a diplomatic-courier flight home?" At this point, with what we were trying to accomplish, I wasn't afraid to ask anyone for anything.

"Oh, I don't think so. I don't really think they are diplomats. I think they just worked at the embassy."

I wanted her to ask anyway, but I didn't press it. I'd try to find out more about diplomatic-courier flights and then pursue it later if I had to.

In the meantime, Yulia went to the airport on Saturday night to meet with Anna, as they had planned. Yulia was frustrated. She wanted to talk with Katib directly, but he would not allow it. He would not allow Anna to give Yulia his contact information. He didn't want to speak with her directly. He was afraid. Afraid for the dog. After the way the traveler had treated her and threatened to kill her, he wasn't going to speak with the lady who came looking for Cinnamon.

Besides, having saved the dog from the unspeakable cruelty that the American threatened, Katib believed the dog was his. He took her without hesitation and cared for her as his own.

Yulia arrived at the airport around 2:00 A.M.—the same time as the flight Cinnamon was supposed to be on began checking in, when Anna was scheduled to work again. But when Yulia got there, Anna was not there. She didn't know why. All Yulia could do was come back again in two nights, when Anna would be there next. Disappointed and a bit angry, she left for home.

Several days had come and gone. I had expected to hear from Yulia before that much time had passed. She was supposed to go see Anna on Saturday. It was Monday night, and there was still no word. I was frustrated and more than a little worried. Suppose the man who took Cinnamon wouldn't give her back? It was a possibility, but I tried not to think like that. We had come so far. We just had to get Cinnamon back.

I went to sleep that night with images of Cinnamon in my head. Just as I was drifting off to sleep, the phone rang. I stumbled out of bed. The phone in our room was unplugged so it didn't wake my husband, who worked nights when he slept during the day. Instead of fumbling in the dark to plug it back in, I charged down the stairs. In my haze, I wasn't fast enough. By the time I grabbed the phone, the call had gone to voice mail. I looked at the caller ID: "unknown caller." I quickly dialed my voice-mail number to see if the caller left a message. It was Yulia. I couldn't believe I had missed the call. I was annoyed with myself but listened for the message.

"Hello, Chris? Chris, it's Yulia. I just came from the airport. I wanted to tell you about my meeting with Anna."

As I listened to the message, I chided myself for being so careless and leaving the phone unplugged.

With an onset of urgency, I raced down another flight of stairs and turned on the computer. With any luck, I might catch Yulia. I remembered that she had e-mailed me her phone number. After we spoke the previous week, I had gotten an international calling card with good rates to Kyrgyzstan. I was ready to use it.

I dialed the access number, then the PIN, then her phone number. Never having called this part of the world before, I couldn't be sure I had the right sequence of numbers. What was the country code? Did they have area codes? Which part was her phone number? It was very confusing. To make matters worse, the line was busy. I tried again.

Each time I called, I had to dial thirty-six numbers. Over and over I tried. If the line was busy, someone must be there. It was only 8:00 A.M. in Bishkek. I kept trying. Still, I had no luck.

Finally, I gave up. I thought I'd e-mail her instead. Chances were, she might still be sitting at her computer and would get my e-mail right away.

> Yulia,
>
> I just missed your call . . . I didn't get to the phone fast enough.
>
> If you get this message this morning please try and call me again.
>
> I tried calling you at the office but the line was busy.

I didn't know it at the time, but Yulia was certainly not online at her computer. She didn't have Internet access at home. She had to go to an Internet café to get online, and she didn't even have an office.

It was Monday night, June 26. Cinnamon had been gone eighteen days.

After my failed attempt Monday night to reach Yulia, I woke up on Tuesday with a new sense of purpose. I tried calling Yulia again. I tried what I thought was her office number. Still busy. I tried her home number. That was busy, too. Each time I dialed,

I pressed thirty-six numbers. Something wasn't right. I knew I was calling a developing country, but still, it couldn't be that hard to make an international call. People did it all the time.

In the old days of the Bell Telephone system, you could just dial 0 and ask for an international operator. I wanted to do that now but didn't know if an operator was still available anymore. I couldn't remember the last time I dialed 0 for an operator. I decided to try anyway.

"Hello, operator?"

"Yes?"

"Operator, I am trying to make an international call, and I'm not having much luck."

I wasn't hopeful but forged ahead.

"I don't want you to dial the call for me, but I'm not sure that I have the country code correct for where I am trying to call. Can you check it for me?"

"What city and country are you trying to call?"

Would she be familiar with Bishkek, Kyrgyzstan? A few weeks before, I didn't even know the place existed.

"Bishkek, Kyrgyzstan." I gave her the codes and the number I was trying to dial. She paused, but just for a moment.

"To dial that city, you must dial 011-996-312, then the line number. You had an extra number in there, which is why your call wouldn't go through," she explained.

I was thrilled. There was a chance I could reach Yulia after all.

It was about 5:00 A.M., my time. That made it about 7:00 P.M. in Bishkek. I could give Yulia another try.

So I grabbed the phone and pressed the thirty-five numbers required to call Bishkek. I didn't get a busy signal this time. The line was ringing on the other end.

"Hello?" was the answer I got.

"Hello, Yulia?"

"Yes," she replied.

"Yulia, it's Chris from the United States," just in case she knew another Chris that spoke English.

"Oh, Chris, hi. Yes, I tried calling you last night." I was surprised how clearly her voice came across the line.

"Yes, I know. I got your message. I didn't get to the phone

fast enough." I made my apologies, then asked, "Tell me. Do you have some news?" I held my breath. I couldn't imagine she would have called halfway around the world if she didn't have some new information for me.

"Yes, yes, I do. I went to the airport again last night, and finally Anna was there."

I listened intently, not wanting to miss anything she might say.

"You see, it was very difficult. When I went to the airport on Saturday night, when Anna and I agreed to meet, she was not there. She had said she would be, and then she wasn't. I thought that was bad, that maybe she wouldn't speak with me."

Okay. I knew this couldn't be the only reason Yulia had called.

"Oh, so what happened then?" I asked, letting her continue.

"So I had to wait two days to go back, because, as you know, that flight that Anna works on is only scheduled for every other day. But she was there this time. I told her that your brother would like to have the dog back, that he is her rightful owner, and that her relative has really no right to keep her."

I was relieved to hear that she had conveyed this message. I felt it was important to get this across.

She continued, "I wanted to talk with him, but still, they are very protective of the dog. After what Matthew [Roberts] had done, they are very worried for her. Her relative would not agree for me to contact him directly."

This, on the other hand, worried me. Anna didn't seem as if she was on our side, and her relative was being extremely evasive. I wondered if Yulia could get through to them. I had to admit, though, that Yulia had made amazing progress in a short time, much more than we had, or perhaps could have, without her. She had gotten the real story. At least we knew that Cinnamon was safe.

Yulia had also found out that the reason Chief Blake had been told that Cinnamon was given to a stranger at the airport was because Anna and Katib had thought that Roberts had sent him, and then Yulia, to look for Cinnamon. They feared for Cinnamon and did not want to return her to the awful man who had threatened to kill her. For that, we were all grateful.

I was anxious to hear what her plan was.

"So Anna is going to talk to her relative again and let him know that your brother wants the dog back. Chris, I have to tell you how touched I am that your brother cares so much for this dog."

It was in that moment, hearing the compassion and gratitude in what Yulia had said, that I realized something very important: that regardless of what country someone is from or what language they speak, people are just people. Up until that point, Yulia and I had conducted mostly businesslike communications. But what she had just said dissolved the façade of rigidity that had been between us. I was unexpectedly warmed that this stranger had taken up my cause so selflessly.

Yulia continued, "I'm sure I don't have to tell you that it is not like that here in Kyrgyzstan. There is a much different mind-set when it comes to animals here. It is a very difficult situation."

I had an idea what she meant. I was sure I didn't want to know more.

Yulia promised to call when she heard from Anna again. I hoped for the best. We had come this far and found Cinnamon. Now we just had to get her back.

The news that Yulia had given me wasn't exactly what I was hoping for, but it was news, nonetheless. It was too early in the morning to start calling anyone, so I typed a couple of e-mails. The first was to Mark. He had e-mailed me already that morning.

Have you heard from Yulia at all? I'm concerned that we haven't heard anything.—M

Had he felt the vibes from Yulia's meeting with Anna?
I typed my reply:

I just got off the phone with Yulia but didn't want to call you this early.

It was not yet 6:00 A.M.

Call me when you get this message.

I knew it would be a while before I heard from him.

The next e-mail I typed was to my friend, Serena, who continued to keep up on our progress to get Cinnamon home. I was considering options again.

Hey, Yulia called me last night at 10:30 . . . I talked to her this morning. It's sort of good news but it's gonna take some doing. Want to fly to Bishkek and bring Cinnamon home?

I love an adventure.

FOURTEEN

CONTINUING MY MISSION, I typed another e-mail to my network of friends and family. I needed some support and encouragement. I was worried about Anna's relative not giving Cinnamon back. Since prayer seemed to have helped us before, maybe it would again.

> Subject: URGENT—Puppy and Soldier update
>
> Hello All,
>
> Cinnamon has been found! But once again I am asking for your prayers for her.
>
> Here is the update . . .
>
> Through the awesome power of prayer and the grace of God, the Animal Welfare Society in Kyrgyzstan was able to locate Cinnamon. It turns out she is with a family who thought she had been surrendered by her owner at the airport.

I purposely left out the horrid details of how the dog handler behaved and the horrible threats he made toward Cinnamon. The e-mail continued,

> This, of course, is not true. My brother was traveling separate from Cinnamon. But, of course, we are grateful that this family stepped in to take care of her.

I then stated that we now hoped and prayed that the family who had Cinnamon would willingly surrender her back to us and that we would find a way to get her home into the United States. I finished with:

I am not sure what will happen or what the answers are, but I'd just like to ask for you once again to **please say a prayer for Cinnamon to somehow find her way home to my brother and his wife.** While I know there are bigger issues than this with soldiers, their families and the war we are fighting, I believe we create and spread joy and love by effecting what little change we can in our own backyards.

I thank you for your thoughts and prayers, and so do my brother and his wife (and Cinnamon, too!)

With puppy love,
Chris

It sounded corny, but that didn't concern me. I felt certain that the first e-mail I sent asking for prayers was a key factor in our finding Cinnamon. So many people were pulling for her. Her situation wasn't as urgent as before, but we needed the help of prayer again, and I wasn't afraid to ask for it. In some ways, I guess I needed the support as well, and so I sent it off.

It was Tuesday morning, June 27. Cinnamon had been gone nineteen days.

Next, I researched ways to get Cinnamon home through contacts who might be sympathetic to our predicament. My mind created all kinds of options and ideas to investigate. I looked into each and every one. I looked up information about the American embassy in Kyrgyzstan, animal-transport companies, and media contacts. I had no idea what I might accomplish, but that didn't stop me. I found two different Web addresses for the American embassy, and I sent them to Mark, thinking we might still find a diplomat willing to help. It was my understanding that diplomats are immune to the restrictions placed on traveling civilians. We'd also heard that diplomatic-courier flights made regular trips in and out of the region. It was a long shot, but if we could find someone willing to transport Cinnamon, the rest would be easy, or so I thought.

Throughout the morning, I also called all my animal-loving friends, who I thought could help. I told them what we were facing and that I hoped for an angel benefactor who either had a private plane that we could use or who might underwrite the cost of transportation for Cinnamon, which could run as high as four thousand dollars. I knew there were people out there who had the money and would be willing to help. I just needed to get a lucky break and find the right connection.

During a break in phone calls, I found an awesome surprise in my inbox. Terri Crisp from Noah's Wish had e-mailed me in response to the "URGENT—Puppy and Soldier update" e-mail I had sent that morning.

Hi Chris:

This is wonderful news! Do you know what the exact price would be to use an animal transporter? Let me know and I will see what we can do.

Wow! I thought Terri might have the answer to my prayers. It didn't hurt to hope, did it? We'd already received one miracle when we found Cinnamon. Were we entitled to two?

Other e-mails had also come in, forwarded to me from friends who received my e-mail that morning.

Why don't you contact Anderson Cooper's e-mail at CNN? Journalists are traveling to and fro all the time. Perhaps one will travel most of the way with Cinnamon! Leave no stone unturned approach, you know!

Chris—If it turns out that he or someone else needs to fly there, please put out an email to that effect. Maybe some of your fellow

rescuers [from Louisiana] will help make that happen. I know I'll
do what I can.

We didn't even know these people. Yet they were sending suggestions and offers to help. It made me feel that what I was trying to do wasn't crazy, as I sometimes felt. It motivated me even
more.

I remembered that a friend of mine knew Oprah's personal
chef. Maybe somehow he could put me in touch with her, so I
could ask for her help. I picked up the phone and dialed my friend's
number.

"Hey, Tony, it's Chris." I'd known Tony for more than fifteen
years. He understood my impulsive and adventurous nature. I
launched into the story.

"You've been following the story of Cinnamon through the
e-mails that I have been sending out, haven't you?" I hoped he
hadn't been deleting them.

"Yeah, I sure have. What's up?"

He sounded enthusiastic, so I pressed on with more details, and
then, "You saw that we found her, right?" He said he had. "Well,
we are at the point where we need to find a way to get Cinnamon
home."

"Okay, go on." He gave me the opening I'd been waiting for.

I took a deep breath. "Well, remember you had said you met
Oprah's personal chef and you knew him pretty well? I was wondering if you knew him well enough to see if he would be willing to approach Oprah to see if she could help." I wasn't holding
back. "I know she's an animal lover, and, well, she has a private
plane and all. Maybe she'd let us use it." Then I shut up. I couldn't
believe I had actually said it, but I had.

"Well, Chris, you know, I'd love to help you, but he's kind of
protective about giving people access to her. It would put him in
a tough spot if he did this kind of thing."

I understood—really I did. That doesn't mean I wasn't
disappointed. I figured Oprah's plane was probably sitting idle in
Chicago, not doing a thing. We'd just needed to borrow it for two
or three days. I was certain she'd help, if only she knew Cinnamon's
story.

I thanked Tony and hung up. At least I had tried. I wasn't giving up that easily, though. Somebody, somewhere would help us get Cinnamon home. It was just a matter of finding him or her.

Through it all, there loomed the stark reality that we still didn't have Cinnamon back. Her future was yet to be decided by the family in Bishkek who was taking care of her that very minute. We all assumed from the start, however, that they'd return her to Mark. We had to. We couldn't let ourselves think any other way. It was critical to keeping us motivated and working toward getting her home.

Although I'm not a big fan of transporting animals on commercial flights, I researched animal-transport companies. Over the years, I had heard my share of horror stories about animals running loose on an airport tarmac or being lost or injured in transit. That was why I had been so enthusiastic about finding someone with a private plane. In a private plane, Cinnamon wouldn't be subjected to flying in a crate in a cargo hold. She'd get first-class service. Unfortunately, we hadn't yet found someone with a plane willing to let us use it.

Pet-transport companies advertise all over the Internet. Many claim to be able to ship your pet almost anywhere in the world and to have experience and excellent records of safety. I assumed they had their own planes and would provide door-to-door service. My assumption proved wrong.

What I found was that the pet-transport companies I'd considered merely offered a service that made the animal's travel arrangements for you. Essentially, they are animal travel agents. The animal would ultimately be on the very same flights it would be on if you made the arrangements yourself. It seemed a high premium to pay when we could make the arrangements ourselves. I wasn't getting the warm fuzzies. In fact, the back of my neck tingled in warning. No, I wasn't going to recommend this as an option unless we absolutely had no other way.

I typed a few more e-mails, looking for options and sending updates to Mark, Yulia, Serena, and Terri. Then, I took a break. I had been at the computer for six hours. It was only 11:00 A.M.

Major Blake Settle poses with Cinnamon shortly after she arrived at Shir Zai. *Courtesy Dave Simpson*

With no real bed, Cinnamon curled up on anything that was softer than the bare ground. *Courtesy Dave Simpson*

Cinnamon being offered fresh bottled water.
Courtesy Craig Lane

Because she had no single guardian, Cinnamon craved the attention of almost anyone who would play with her.
Courtesy Craig Lane

Not generally welcomed in the barracks, Cinnamon was sometimes allowed in for a nap. *Courtesy Paul Barkley Hughes*

Master Sergeant Rowan Panganiban poses with Cinnamon. *Courtesy Dave Schlosser*

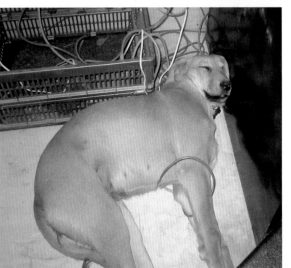

Shortly after Mark met Cinnamon. This the first image that h sent of her to Alice.
Courtesy Mark Feffer

To find relief from the heat outdoors, Cinnamon sleeps under an office desk
Courtesy Paul Barkley Hughes

Captain Craig Lane receives a nuzzle from Cinnamon. *Courtesy Craig Lane*

Just outside the door of Mark's office, Cinnamon sits in one of her favorite spots. *Courtesy Mark Feffer*

Cinnamon was never picky about her choice of where to lie down. Most spots were softer than the gravel-covered ground on base. *Courtesy Mark Feffer*

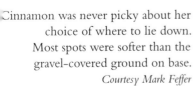

Cinnamon takes a break from begging food from the soldiers at a weekly barbecue to investigate the camera.
Courtesy Mark Feffer

A telltale sign of a puppy ready to play, Cinnamon gives a puppy bow.
Courtesy Mark Feffer

Likely teething when this photograph was taken, and frequently left to entertain herself, Cinnamon finds a way to ward off discomfort and boredom.
Courtesy Mark Feffer

Cinnamon escaped the cold of the Afghan winter by curling up in front of the heater in Mark's office.
Courtesy Mark Feffer

As a soldier cleans his M-60 machine gun after a mission, Cinnamon looks on and seems oblivious to the war going on around her.
Courtesy Mark Feffer

Cinnamon shares the spotlight with Mark after her entr into the middle of team meeting.
Courtesy Mark Feffer

As if a sign from above, a rainbow over Camp Shir Zai greets soldiers returning from a mission and a brush with death.
Courtesy Dave Schlosser

Team Juliet 6 and Cinnamon out-side Camp Shir Zai. Since they are outside the gate, Commander Don Plows holds on to Cinnamon to ensure she doesn't run off. (Some faces hidden for security purposes.)
Courtesy Mark Feffer

After lunch, I took up my station back at the computer. I queried for my e-mail. When it came in, something odd caught my eye. The subject line,

Our dog!!! Kirgyizistan [sic], Bishkek!

Who? What?, I thought. My heart picked up pace with the familiar rhythm of anticipation and anxiety all at once. I read at Mach speed.

Hello, madam!

My name's Katib! I'm that man who took your beautiful dog. Just several days ago we have known that the man who has left the dog in Bishkek was not his owner.

It's pity story because he really wanted to kill the dog when a line's stuff [airline employee] refused to accept the dog to the plane [sic].

I had heard it several times before, but I still felt shock and rage at what Roberts threatened to do to Cinnamon and how he had treated her.

I say you that your friend wanted to kill your dog and at the end he left her! As only I heard about that I decided to save that poor dog and took at hom [sic].

We had heard this from Yulia, and it was comforting to know that Cinnamon was being taken care of.

Now she lives with me at my home and all members of my big family love her. I want to say that I love her very much and I spend time at nature with her. I think your dog has good conditions at my home!

p.s. I send to you photo of your dog. She is very happy with me and she is at my heart. And please send me your answer or your opportunity.

Hmmm. Something didn't seem right. Just what was Katib trying to tell us? I opened the pictures, and then I understood. The pictures showed Cinnamon surrounded by Katib's three young children. They were smiling and hugging her. Their bright eyes were sparkling.

It was plain as day—Katib wanted to keep her. Why wouldn't he? He had saved Cinnamon's life and took her into his own home and cared for her. He was showing us the picture of Cinnamon with his kids. They looked so happy. It was easy to see.

I was very unsettled. I wrestled with giving Katib the benefit of the doubt, but his wish to keep Cinnamon seemed pretty clear. My anger kicked in over how unfair the turn of events had been to Mark. Then the all-too-familiar knot in my stomach tightened.

I tried to keep my cool. I had panicked when I read Katib's e-mail and saw the picture he'd sent. I couldn't afford to lose my perspective. I had to talk to Mark. He was a stabilizing force and would know what to do.

While we still didn't know if Katib would return Cinnamon, Mark thought it would be a good idea to contact Chief Blake. He wanted to give him the news and to see if he could help.

Chief,

Great News!!! We found Cinnamon!!!

My sister contacted an international pet rescue organization who has an affiliate organization in Bishkek. They made contact with Anna (the Turkish Airlines employee), who stated that she didn't give Cinnamon to a "stranger," but rather, she gave her to her cousin. We've made contact with the cousin, and though he and his family have grown attached to her, we have asked them to consider giving her back.

Can you make some inquiries into how I might get her home to Baltimore? I have some buddies who will be flying through Manas. If you could SOMEHOW get her onto one of their flights, that would be great. We will of course be paying the fees for the pet transport company, but if we could get permission to have her fly on a military flight, that would obviously be a help. I don't expect that will be allowed, but I'm thinking it's worth asking.

The pet rescue contact is also making some local inquiries about pet transport for us.

Please get back to me as soon as possible. I don't know when these guys are coming through Manas. I also want to get back to the folks who have Cinnamon quickly to see what they have decided.

Thanks for everything.
Mark Feffer

Chief Blake was happy to hear that Cinnamon had been found. After everything that Mark had been through with this dog, he was glad for him. He, too, had animals at home and knew what they meant to a family. In fact, at Christmastime, just before he deployed, he had gotten two puppies, Sprinkles and Tinkerbelle, one for each of his daughters. Sprinkles, the littlest one, had been sick and was hospitalized for days. He and his family worried day and night about her, not sure if she would pull through. So he knew a bit about what Mark was going through. For Chief Blake, there was no decision to be made. He would do whatever he could to help Mark get Cinnamon back and get her home.

The first thing Chief Blake needed to do was to brief his superiors on base about the most recent development with Cinnamon. He told them the real story of what had happened with Roberts at the airport. Major Mark Anarumo was the commander at Manas

Air Base and Chief Blake's boss. He'd just come from the day's briefing. He'd been frustrated by the news that Chief Blake delivered the previous week, that the civilian dog that had shown up on base was not out of the country, as he had thought. Now, he was shocked when he heard what happened at the airport: how a DOD dog handler had threatened to kill the dog and that the airline employee had taken pity on her and agreed to take her in.

Chief Blake also told him that the navy officer who adopted the dog was trying to get her back. The situation put Major Anarumo in a tough spot. Technically, the dog was not his problem. After the initial security case of her being on base was closed, he could have washed his hands of her, but he felt bad for the officer.

Anarumo had been stationed on bases in foreign countries enough times to know that there was always something that fell outside the rule books. Surviving on a base such as this required thinking outside the box. Major Anarumo had been trained by the air force to do just that. He'd trained his men to do the same, to be risk takers when required. He trusted his men to handle these situations and act appropriately. Besides, what were the odds that this dog was found after everything that had happened?

So he didn't have to do it, but Major Anarumo wanted to help make things right for Cinnamon and for Mark. He gave Chief Blake the latitude he needed to help Mark out. He told Chief Blake, "Yeah, go ahead. Do what you have to do. Help the guy out. Do whatever you need to help get Cinnamon out of Kyrgyzstan and back home to Mark in the U.S." Then he continued, "But remember, this isn't your mission. Make sure you get everything else done that you have to get done"—which is exactly what the chief and his partner, Sergeant Kamrad, did.

Like Mark and I, Chief Blake operated under the assumption that Katib would return Cinnamon. He began to pursue getting Cinnamon's health certificate and the paperwork required for her to travel. The chief appreciated having the assistance of the commander's interpreter, Maria, and learned what a huge advantage her help was.

To wade through the complicated process of securing what was needed, Maria made contact with her friend, Natalie, who was a local veterinarian. Natalie was part of a local canine project that trained local dogs and handlers. The handlers from Manas helped out with the project. Natalie told Chief Blake and Maria that, while Cinnamon previously had all the necessary paperwork to fly out of Afghanistan, it was useless in Kyrgyzstan.

Natalie went on to explain that Cinnamon needed Kyrgyz paperwork in Russian, the local language, and it needed to be secured from the appropriate Kyrgyz government offices, where they would have to pay a fee for each document. The chief would not have known any of this without Maria and Natalie. He would likely have tried to use the same documentation that Mark had provided Roberts, which would have resulted in Cinnamon's being turned down for her flight home. Chief Blake was grateful for their help and for this important piece of information.

The e-mail I'd received from Katib upset me more than I admitted to anyone. It was hard to consider that, after we had located Cinnamon, Katib might not agree to give her back. I knew that he had saved her and was caring for her, but Cinnamon already had a home. Katib had to understand that Cinnamon belonged to Mark. She wasn't just a stray dumped off somewhere. She had a loving family waiting for her, and they wanted her back.

I tried to stay rational about Katib's e-mail, but then I suffered another emotional setback. It hit me hard. I felt I couldn't get a break. In the replies I got from the request for prayers I had sent out earlier that day, there were a few that stood out from the rest. Mixed in with the suggestions about how to get Cinnamon home and how to raise money to pay for Cinnamon's flight were e-mails like this one:

. . . if Cinnamon is living in a loving home, why not just let him [sic] stay where he's at and avoid the stress of a 12+ hour flight. If this Sailor has room in his home and heart for a dog, why not adopt locally? He can save two lives—Cinnamon's and one

other—by letting Cinnamon stay where he is and adopting
another "Cinnamon."

I tried not to let the messages upset me. I knew these people
were just trying to help, but I was hurt and confused. How could
they suggest such a thing? They didn't know Cinnamon or the
close bond that she and Mark share. They hadn't seen the images
of poverty in Kyrgyzstan that had caused Alice pause. And Cinnamon's life would not be what Mark intended, complete with a
nice cushy bed to sleep on and lots of fun toys to play with. She
wouldn't be pampered and doted on with lots of yummy treats
just for being adorable. While the family that had taken Cinnamon seemed to have good intentions, life for a puppy would
be difficult in Kyrgyzstan. Pets in Kyrgyzstan were lucky to get
a meal once a week. They were lucky to live from one day to
the next.

Leaving Cinnamon there was not an option. We had to do
everything we could to get her back, to get her to the U.S. She
belonged with Mark and Alice. I focused on the other more positive e-mails. I had to.

Figuring out how to reply to Katib was tricky. It seemed he had
been asking if he could keep Cinnamon, so I had to impress upon
him that, indeed, Mark and Alice wanted her back. She was not
really his to keep, but Katib had rescued her; he had possession
of her. Thinking Roberts had sent Yulia looking for Cinnamon,
Katib had been cautious with her in the beginning. I understood
why, but if he decided to keep her now, there would be little we'd
be able to do. It would be over.

I took the liberty of responding on Mark's behalf. I knew full well
that he wanted Cinnamon back. So after some careful thought and
more than a little apprehension, I took a deep breath and typed.

Hello kind sir,

We are so very grateful that you took this beautiful pup into your
home and cared for her. When we heard what the man at the

airport did with her, we were shocked and devastated. We had no idea he would act so cruelly toward her and the people at the airport. Our first concern was that Cinnamon was okay and being well taken care of and we were so relieved to finally find out that she was okay. Thank you for opening your home to her.

I have forwarded your email and pictures to my brother . . . he is her owner. He raised her from a puppy for over 6 months and so is very attached to her and wanting to have her home.

I believe that he or I will email you very shortly with his decision about what to do. We understand from your relative Anna that you would be willing to return her to us if that is what we'd like to do. It is a very hard thing to deal with so I am hopeful that you understand.

Again thank you for your understanding and kindness in this very difficult situation.

My heart pounded in my chest. I said a prayer and hit the SEND button.

I'd finally calmed down when I talked to Mark about Katib's e-mail. Mark and Alice had not been surprised by it. Katib had been kind enough to take Cinnamon in. Why shouldn't he want to keep her? But, at the same time, they wanted her home. For Mark, it was not an option to leave Cinnamon in Bishkek. He knew the conditions there. It was not what he wanted for Cinnamon.

Initially, however, Alice had considered leaving Cinnamon with Katib and his family. She had worried about Cinnamon every day since she disappeared. When she'd heard that Cinnamon was safe with a local family, she was elated. Alice had prayed for Cinnamon and for guidance about what to do when she found out Katib had her. *Dear God, if it's meant to be that Cinnamon stay with this family, then so be it. I just want to know that she is safe and okay—that she's not starving or lying dead somewhere on the airport tarmac.*

Afterward, she had thanked God that her prayers for Cinnamon's safety were answered. When Alice saw Cinnamon's picture, however, she felt differently. "Oh, there's my girl," she said out loud when she opened the picture. She had grown to love her so much and felt such a strong bond with Cinnamon.

And while others who looked at the picture of Cinnamon with Katib's family saw a happy family scene, Alice saw something different. Cinnamon's collar was gone. She'd had it on when Mark loaded her into her crate. It was blue with yellow flowers on it. Now around her neck was a thin clothesline of no more than a few feet long. Was this how she spent her days? Was she tied up in the yard on a short piece of string all day? It didn't seem safe, especially since it looked like she now had no ID tags. What if she got loose and wandered off?

Mark and Alice wanted Cinnamon home. They wanted to give this vivacious little puppy the life they felt she deserved after the rough start that she'd had. They knew such a life would be difficult for her to have if she lived in Bishkek.

Mark had also reassured me that I'd said the right things to Katib. I hoped he was right. I didn't know what I would do if my response to him tipped the scale against us. I was sick with worry but tried not to dwell on it. There was still more to do.

In the interim, Mark had been working on his own options for Cinnamon's travel. He knew a multitude of guys who were serving in Afghanistan and whose deployments were coming to an end. Perhaps somebody was coming through Kyrgyzstan who could travel with Cinnamon. A lot depended on if he could get authorization for her to fly on a military charter or whether a serviceman could fly on a commercial flight. He inquired of everyone he could think of.

After talking with Mark, I was inspired with another idea. Why hadn't I thought about it before? Perhaps Terri Crisp's original idea to contact the media wasn't a bad one, but we could use a different angle. This war was a different war than those in the past. There were reporters embedded with troops everywhere. Perhaps there was a journalist going over to Afghanistan or one coming home. Surely somebody was an animal lover and could bring Cinnamon home with them. What a story that would make.

I typed an e-mail to Mark.

Hey,

Do the military guys over there have any embedded reporters?

Perhaps there is a journalist that is coming this way that would be willing to bring her. Worth a try . . . throw the spaghetti and see what sticks.

I felt brilliant. I was sure that to my brother, the skeptic, I appeared ridiculous. I didn't care.

Thinking it would be easier to get the attention of my local news station than that of a national cable show, I looked up the e-mail address for the local CBS affiliate. Maybe someone there could help.

Dear Judy,

I watch you on the morning news and have seen your morning pet segments . . . so I know you have an interest in our furry little friends.

I gave her the details, and then forged on.

. . . is it possible that CBS has any journalists or crews in Kyrgyzstan that might be coming to the U.S. this week? Would you be able and willing to find out and perhaps someone could bring her home . . . or perhaps advise me how to go about presenting this to them and putting me in touch with the right people.

Thanks in advance for whatever you could do.

It was a long shot, but so what? My feelings were summed up in one line in an e-mail of options I'd sent to Mark.

Call me crazy, but I was hesitant to contact Noah's Wish in the beginning and look where it got us!

On Wednesday morning, I opened an e-mail that had come in from Stephanie Dawes, from the WSPA. She was excited that we had found Cinnamon and wished us luck with getting her home. I took her continued interest as an opportunity and e-mailed her.

We are looking at pet transport companies. Any suggestions on who to use?

Any other creative ideas would be most welcome.

We are also looking into seeing if there are any journalists traveling from that area that would be willing to bring her back. Do you have any connections?

I was shameless and I knew it, but I was on a mission to get Cinnamon home. All I needed was one person to take notice, one person to care that this puppy needed a ride home. Okay, so it was a seven-thousand-mile ride, but just one champion would be all it would take. If we could find someone already in the Middle East willing to bring Cinnamon back, it would spare one of us from having to make the fourteen-thousand-mile round-trip ourselves. So I asked anyone and everyone who I thought could help. We had found her when we thought we never would. How hard could it be to get her home?

Then I heard from another Good Samaritan. She'd responded to the e-mail update I'd sent asking for more prayers for Cinnamon.

Yay! I'm so happy to hear she has been found safely! Sadly though, unless you can get Cinnamon to London or Amsterdam next week, I won't be too much help in getting her back to the States :-(

Let me know if there's anything else I can do,
Emily

I'd met Emily in Louisiana, when we both had volunteered for Noah's Wish. She was a second-year veterinary student who provided medical assistance to the animals at the shelter, and she was one of the most hilarious people I'd met. We stayed up many nights laughing ourselves silly while she should have been studying and I should have been sleeping. Emily had been vacationing in Amsterdam. If we could get Cinnamon to her, perhaps she could bring her home.

I knew she'd agree to help if she could. I let Yulia and Mark know that I'd found a helpful traveler, but Yulia promptly reminded me,

We can't fly her through Europe. There is a 6 month quarantine requirement.

Of course, how could I have forgotten? Cinnamon would not only be quarantined if she traveled that route but she would also be required to have a rabies-antibody test done when she arrived. European countries do not accept a test done in Kyrgyzstan. If she failed the test, they'd either send her back—or worse, they'd euthanize her. No, Emily wouldn't be bringing Cinnamon home from Amsterdam.

I hadn't heard back from Katib yet. It wasn't even a full day since I had e-mailed him, yet I was on edge. But thinking more about it, I felt this was good. It gave me the chance to send him another e-mail. I had to let him know that, yes, Mark definitely wanted Cinnamon back. I knew that all along, but I hadn't stated that clearly in my first e-mail to him. I was being cautious with Katib. I didn't want to rock the boat. I was never a skilled negotiator, and unfortunately now was the time I needed razor-sharp skills. I wasn't all that confident. I began to type anyhow.

As I typed, I remembered what I had felt when I first began

working with Yulia. People are just people. They are really no different than we are. So I just typed from my heart.

> Hello Katib,
>
> We understand how well you and your family have been taking care of Cinnamon and that you have grown to love her. But as my brother raised her from a puppy for so long he is looking forward to being reunited with her. I know it will be difficult for you to see her go, but know that she is going to have a wonderful life with my brother and his family.
>
> We are working right now on her travel arrangements. Your relative Anna knows of my contact Yulia Ten who is helping us. Yulia will be contacting you via email to make arrangements and a time to pick Cinnamon up from you. We would like to do this very soon.
>
> Please understand we know this is difficult for everyone. My brother would like to help you and your family find another puppy for your own, if you would like for this to happen. Please let us know if you would like to do this.
>
> With much thanks.

This was a difficult situation for everyone. This was the man who saved Cinnamon, and it was obvious that he and his family cared for her, but so did Mark and Alice. We tried to offer a solution that would work for everyone, that would make everyone happy. We felt what we offered would do that, so we waited for his reply.

It was Wednesday, June 28, twenty days since Cinnamon was gone.

Wednesday morning in Kyrgyzstan Chief Blake had a lot to do. The e-mail he'd gotten from Mark that Cinnamon was found set him in motion. Having briefed the leadership on base with the latest on Cinnamon, he was relieved at their response.

Everyone felt bad for Cinnamon and Mark, including Chief Blake. Mark had done the best he could to get Cinnamon home. He'd done everything right, but he'd been deceived. He'd been lied to by the dog handler, a man whose work servicemen's lives often depended on. It just wasn't right. In fact, Chief Blake was infuriated by it. He was thankful when his boss gave him the latitude he needed to help Mark with Cinnamon. Blake knew that Mark had gotten lucky this time.

I sent Chief Blake an e-mail giving him the status of getting Cinnamon from Katib and asking him to help Yulia with arrangements. They needed to pick Cinnamon up and figure out who would care for her until she boarded her flight home. All the while, her transportation was still undetermined.

The chief filled us in.

Hello all,

It is great news that Cinnamon has been found. I have talked with our K-9 guy today, and he will help arrange for the vet check and papers (we have a local vet that we use; she is very good and very reasonable). . . . I do need to know if they still have the crate for Cinnamon. My interpreter is on vacation until Monday, so I will work the base issues this week and have her help make contact with Yulia when she is back on Mon.

I am sure there will be more questions once I start talking with folks here. I will talk with the ATOC [Air Terminal Operations Center] folks and see what I can arrange. I will need to know dates as soon as Mark finds out when his friends are coming through Manas, and if it is a charter or rotator. I will also check with the pet shipping companies, maybe Yulia can recommend one that is reliable. I will work both ways of returning her and see which will work the best.

Mike Blake

———

The situation with Cinnamon was not like any other animal-welfare case that Yulia had handled. She felt pulled in so many directions. The more she learned about the situation, the more difficult it became.

She knew that Katib had no right to keep Cinnamon. Mark was, in fact, her rightful owner, but there are no real ownership laws in Kyrgyzstan governing animals and animal rights. The few laws that do exist are not enforced very well.

Yulia felt torn by the situation. While she wanted to help Mark get Cinnamon back, her first concern was for Cinnamon. She thought that perhaps Cinnamon had found her new home with Katib and his family and that it might be better for Cinnamon to stay with him. Yulia had been involved several times in transporting animals to the U.S. and knew how stressful the travel could be. She'd witnessed a case where two cats that had flown to the U.S. were deceased when they arrived. The airline that flew them took no responsibility for their deaths. In two other cases, animals were lost during the very same flight from Bishkek to Chicago that Cinnamon was originally supposed to be on. Fortunately, they were eventually found, but it was a very long and stressful flight for them to endure. Yulia didn't think it would be good for Cinnamon to go through anything like that.

But Yulia also had compassion for Mark. She knew that Cinnamon belonged to him, and she was impressed by his love and devotion for her. It was something that she rarely saw in Kyrgyzstan. I later found out that she was also taken with my patience and persistence and my love for my brother. Yes, Yulia was in a predicament, but her priority was Cinnamon's welfare. Ultimately, she felt that she must find the best solution for Cinnamon.

Yulia thought long and hard about what to do.

As hard as I tried, securing Cinnamon's transportation was worse than challenging. I just couldn't make any headway. I thought

I was being creative, but nothing I researched yielded any con-crete way to get Cinnamon home. To make matters worse, Mark hadn't replied when I sent him information about the embassy, about trying to contact journalists, or even about Terri's offer to help with transportation. I was discouraged. I did my best to let it roll off my shoulders.

I hadn't heard from Katib or from Chief Blake either. What was going on? It made me feel like I wasn't needed anymore. I guessed maybe my job was done. What I failed to remember was the ten-hour time difference between Vermont and Kyrgyzstan and that everyone was simultaneously working on their own solutions for Cinnamon's transportation.

On the heels of this frustration, I was dealt a worse blow. On Thursday morning, I opened my e-mail and found a message from Yulia. I read with horror.

> Hi Chris,
>
> I have read your letters and as I understood, Cinnamon is in good hands.
>
> Forgive me for what I will say, but I am always on the animals' side.
>
> I do understand that your brother loves Cinnamon very much, but sometimes it is an act of love to leave a situation like it is.
>
> It will be very stressful for the dog to be moved from the family first to the kennel where she will be kept for some time then to the air-plane and please remember that any flight she will take won't be a direct flight—one or two stops on the way when Cinnamon will be moved to another airplane. It is a lot of stress not to mention the flight itself.

I couldn't be reading right. My head spun. What was Yulia sug-gesting?

> Please think about this situation and give my telephone number to . . . your friend at the kennels . . . and if you decide to check

how Cinnamon lives in this family and if you'll decide to take her to be return to your brother.

Blessings, Yulia

My heart dropped. My stomach churned. This was not good news. Yulia was actually suggesting we leave Cinnamon in Kyrgyzstan with Katib. She was our ally from the start and had agreed to help us, but was now turning against what we were trying to do. I felt that Yulia was trying to deter us from bringing Cinnamon home.

If Yulia was not in our corner, the entire effort to convince Katib to give us Cinnamon back could be derailed. What would we do then? There would be little else we could do. I reread her e-mail.

As hard as it was to admit, what Yulia was saying made sense. The trip would be difficult on Cinnamon, with all the moving around, being uprooted again, and the long flight home. I couldn't fault Yulia. She was just looking out for Cinnamon.

It was still a hard reality to face, that perhaps it did make sense to leave Cinnamon with Katib. The only comfort was knowing that she was in a decent home with a family that said they loved her.

I had to talk to Mark.

Yulia's e-mail had hit us hard. I was shocked, and Mark was angry. We believed that once Yulia had found Cinnamon, it was just a matter of reasoning with Katib. We thought that he would understand that Cinnamon was not just a stray, that she had a family who loved her and wanted her with them. We felt that the odds had finally been in our favor. The e-mails we had gotten from Katib and Yulia, however, changed that. They put us in a new state of panic. Getting her back was still no sure thing. It could go either way.

This also made the time waiting to hear back from Katib seem like an eternity. I couldn't wait anymore. I had to do something.

I thought carefully about what I would say to Yulia before I typed a reply to her e-mail. The words finally came.

Hi Yulia,

Yes, I do understand how you feel. We know that it will be a difficult time traveling for Cinnamon and arranging the travel issues. My brother feels it is best for her to be returned to him and since he is really her owner it is up to him to decide. They have considered leaving her there. Please do not think that they have not looked at this option. But he knows her very well, and loves her enough to have been working to find her through extremely trying circumstances and now to try and find a way to get her home. I am sure he would not do this if he felt that it would harm her.

Have you made contact with Katib? I am a little bit concerned that I have not heard from him. I emailed him as you had seen but he did not reply. I will send him your phone number today.

I also sent Chief Blake your phone number, but I don't think he has access to making local calls every day. Perhaps you have already emailed him.

It may be possible that Cinnamon will travel on a military flight, in which case most of the issues you mention will go away. We realize the travel issues with bringing her through Europe so we will not be considering that as an option. I will let you know as soon as we find out how we will get her home. Of course we won't be able to make final arrangements until you and the Chief pick her up and we know the soonest date she can travel.

Please let me know when you have spoken with Katib.

Most grateful,
Chris

I sent it off, not knowing when she would be on e-mail next. I couldn't take the chance that her thoughts about Cinnamon's staying with Katib would solidify. So I decided to try to reach her by phone.

I picked up the phone and began dialing the long sequence of numbers that would connect me to this faraway land. Thirty-five digits later, the call rang through. The line opened on the other end to a voice speaking a language other than my own.

I spoke into my end of the line, "Hello? Yulia please. It's Chris." And then, as an afterthought, I added, "From the United States."

I had no idea if I had dialed the right number or if the woman on the other end understood what I said. I hoped for the best. The line went silent momentarily. I could hear my own breathing.

"Hello, Chris?"

"Hi, Yulia. How are you?" I always felt compelled to begin with the pleasantries. I was conditioned for it, but in light of Yulia's last e-mail, it now felt silly.

"Yulia, I got your e-mail."

"Chris, yes, I am sorry. Please understand that this is very difficult, but we have to think of the dog."

I knew her heart was in the right place. I had to find the words to help her understand that we were thinking of Cinnamon as well.

"Yulia, please do not be sorry. I completely understand." It was hard, but I really did understand. I continued. "We are so grateful about your concern for Cinnamon. We want you to know that, of course, we have considered leaving Cinnamon where she is. We realize that another change in homes and the long trip to the U.S. will be difficult for her. But Mark knows her very well, and he would certainly not put her through all this if he felt it would harm her in any way."

"Yes, I do understand," Yulia replied. "And, Chris, I want you to know that I think it is so wonderful how much your brother loves this dog. It is not like that here in Kyrgyzstan. There is a much different view on animals than you have there in the United States."

Yulia confirmed what we believed about animals in Kyrgyzstan: that they have low status as domestic pets and are not nearly as well regarded in the family as they are in the U.S. Wanting to make Cinnamon part of their family and give her a loving home were two of the main reasons that Mark and Alice decided to adopt Cinnamon in the first place.

I held my breath. Yulia's continued cooperation was critical to getting Cinnamon back from Katib and to the U.S.

Yulia then offered, "I will talk with Anna again and have her relay to Katib what you have told me. I'll let you know when I hear back from them."

The time difference between the U.S. and Kyrgyzstan made communications slow and difficult. There was always a wait between e-mails and phone calls. Also, Anna worked at odd hours and only every other day. It made Yulia's job of talking with her slow as well. At this point, there was nothing else I could do. I had to continue to believe that she would help us. I had to continue to believe that Cinnamon would make her way home.

It was Thursday morning, June 29, at 6:29 A.M. Cinnamon had been gone for twenty-one days.

FIFTEEN

FINDING CINNAMON A ride to the U.S. continued to be a difficult task. The never-ending obstacles were painful reminders. Chief Blake looked into every option he could think of.

One of the first he'd considered was to get Cinnamon on a military flight home. There were plenty of guys coming through that were heading to the U.S. He knew it would be a long shot. Cinnamon shouldn't have been on the military flight from Kandahar to Bishkek in the first place. It was against regulations to transport personal items on the C5 and C17 airplanes that the military used to airlift personnel and equipment. But he knew that there was a procedure to get a waiver. He considered the option.

The further he looked into it, though, the less he thought it would happen. The waiver had to be approved by a general. Even if he could get one to agree, it could take months. It wasn't a great plan for Cinnamon. There had to be another way.

The daily challenge continued for me as I did what I could to grease the wheels and keep things moving. We operated under the assumption that we would succeed in getting Cinnamon home. There was a multitude of details to take care of. I did whatever I could to be helpful to Yulia and Chief Blake. They were really in the driver's seat. It would ultimately be up to them to get Cinnamon home.

I forwarded Cinnamon's health and rabies certificates to Yulia. Mark originally had them done when she was supposed to be coming home the first time. We thought it would help Yulia secure the new documentation she would require when Cinnamon finally flew home. At the time, we didn't know what Natalie, the local veterinarian helping Maria, had told Chief Blake about Cinnamon needing official Kyrgyz documentation.

I wasn't sure she had them, so I also gave Yulia Katib's and Chief Blake's e-mail addresses. They would all eventually have to be in touch with one another to get Cinnamon back to Manas. In my mind, the sooner the better.

At the end of my e-mail to Yulia, I wrote,

> I will let you know if I hear anything further from Katib. So far I have only gotten his first email. So far, he has not replied since I emailed him back yesterday. Please let me know if you make contact with him.

I was desperate to hear something from someone.

Yulia felt bad about the e-mail she had written to me, but she knew she had to think of Cinnamon's welfare and what was best for the dog. Also, negotiating with Katib to surrender Cinnamon was taking its toll on Yulia. She felt like a psychologist trying to guess what he was thinking, and she felt inept at the job.

Yulia knew that Katib lived a simple life. He worked for Turkish Airlines and earned a modest income. To supplement his earnings and support his family, Katib worked his land. Things were often very tight, and when Cinnamon arrived, they got tighter. Yulia remembered that Mark had originally offered a reward for Cinnamon's return. Perhaps, she thought, he would honor that and Katib could collect the money in exchange for Cinnamon's return. It was an arrangement that would benefit everyone.

Yulia made a mental note to ask me about it.

Later that night, as I usually did throughout the day, I headed to my computer to check for any news. Instead of the typical spam e-mails or the disappointment of not hearing from anyone, I found a familiar subject line that made my heart skip.

Re: RE: Our dog!!! Kirgyizistan [sic] Bishkek!

A reply from Katib. I hesitated just a moment before I opened the e-mail. I wanted to read what he said, but I didn't.

Hello madam!

Did his exclamation point mean good news? My heart pounded in my chest.

Yes I understand you and I want to help your brother. I'm hunter and I have one dog for hunting.

Infect (sic) I like animals and really loved your dog but I want to say you (sic) that it's hard to have two dogs.

I was overcome with emotion and cried with happiness.

My children also loved it but I think in my condition it will be better to return it to you. I will try to explain it to my kids. They are so happy they play every day that is why I can understand how much you also can loved that dog!

Your sincerely Katib!

Sweet relief. The tears continued to stream down my face.

I called Mark immediately after I got Katib's e-mail. I had to let him know I'd heard from Katib and that he was ready to give Cinnamon back. I was elated. I thought Mark would be too. But Mark is a realist, and that overshadowed any joy he may have felt. Mark was relieved but reminded me that we still had a lot to do in order to get her home. We also agreed that we'd be much happier once she got safely back to Manas with Chief Blake. Cinnamon wasn't home free yet. I was celebrating before the prize was in our hands. Mark set my feet firmly back on the ground.

I couldn't blame Mark for his reaction. He had been burned so badly trying to get Cinnamon home in the first place, and we were still a long way from success.

When Yulia and I finally spoke about what had happened to convince Katib to return Cinnamon to Mark, I couldn't believe my ears. It seemed fate had intervened on our behalf.

"Well, you know, Katib is a farmer"—Yulia filled me in on what she had learned—"and apparently Cinnamon killed some of his chickens. Three I think."

"Oh my gosh," was all I could say.

"This is a problem," Yulia went on, "because, as you know, Kyrgyzstan is not a wealthy country. People raise their own food here. Cinnamon probably learned how to do this while she was fending for herself in Afghanistan. But it is not a very good thing for her to take food away from his family like that."

I was stunned. We were lucky that Katib hadn't killed Cinnamon on the spot. It gave us another glimpse of the heart he had for Cinnamon. I was also a little amused. Cinnamon had been up to her antics again, just being a puppy. She probably had just been playing or trying to fill her empty belly.

The issue of getting Cinnamon back on base and to the U.S. became ever more pressing. Chief Blake got word that he was scheduled to rotate out of Manas and head back to the U.S. himself. It made us all very uneasy. Who would coordinate the details of Cinnamon's return and transportation if the chief left before it was done? We had conquered so many obstacles up to that point, but it seemed there was always another one in the way. What other complications would arise? Granted, we had made headway trying to reunite Cinnamon with her American dream, but it would have been nice to have clear sailing for a change. Apparently that was not to be. We couldn't afford to let our guard down. No, there was still a lot to be done and little time to do it.

Chief Blake found out that there were several animal-transport companies that operated in the region. Servicemen who adopted dogs from the area used them to transport their dogs home. Unfortunately for Cinnamon, he also discovered that they did not fly from Kyrgyzstan. The option was another dead end.

Now that Katib had agreed to give Cinnamon back to Mark, we had to make arrangements to get her back to Chief Blake at the base. While Mark and I wanted to help coordinate the details, it was really up to the chief and Yulia. I gave each of them the other's contact information and asked them to connect.

Hello Chief Blake,

Chris Sullivan here . . . Mark's sister.

Yulia Ten at the Kyrgyz Welfare Society is the woman who found Cinnamon for us. She is very happy to have your help and involvement in working the logistics to get Cinnamon back to the U.S.

While everyone is trying to figure out the transportation issues, the next step is to pick up Cinnamon from the family that has her. Yulia will be making the arrangements but will require your help on a few levels.

Perhaps going with her to get Cinnamon (not certain about this), but most certainly to take and care for Cinnamon until she can be flown out.

I think it's best if you and she make direct contact to handle the details.

I have also given Yulia your email address. Yulia does not have an Internet connection at home so sometimes it takes her a while to respond to email. For that reason and because I don't have a phone number for you, would you make the first call to her? I think this would be the quickest way for you two to make contact.

Several days had passed when I found out that they hadn't connected. I missed the part in the chief's previous e-mail saying his interpreter was unavailable until Monday. Apparently, I had forgotten to let Chief Blake know that Yulia spoke English. As a result, the waiting made me more than a bit antsy. It was nearly impossible for me to step back and let Chief Blake and Yulia make this happen. I prodded Chief Blake just a bit.

Mike,

We were awaiting the final word that the family with Cinnamon would indeed surrender her. I did get an email from them this morning, much to our relief, that they are ready and willing to do this.

I spoke with Yulia earlier today (Friday) to let her know. She is happy to help with the arrangements. She is looking forward to having your help in physically moving Cinnamon around. . . . whether this includes the initial surrender from her current caretakers or not, I am not certain. I know for sure she really could use your help with getting her to the airport when her final travel arrangements are in place.

She indicated there were some issues around paying for "transportation." I am not really sure what she meant. I am certain once you make contact it will all be much clearer. Of course, Mark will be covering any expenses involved. And I am hoping that whatever she needs will not be any trouble for you to accommodate.

In an earlier email, I gave you contact numbers for her. The only number that is valid to reach her is her home # which is 312. . . . You may reach her there almost anytime. Please ignore the other number I gave you. Also, she must go to an

Internet cafe for email access, so that is not a very quick way to
get her.

Thanks for all your help. Let me know if there is anything you
need from me.

Best regards,
Chris

In the meantime, Yulia was still feeling some resistance from
Anna and Katib in getting Cinnamon back to the base. While
Katib's e-mail indicated he believed giving Cinnamon back was
best for everyone, Yulia reported that he seemed reluctant to actually put a plan together to get Cinnamon to Manas—another issue that made me nervous. Until Cinnamon was with Chief Blake,
there was no guarantee we'd get her back. We couldn't count on
anything.

I spoke with Yulia Friday morning, and she asked me to contact
Katib on her behalf. She said that he was troubled about something and thought, perhaps, he needed reassurance that he could
trust her. It was frustrating that he'd agreed to surrender Cinnamon but was still holding back like this. We couldn't be positive
what the issue was, and I wasn't certain that my encouragement
would help. I typed another e-mail to Katib.

Hello again,

I thought I would write again to explain about Yulia Ten being
involved and helping us with Cinnamon. She has been very
helpful in talking with your relative Anna and finding where Cinnamon is when we thought we would never again know where
she was or what happened to her. You can very much trust her
in taking very good care of Cinnamon and helping us get Cinnamon safely back to the U.S. So that is why I wanted to put you
in touch with her and why I gave her your email address. I hope
you didn't mind that.

Please know that she is very happy to work with you and will be very kind to everyone involved. So then when you and she can talk on the phone or by email you together will make arrangements for her to take Cinnamon.

Please tell us how and when this can happen. Is it best for you to bring Cinnamon to her or would you prefer that she come and pick Cinnamon up? Whatever is best for Cinnamon and for you we will most definitely work to accomplish. And Yulia's number is 312. . . . The number I gave you in my last email was not the correct number.

I look forward to hearing from you again about what arrangements will be made.

And I hope that you enjoy your day.

Very sincerely,
Chris

It was Friday morning, June 30, twenty-two days into Cinnamon's detour on her way to the U.S.

While Mark, Chief Blake, Yulia, and I were working to get Cinnamon back to the base and home to Maryland, Alice was busy with another mission. A week before Mark came home, she decided it would be fun to throw him a welcome-home party. Mark kept her updated with all that was going on with Cinnamon, but her days consisted of compiling a guest list, sending invitations, finding a caterer, making centerpieces, and overseeing all that went along with party planning. Mark had served his country and deserved to celebrate being home with his friends and family with festive merrymaking in his honor. Unfortunately, Alice left herself little more than a few weeks to pull together what seemed like planning a wedding. She was frazzled. She was consumed. She had time for little else.

Mark was grateful for all her efforts. He looked forward to the party, hoping it would be a chance for him to reconnect with loved ones. It could also help him relax and unwind, which he'd been having trouble doing since he returned. The aftereffects of his deployment were noticeable, and Cinnamon was still not out of the woods. And while he thought the party would be fun, it would be a bittersweet homecoming celebration without Cinnamon.

I found it difficult checking into flights to and from Kyrgyzstan. The flights don't leave every day, so one must know which days to ask for, which I didn't. It was time consuming not only to find a flight with a price but also to compare itineraries.

Nonetheless, I finally came up with some benchmarks. I sent them to Mark in an e-mail.

Just for kicks and grins I checked ticket prices. . . .

Bishkek to JFK round trip is $1258

JFK to Bishkek round trip is $2561

Not including Cinnamon's ticket.

No word from anyone today on my end.

Happy 4th!

I tried to sound jovial. Mark's replies in his e-mails at that time were brief and unanimated. I wanted to cheer him up. I knew he was having a hard time dealing with Cinnamon's ordeal and the aftermath of his deployment, but I also realized it was likely worse than I could imagine. Still, I had to try.

Chief Blake continued to work on Cinnamon's transportation arrangements, assuming she would be returned. He, too, had yet to succeed in nailing anything down, though. He never seemed to question, however, that he'd find a way to get her home. But until she was on U.S. soil, he knew that anything could happen, and he was concerned that his departure from Manas had been moved up. If we didn't get Cinnamon out of Bishkek soon, it was likely he'd be gone before Cinnamon could fly out. My anxiety was also building. Someone else was in the driver's seat, and I didn't like it. It was hard to admit, but my part in getting Cinnamon home was done. I had to let the rest of the details go to someone else. I just hoped and prayed that the chief was up to the task.

In the meantime, Yulia had made another suggestion. She offered to fly to the U.S. to bring Cinnamon home. She had made the trip before with another dog. We were stunned at her generosity. Of course, Mark would pay her airfare, but it still was quite a commitment of time and effort on her part. She'd also have to get a visa, which required a waiting period of several weeks. That meant that Cinnamon would remain in Kyrgyzstan for that time. Since the chief's deployment was coming to an end, the questions came quickly. Who would take care of Cinnamon after the chief left? Would anyone be willing to take responsibility for her as Chief Blake had? She still needed her exam and health certificate updated, and she wasn't on base yet. Even with all the added questions, Yulia's flying Cinnamon home was definitely an option worth considering.

By Wednesday, July 5, my nerves were shot. Neither Mark nor I had heard anything from Chief Blake, Yulia, or Katib for seven days.

Mark apparently felt the same way I did. I got an e-mail from him early that morning.

Subject: Any word from the chief?

Any news? Now I am getting antsy not having heard anything.

He had also e-mailed the chief.

Chief,

The latest I've heard from my sister who is in contact with Yulia is that she requested your help in arranging transportation for Cinnamon to the base. I'm not sure what the issue is. Have you been able to make contact with Yulia? I'm guessing you haven't gotten permission for Cinnamon to fly on the rotator . . . ?

My latest and probably best plan is for Yulia to accompany Cinnamon on a commercial flight from Bishkek to the States. She has done this in the past, and has agreed to do it for us. If you could help her with the transportation arrangements and all the required paperwork that would be a big help. She speaks English. You should have her number.

. . . I will do what I can from this end.

Thanks,
Mark Feffer, LCDR, USN

Then, I nudged Yulia.

Hi Yulia,

Just wondering if you heard from Katib or the Chief today?

Or maybe you were able to talk to Anna.

My brother is very appreciative of your offer to fly Cinnamon home. That is a possibility. I guess we have to get her from Katib first.

If you talk to Katib or Anna, can you see if they still have her crate?

Regards for the day,
Chris

Finally, by midday, Mark heard from the chief.

Sir,

I talked with Yulia and am coordinating to get Cinnamon to the base. I now have help from OSI [Office of Special Investigations] (they can go off base without all the red tape) who is going to pick up Cinnamon and return her to base. I will be calling Yulia in the morning (my time) and would like to make this happen on Thur.

I need to know a couple of things, is Katib expecting any reward before we can pick Cinnamon up? Are any of the individuals you know that will be coming through going on a contract plane? The regular rotator we will not be able to use, however with a contract plane we might be able to work something. If I remember right, when you left you had talked with the charter company and they didn't have a problem with it. If that is accurate, I might be able to work that angle. I am also checking with an animal transport service, there are a couple that state they cover Asia.

I have a vet set up for the Health certificate, so once a date is confirmed (it is only good for 10 days) I will arrange to have that done.

Yulia told me that the 26th is the soonest she could get out with Cinnamon, so depending on how you want to work this, we can use that as our first or last resort, just let me know. When I have the info on the charter and transport company we will talk and you can decide which you feel is the best way to go.

I will let you know as soon as we have Cinnamon on base.

Take care,
Mike Blake

Despite the fact that things seemed to be moving forward, they weren't moving fast enough for Mark or me. We were anxious.

At every turn, things had threatened to go wrong. We were constantly on edge, thinking that fate could turn against us again at any moment. I was concerned that Katib seemed reluctant to communicate directly with Yulia. My conversations with Yulia had given me an idea why.

Back to the keyboard I went.

Hello Sir,

Good day. And I understand that arrangements are being made to have Yulia receive Cinnamon from you. We are so thankful for all you have done. I hope this is not too forward, and to say thank you we would like to cover the expenses that you have incurred in taking such good care of Cinnamon. How would we go about getting these finances to you? I really don't know how to send funds to Kyrgyzstan. But for certain we will be glad to cover these costs for you. And also if you would receive it there is a reward that was offered for her safe return and you would of course be in receipt of this.

So please know that we are happy to say thank you in this way. It would be most helpful if you could kindly call Yulia today. Her number is . . . She is having help in getting Cinnamon and they are able to do this on this very Thursday. She can also tell me how to send you the reimbursement for Cinnamon. So do please phone her.

Thank you for your help,

Sincerely,

Christine Sullivan

I had hoped that Katib didn't think I was being too forward. I worried about it, though, thinking that he might because of cultural differences. Although he had sent e-mails to me, he seemed to ignore the issues or questions I raised in them, writing as if he hadn't received my e-mails at all. It was frustrating and time-consuming. I needed to be sure Katib knew that Mark was more than willing to reimburse him for the cost of caring for Cinnamon and to give him the reward money. We hoped our efforts were enough.

Days had passed. It was Wednesday, July 5, twenty-seven days since Cinnamon should have been in the U.S.

On Thursday, Mark and Chief Blake continued their attempts to find a way to get Cinnamon home. Mark knew some of the guys from Kandahar that would be coming through Manas. They knew Cinnamon and had heard what had happened to her. Mark was sure they would want to help bring her home. He e-mailed several of his contacts.

> Do any of you guys know if your flight to the States is a contract flight? Mine was a contracted flight operated by OMNI Air. When I spoke to them, they said they would be happy to let you take a dog. They do it all the time.
>
> If you are on a contract flight, we might be able to get Cinnamon home on that flight with you.
>
> Please let me know.
> Thanks.

With all the details being addressed and options being considered, it was very confusing. The questions kept coming. Was anyone coming through that would take her home? There were plenty of personnel traveling through Manas, since it was a stopover base, but were they flying home on a military flight or on a contract flight?

Could she fly on a charter flight? The charter companies said yes, as long as the military agreed. A charter flight was not technically a military flight, but it was subject to military regulations. No one with the military wanted the responsibility of saying yes.

Could they find someone to take her on a commercial flight?

If so, it would have to be a civilian contractor, since military personnel couldn't change their flight itinerary to fly home on a commercial flight. Could we trust another contractor to get the job done after what Roberts had put everyone through?

How much money was Katib expecting to cover his expenses? No one knew this yet, since Katib had not replied to my last e-mail yet. Also, we didn't know how Mark would get the money to him.

Who was actually bringing Cinnamon to the base? Yulia or Katib? Or was the chief going to get her? Yulia was hoping that the chief would go get Cinnamon. She didn't have her own car, so that would be easier for her. The chief, though, was hoping that Yulia would bring Cinnamon to the base, since going off the base presented more obstacles for him. Because it was unofficial business, he couldn't use a military vehicle. Whose vehicle could he use? Would it be big enough to fit Cinnamon and the crate inside? The thought of coordinating all the details made my head spin and my stomach ache.

Midday we got an update from Chief Blake.

Hello all,

If Katib can bring Cinnamon to the airport that would be great, if not I have arrangements to pick her up.

I tried to call Yulia today and could not get through; don't know if it was my phone or hers, but if I don't hear from her by lunch Fri. I will try to call again.

I also have everything set up with the kennels, the commander is aware and has no problem and the K-9 guys are more than willing to help, so this will not be a problem.

Just let me know how much you want to give [to Katib] (it is 40 som to $1 approx) I will need to cash a check so I have it on hand

Mike

While we still couldn't relax, it appeared that Chief Blake was on top of things.

Another day went by. The wait felt interminable. Cinnamon's fate seemed to be in Katib's hands. Finally, in the middle of the night on Friday, July 7, I received an e-mail from Yulia. I opened it that morning.

Dear Chris!

It was like a detective story. I've tried to reach Anna at 2 A.M. at the airport and the man that started to ask me why do I need her was Katib himself. And we talked finally. He said that he would like to get 150$ (sic) as a compensation of his expenditures. And he is ready to deliver Cinnamon right to the gates of base. I will call Michael and we'll try to arrange this. I have Katib's phone number and can contact him any time. Please contact Michael too to arrange the financial part. I am so glad that we are moving at last.

Hope that we are very close to a happy end.

Best wishes, Yulia

Whew! Our fears that Katib was being evasive seemed to be fitting. Before he identified himself to Yulia, he asked all sorts of questions, posturing as if he were protecting Anna or had something to hide. Yulia wasn't sure what to make of it but was relieved when she finally learned his identity. We also knew in our hearts that if it weren't for Katib, Cinnamon's fate would likely have turned out much differently. Fortunately, he came through and agreed to help Yulia get Cinnamon back to the base. We were close to our goal but not there just yet.

Chief Blake continued to chase down travel options and kept Mark updated through e-mail. Coordinating phone calls was difficult. The time difference proved challenging. And, of course, Chief Blake had a real job to do. He was doing all he could for Mark and Cinnamon, and then some.

Throughout the day more details fell into place. Mark and Chief Blake worked out the details of Katib's reward and how to get it to him. Then, Mark received another update from the chief.

Sir,

. . . I talked with Yulia today and she is going to call me and let me know what time on Monday. She also said that she could be there on Monday and I gave her directions to the Joint gate that we have. . . . I will e-mail you as soon as I have Cinnamon.

We have everything I can think of covered on this end. . . . I will keep you up to date.

And then the best e-mail I'd received up to that point:

Dear Chris!

We are going to get Cinnamon on Monday at 11 A.M.

Yulia

We finally found out all the details that were in place for Monday's transfer of Cinnamon.

Yulia would pick up Cinnamon and meet Chief Blake at the joint gate between the air force base and the public airport. She'd found out that Katib still had Cinnamon's crate, and they would bring that along.

To compensate Katib for his expense in caring for Cinnamon and to make good on the reward originally offered, the chief would give Katib money for himself and for Anna, who was not expected to be there that day.

The plans were set. We needed only to wait to hear of their success.

It was Friday, July 7. Cinnamon was twenty-nine days overdue. Was it possible she was almost home?

Over the next few days, Chief Blake and Mark spoke over the phone. It was the weekend, so it was a little easier to coordinate calls. But at this point, all we were doing was waiting and hoping that Cinnamon was delivered to the chief safe and sound. The calls were merely to reassure Mark that all was well. He worried like a mother hen.

SIXTEEN

ON MONDAY AFTERNOON, you would think we were waiting for the stork to arrive. In some ways we were. Cinnamon was our baby. We couldn't have anticipated her return more. When the phone rang, once again I held my breath.

Chief Blake and Yulia had finally connected to get Cinnamon back on base. They had considered a few options. None were very easy.

Yulia had offered to go get Cinnamon from Katib, but since he lived outside the city and she did not have a car, it was not a great choice. How would she get the dog and her crate on a bus? Of course, we reassured Yulia that we would reimburse her for any expenses she'd have transporting Cinnamon. Perhaps she could take a cab.

Chief Blake also had a plan to go to Katib's on his own time. This, too, presented its own set of challenges. Because it was unofficial duty, the chief could not use a military vehicle to make the drive, and any vehicles available to him were on the small side, to say the least. It was questionable how he, Maria, Cinnamon, and her crate would all fit into such a small car. If it turned out that was their only option, the chief promised he would make it work.

In the end, Katib brought Cinnamon to the airport himself. He met Yulia, who arrived by bus, at the joint gate between Manas Air Base and the commercial airport. Since Katib worked at the airport, he traveled there on a regular basis anyway. Yulia was shocked when she saw Cinnamon. Katib had brought her in the trunk of his car, where he often transported his own dog. Cinnamon was visibly frightened when he let her out. Katib was undaunted when Yulia explained the dangers of what he had done. She believed he did not mean her any harm and that he didn't know it was unsafe. After witnessing this, however, Yulia was relieved for the first time that Cinnamon would live with Mark in the U.S.

Yulia then spent a few minutes taking Cinnamon for a short walk while they waited for Chief Blake. It was the first time that she had met Cinnamon. Up until then, she had only seen Cinnamon in pictures. Yulia was taken with how beautiful and affectionate Cinnamon was.

Chief Blake went to the gate at the prearranged time to meet Yulia and Cinnamon. Kamrad and the kennel master went along with him. The chief saw them first. They were just outside the gate. He walked out to meet them. Cinnamon recognized him instantly. Her tail wagged, and she tugged on her leash, dragging Yulia right over to him. Everyone laughed as she jumped on them and licked their faces, as if to say, "I've missed you guys so much!"

It was clear that Yulia had found the right dog. Everyone was smiling and glad to see her. Katib had told them all about how he came to have Cinnamon, how angry his wife was when Cinnamon hunted their chickens, and how hard it was for him and his children to give her up. Like everyone else who had met her, they had really fallen for her.

Everyone lingered, talking, for about thirty minutes. Yulia had taken the opportunity to connect with the kennel master. It was an important contact for her work at the Animal Welfare Society of Kyrgyzstan. In the end, she received some generous donations of used kennels and other supplies that she would put to good use for the animals that she helped.

Before everyone parted, they took pictures of the happy reunion. It was gratifying for Yulia to know that Cinnamon was on her way home. The chief and his friends promised they'd take good care of her.

My phone kept ringing as I held my breath. I anxiously picked it up. I hoped it was the call I was waiting for from seven thousand miles away.

"Chris, it's Yulia. Cinnamon is back on base. It definitely was her. She was so happy to see the guys there."

I flopped down in my chair and let out a huge sigh of relief. The weight of the past several weeks, since Cinnamon went missing, was lifted. She was finally back with the chief. I bubbled over with my thanks to Yulia. I was so happy. I had to call Mark.

"I just got a call from Yulia. Cinnamon's on base with Chief Blake. They did it."

He was relieved, but you could tell things had taken their toll on him.

"That's great. We still need to get her home, though."

It was hard for him to celebrate just yet, after what had happened with earlier attempts to get her home. But I was happy that she was back in the chief's hands.

And later that day in an e-mail, the chief wrote,

We have Cinnamon on base, and all is well.

Sorry I did not email earlier, very busy day.

I will email in the A.M.
Mike

It was short and to the point. He had lots to do for his real job, and he was wrapping up, anticipating his own return home. His job here was almost done—almost. Cinnamon still needed a ride to the U.S.

The third and final option that Chief Blake had explored for transportation was to find a local serviceman or contractor to take Cinnamon to the U.S. There was no shortage of them. Most anyone heading back home from the region had to pass through Manas. He and Mark queried anyone coming through.

Having had the support of so many people through e-mail, I felt compelled to let everyone know the good news. This was one update that I was happy to be writing.

Hello Everyone!

The news we have been waiting for!!! Cinnamon is back with our American friends in Kyrgyzstan! We are so grateful for all your thoughts and prayers.

We are still facing the challenge, however, of getting her to the U.S. We have a number of options, but they all present their obstacles . . . some tactical, logistical and financial. We are still working it all through and hope to have her home in a few weeks. Anyone who has any ideas, suggestions, or connections, we welcome all your thoughts and ideas. And, of course, keep praying!!!

Please know, we definitely considered leaving her with her new family over there. There were some issues, however, and the family decided that it would be best for her to be returned to my brother (for one, she was killing their farm animals . . . yikes!). We are so grateful for their compassion and the care they gave her. (This is not generally the case in their culture.) And we could not have done it without the help of Yulia Ten, the head of the Kyrgyz Welfare Society.

Thank you for all your prayers and well wishes. This is one story on its way to a happy ending!

Many thanks and puppy love,
Chris

The support, suggestions, and offers to help came flooding back to me.

Will keep praying! cannot wait to hear of Cinnamon's reunion with your brother. Miracles happen and we've already seen a few. What about your Congressman?

This is awesome news!!!!!!!!!!!! I will send out to my crew and see if anyone has any ideas to offer. Do you know what it would cost to bring her back? Maybe we could get a fund going?

I am so happy to hear the good news. You have been so patient. I am sure you will also overcome this last hurdle.

Chris I'm doing happy dances all over the joint.

Hi Chris, Great news on Cinnamon. Here's some contact info I dug up for Best Friends. . . . I am also going to contact my friend Cindy that went out to Utah for a course and she may know of some contacts. . . . Please stay close in touch.

I know I'm willing to send a donation. Let everyone know if that's the option you choose.

Have you contacted Best Friends Animal Society? . . . If anything, I would ask them to put it on their website, which hundreds of thousands view. You could email Amy. . . . She is a writer for their website.

Wow, lots of logistics to overcome huh? Okay well it has worked out so far, so I will keep praying and visualizing Cinnamon coming off the plane into your brother's arms.

Amazing. Absolutely amazing. :-)

It was Monday, July 10. Cinnamon had been gone thirty-two days, and she was almost home.

An e-mail I received from Yulia the next day summed up what I had come to learn myself.

It is great that Cinnamon now has so many friends all over the world. :) All the best, Yulia

She truly did, and we would never have gotten this far without every single one of them.

Chief Blake and Sergeant Kamrad cared for Cinnamon as best they could. They set up her crate in a kennel in a secluded section of the base. Their superiors had agreed to let her stay there, but they didn't necessarily want it advertised. Blake and Kamrad took turns walking Cinnamon. They fed and walked her in the morning and evening. They didn't always have a chance to get to her during the day. She was more or less on her own. They worried about her constantly. She wasn't used to being cooped up all day, and she wasn't used to being alone. Sure, she was independent, but she was still just a puppy. They did their best, but they still worried.

One morning, when the chief headed over to Cinnamon's kennel, he noticed that since he'd last seen her a soft blue blanket had turned up in her kennel. *Who put that there?* He wondered, but it really didn't matter. He was happy someone had thought enough of her to give her a soft bed to sleep on.

Another day, Chief Blake headed over to walk Cinnamon. His heart skipped a beat when he noticed she wasn't there. Her kennel was empty. *Where in the world had she gone now?* How would he call Mark and tell him that he'd lost Cinnamon himself this time?

Before he worried too much, Chief Blake looked up and noticed Cinnamon's leash was missing, too. Apparently, someone had taken Cinnamon for a walk, and as Chief Blake found out over the next few days, quite a few people took Cinnamon out and played with her. She was the only dog at the kennels that they were allowed to play with. So Cinnamon, he came to find out, spent almost more time out of her kennel than she spent in her kennel. And that was just fine with the chief.

Over the next few days, Cinnamon's outings became more frequent and took her farther and farther around the base. Even though the base leadership wanted her presence kept low-key, more people found out about her. Cinnamon quickly became somewhat of a celebrity. Everyone wanted time with her. She was a morale booster to many of the men and women while they served their deployment. She made everyone feel good. She was like a little piece of home for many of the troops who had pets of their own. They missed their pets, and she comforted them, even for just a little while.

Chief Blake was relieved. He had been trying to keep Cinnamon's presence on base on a low profile. Since the word was out now, he no longer had to worry about who knew she was there. This allowed him to feel comfortable walking Cinnamon, so he, too, ventured out with her in tow. He enjoyed Cinnamon's company and watching her explore her new surroundings on base. One day, as the chief strolled with Cinnamon, a grasshopper popped out of nowhere and caught her attention. In a moment, she pounced on it, startling the little critter. Cinnamon had found a new game to play, and she played with the insects whenever she could. In fact, each time Chief Blake took Cinnamon out for exercise, she engaged in this simple yet mesmerizing new game that she learned.

The biggest surprise admirer of Cinnamon's turned out to be a crusty colonel who was mostly feared at Manas.

Jim Kamrad commented about it to Chief Blake one day.

"Did you see who was walking Cinnamon this morning? He even had a smile on his face."

"No, way." Blake grinned. "Not the colonel. He never smiles."

Cinnamon not only brought a smile to the colonel's face but also quickly climbed into his heart. As one of the leaders at Manas Air Base, Colonel Arnold Holcomb walked the base frequently. He liked to know what was happening, so he made it a point to have his eyes on things. Walking behind the Security Forces building one day, he was surprised to see a dog in a cage all by herself. She had not been with the military working dogs, and she certainly didn't look like one. They were mostly German Shepherds, and she looked more like a Lab/Greyhound mix.

The colonel asked around about her and found that leadership on base had unofficially given the nod to her being there. Based on what he had learned, he was also satisfied that she would likely be gone in a week or less.

Like many of the service members who had cared for Cinnamon, the colonel had been an animal lover since he was young, and he missed his own two dogs back home. He quickly took advantage of Cinnamon's being there to provide the love, fun, and comfort that deployments generally lack. When the colonel first approached Cinnamon, she was sweet and friendly. She looked up at him with gentle and caring eyes. And when Colonel Holcomb looked back into Cinnamon's eyes, he could tell how kind she was. He knelt down next to her and hugged her close. Cinnamon seemed to enjoy the affection just as much as he did. He hugged her like this often, and she let him do it as long as he liked, leaning into him and just standing there next to him. Cinnamon quickly endeared herself to the colonel.

Colonel Holcomb worried that Cinnamon would be lonesome because she was separated from the other dogs on base. So he tended to her regularly, making sure she had food and water and visiting her each morning and night. The colonel also added a blanket to Cinnamon's kennel so she could curl up on something soft. As an early riser, Colonel Holcomb would jog daily while it was still cool and quiet on base. He found that Cinnamon enjoyed this morning routine as well. And while Colonel Holcomb would run at a brisk pace, with her extremely long stride Cinnamon was barely speed walking.

While on one of their many long, relaxing walks together, the colonel and Cinnamon stopped to visit several Security Forces troops. It was a very hot, sunny day, and the men had gathered under a gazebo to stay cool. In her calm and confident manner, Cinnamon walked up the stairs, directly to one of the men sitting in the shade and jumped into his lap like she was a five-pound Chihuahua. She was so big by that time that her legs hung over his lap, sticking out in all directions. They all had a good laugh over yet another of Cinnamon's unassuming tricks.

The colonel realized quickly that he was not the only one so fond of Cinnamon. When word spread that Cinnamon was there, many others had taken to visiting with and walking her. Since he genuinely treasured his time with Cinnamon, the colonel swiftly laid claim to walking her every morning between 6:30 and 7:30 A.M. He'd tell anyone who tried to challenge it, "That's my time with Cinnamon. Don't even think of taking her out then." The colonel's reaction was typical of the positive effect Cinnamon had on the military members. Even he had given in to her charms.

Not knowing which option to get Cinnamon home would work out and having hit obstacles with every single one of them, we had to keep working. Mark e-mailed the chief and others trying to help with his updates at every turn. He was a nervous parent planning for every contingency on behalf of his child.

> Guys,
>
> We've finally gotten Cinnamon back on base at Manas AB. . . .
>
> We're not out of the woods yet though . . . I'm working trans-portation to the States, but I'm getting the runaround. ATA, the charter airline company . . . says that they have no problem with taking her, but that they want to be told by the USAF Passenger Reservation Center at Scott AFB that it's OK. I spoke to the PRC [Personnel Readiness Center], and they told me I needed to speak to the Policy office at AMC [Air Mobility Command]. The Policy office told me they have nothing to do with waivers. I'm kind of stuck at this point, although the Policy office said they'd send me the info I needed to get the waiver. Apparently the DOD doesn't allow pets to travel unless it's under permanent orders. . . . The problem is that I haven't been able to get to someone who's willing to listen to our story and say "yes."
>
> I can still get her home commercial, but I have to wait a minimum of 3 weeks for my contact in Kyrgyzstan to get her visa . . . I have considered flying there to get her myself. We'll see what happens.
>
> Anyway, I'll keep you posted.

We pressed on. We just needed to find the right option, at the right time, with the right person to bring her home. We couldn't afford to let any thoughts that she wouldn't make it home enter into our minds. We all worked furiously on the alternatives. We had people from all over the world volunteering to help get her home. But in the back of our minds, we knew time was of the essence. Chief Blake would be rotating out in just a few weeks. Who knew what might happen to Cinnamon then? We didn't want to find out.

Mark began thinking that perhaps the best way for him to get Cinnamon home was to fly to Bishkek himself to get her. It made sense. It wouldn't be easy, but it would calm his concerns about anything else going wrong. He had tremendous guilt about having trusted Roberts after what Roberts had done, and he worried that the same thing, or worse, could happen with just about anyone else.

Mark checked into flights to Bishkek. It would be a grueling trip. He had just finished the long journey home. If Mark headed back to Bishkek now, he would travel for close to fifty hours there and back; plus, it was unlikely that he would be allowed back on base. While he was technically still on active duty, his deployment had ended. He couldn't just show up and expect to be allowed on base and be given housing. It didn't work like that. It would take some doing. Perhaps having Yulia fly to the States was a better plan. He e-mailed the chief.

> Do you think I'd be allowed to stay on the base? I can bring a uniform if needed. By the time I fly, I will no longer be on Active Duty. I am a Reservist. Obviously I won't be traveling under orders.
>
> I'm also going to make some more calls to try to get approval of her on the flight.

Just a short time later we heard from Chief Blake. He was tending to the minute details that required attention from someone like himself, someone who is dedicated, competent, and thorough. We learned that he thought he'd had a flight for Cinnamon that would leave in just three days.

> Sir,
>
> I won't know anything for sure until tomorrow (Thur), however I may be able to get Cinnamon out commercial on Sat this week. I am awaiting confirmation. . . .

If all goes well

1. I will get her to the vet for her paperwork

2. I will need to have you pay for the transport cost . . .

3. I will escort her to the plane to ensure she gets on . . . If there are any problems I then can immediately take her back on base

4. You will need to be at her destination point to pick her up. . . .

5. I don't foresee any, but if there are any expenses, just reimburse him [Cinnamon's escort] at the destination

He filled us in on a few more details, and then, as we came to depend on Chief Blake, he offered another option.

If neither of these works out I am calling another individual, who is known to have connections and may be able to help.

Lastly, he cautioned Mark against staying on base.

As to your earlier questions of staying on base and such, right now I don't even know if I could get you on base, so I would rather have that as a last resort right now.

He didn't say much about why, but we read between the lines. Something was going on that he couldn't tell us about. We learned later on, which we confirmed through our own research, that there had been an incident at the American embassy. Two U.S. diplomats had been kicked out of Kyrgyzstan under questionable circumstances. Because of the resulting tenuous diplomatic relations, the chances of Mark getting into the country or Yulia getting an approved visa to the U.S. were highly unlikely at that time. Our options for Cinnamon were dwindling.

Mark felt he had to keep his finger on the details, not that the chief needed anyone to remind him to be meticulous with planning for Cinnamon's travels but to be sure that all bases were covered and nothing would go wrong. Still the worrisome parent, Mark replied to Chief Blake.

That would be FANTASTIC. Whatever you need me to do, just let me know.

Please make sure that the airline knows she's coming. When we finally made contact with Turkish Airlines, we found out that there was nothing wrong with the cargo hold heaters. They refused Cinnamon because Roberts didn't have a "ticket" for her. They said he couldn't go back out to the ticket counter to buy the ticket for some reason. So, just make sure whatever airline it is knows she's coming and knows the crate dimensions.

I have my cell phone with me. Call me ANYTIME. . . .

I can be at JFK with about six hours notice. Baltimore is no problem.

Thanks for everything.
Mark

On Wednesday, July 12, Cinnamon had been gone thirty-four days and was now a day closer to being in her forever home.

The plans for Mark's homecoming party had been coming together. It was scheduled for Saturday, July 15. I would be heading to Maryland for it by the end of the week. But with news that Cinnamon might be coming home on Saturday, I reconsidered my travel plans. We didn't know what airport she'd be coming into. It could be Baltimore or JFK. I e-mailed Mark.

Mark,

Perhaps I should wait to make my travel plans this week until we hear back about this. I could easily pick her up at JFK and bring her down. . . . I'm coming through anyway.

I was a constant planner. I'd be passing right by JFK to get to Maryland. Wouldn't it be fun, I thought, for Cinnamon to be home in time to be at Mark's homecoming party? And, of course, I wanted to be in on welcoming her home. Surely it could work out. It was just a matter of timing. Plus, I truly believed that Mark deserved such a capstone to his time served in defense of our country. I knew it was corny, but that's just me.

To keep Yulia in the loop, I sent her a message also. We'd have been nowhere without her. I was certain she was waiting for good news of Cinnamon finally making it home.

Hi Yulia,

Keep your fingers crossed for good luck . . . Cinnamon may be flying home on Saturday!

I will let you know what happens.

Her reply made me smile.

Dear Chris!

I am so glad and I will better pray—fingers probably will not help :-)

Mark was plagued by the slow movement of the travel plans. He was home now. He had nothing much to do but relax and recover from his deployment. Chief Blake, on the other hand, still had military responsibilities to answer for, and the time difference made communications slow and difficult.

On Thursday morning, July 13, Mark received an update from the chief.

Sir,

Sat did not work out, the individual was booked on British AW and could not switch Airlines. I have 4 more options lined up.

The man was amazing. He was a machine—a machine with a heart of gold.

> JFK is the destination that Turkish AW would fly into in all cases . . . they need 2 day notice. They state they have to coordinate with JFK prior to shipping . . . I also need a day to get the vet papers.

He went on to confirm that getting a waiver to put Cinnamon on a military flight was not possible because they were not set up to secure live cargo. Also, while she could fly on a C5, she could not do so without the proper permission. Essentially, he was confirming what he'd already suspected—that the military flights were not an option. But he had dug in, and dug deep, to see what he could come up with for Cinnamon.

> I keep digging for options to see what turns up. Also I will be rotating out in 6 weeks, but may get pushed up to 4. . . . I need to send her before the new crew starts arriving and I leave.

> Email me back when you get this, I tried to call earlier but it went to voice mail and then wouldn't let me leave a voice mail.

Mark did his best to relax, but the uncertainty of getting Cinnamon home successfully weighed on him almost all the time.

SEVENTEEN

MARK'S PARTY WAS coming up fast. I decided to break up the trip to Maryland, stopping to visit my niece in Connecticut and then continuing on to Baltimore by train. I'd made the long car ride to Maryland more times than I'd planned in the previous year. Another twelve hours in the car by myself was not something I looked forward to. I'd get to Maryland on Friday night with enough time to settle in and enjoy Mark's party on Saturday. There was nothing left for me to do to help get Cinnamon home. It was out of my hands. It was hard to admit, but my job was over.

Chief Blake kept up the search for someone to take Cinnamon home. He hoped luck was on his side when he thought he'd found a suitable candidate. Michael Thomsen was a radio technician with a U.S. defense contractor. He had been in Bishkek since February 15. His job was to maintain and repair the radios and network used by the allied forces. As a contractor, he was scheduled to be in Kyrgyzstan for a year, with just one leave to visit home.

Mike had been in Bishkek just four months. He wasn't due for leave for another three. He had a new son at home that he hadn't seen since the baby was two weeks old. The stress of his job and being gone from his family was getting to him—more than he had expected. To make matters worse, he and his partner at work hadn't exactly gelled as a team. The stress mounted.

Mike came in from work one day, needing to blow off steam. He sat down with a buddy and vented.

"I really could use a vacation," Mike told his friend. "I'm not sure how I'm going to wait until September before I take leave." He hadn't planned on taking vacation until then. Plus, if he waited, his company would pay for his ticket home.

"Well, would you be interested in a free ticket home?" his buddy asked.

Mike looked up in surprise. "Is this a joke or something?" It had to be.

"No, it's no joke," his friend told him. "There's a naval officer stationed in Afghanistan who adopted a dog. I guess the dog got stuck here in Bishkek. He's willing to pay for a plane ticket in exchange for someone to bring the dog home."

It was a no-brainer but seemed too good to be true. Mike asked his buddy for more details. "So this is for real, right?"

"Yeah, Chief Blake from the security team asked me if I could do it, but I can't take vacation right now. You should go talk to him about it."

The contractors didn't generally spend much time on base. They were civilians, and so they lived downtown with the locals. It was incredibly good fortune that Mike's buddy had known about the free ticket Mark was offering. For Mike, encountering this opportunity seemed like the answer to his prayers. Somehow, he felt it was meant to be.

Later that afternoon, he went to the security offices at Manas. Chief Blake filled him in on the story of how Roberts had been hired by Mark to take Cinnamon to the U.S. but had abandoned her in Bishkek. Then, after thinking that she was lost for good, they had an incredible stroke of luck and were able to find her and get her back. Now, they needed someone to bring her home.

Mike was shocked. Living downtown, he saw what it was like in Kyrgyzstan on a daily basis. He saw how people lived. It wasn't a pretty sight. It wasn't like back home. While the city was developing, it was still very depressed and very dirty. Dogs ran loose all the time. To him, it was almost inconceivable that they found Cinnamon alive and well in those desolate conditions.

Chief Blake explained the deal to him: "Mark will pay for your round-trip ticket. All you need to do is ensure the dog makes it to the U.S. safely. You interested?"

Was he interested? Chief Blake was kidding, right? If all he needed to do was to take care of the dog and get her home, you bet he was interested. There was no question about it. Mike needed to get home to see his family. He believed, without question, that he was in the right place at the right time to do the right thing.

They say that you make your own luck, and with his persistence, Chief Blake may have indeed done just that.

Once Michael Thomsen had agreed to transport Cinnamon, they had a lot to do. They had to book his flight, ensure Cinnamon could get on the plane, and arrange for her health exam and travel documents. It was all slowgoing.

First, Chief Blake called the airline to see about a flight. By the time he and Michael were able to get to the airport, the ticket desk there was closed. They were frustrated. They had told the airline ticket agent they'd be coming that afternoon to book the flight. The agent never thought to tell them that the counter would be closed by the time they'd get there.

Plan B took them to downtown Bishkek. Getting there wasn't the easiest thing to do, but having lived downtown, Mike Thomsen knew of a travel agency there. They could make the arrangements through the agency. Once they got there, they were able to book Mike and Cinnamon's flight. The chief would have to arrange with Mark about getting the flight paid for and then return to do so.

Once Cinnamon's flight was confirmed, the chief could make arrangements to get her health certificate. Maria and Natalie, her veterinary friend, walked him through everything that needed to be done. Maria had been invaluable in helping Chief Blake make his way to all the government agencies required to put their stamp of approval on Cinnamon's travel.

It took Chief Blake and Maria the better part of a day to get everything done. Most important was to get permission to take Cinnamon out of Kyrgyzstan. The government had to be certain that she was not considered a national asset. It seemed an ironic necessity, given everything that Cinnamon had been through. Lastly, they had to make the rounds to get her health certificate and travel documents and to pay the fee associated with each piece of paper.

Chief Blake was glad once it was all done. It was late, but he e-mailed Mark, certain that he would want to know the latest.

Sir,

We have the flight booked; I will get all the details tomorrow. It will be an Aeroflot flight on Tue. . . .

Cinnamon will see the vet Mon morning for her paperwork.

Even though the chief had gotten the paperwork from the government agency that supplied it, Cinnamon still needed to see a veterinarian to have it filled out. Chief Blake would get that done in the next few days.

There was another detail that the chief had not planned for, but as Cinnamon's travel date drew closer, he felt it needed to be taken care of. Seven thousand miles away, Mark and I had thought of the same thing, but neither of us said anything about it. It was just too hard to admit, and how would we bring it up anyway?

How did we know that we could trust Michael Thomsen? We had no idea who he was. Hadn't we trusted Roberts with Cinnamon? And look what he had done. How did we know something similar, or worse, wouldn't happen at the hands of Michael Thomsen? Ultimately, we really didn't.

The issue took care of itself.

"Chief Blake," Mike started, "I just want you to know I'll take good care of her."

The chief stopped and looked up. He listened intently.

"I mean, whatever happens, I won't leave her. If she doesn't get on the flight, I don't get on the flight. I can imagine you guys must be worried it'll happen again. But it won't."

Like Mark and me, the chief hadn't wanted to bring it up. How could he? It was baggage from Roberts, but Michael Thomsen had sensed that everyone was worried about Cinnamon's making it all the way home this time. Mike reassured the chief that he'd make sure that it happened.

The chief was silently relieved. He knew Mark would be, too. Mike was the right guy to get the job done.

Saturday was a busy day for Mark and our family. The last-minute arrangements were being made for Mark's homecoming party, and since Alice had decided to do just about everything herself, it had become overwhelming, to say the least. She wasn't one to necessarily ask for help, but as the day of the party drew near, Alice had no choice. She just couldn't do it all herself—plus, our family wanted to help.

So, we all pitched in. First, the party hall had to be set up: tables, chairs, decorations, centerpieces, linens, beverages, all had to be brought in, set up and arranged. While Mark and Alice appreciated the crowd of people that had offered to help, having so many people created a bit of mayhem. Each person had his or her own idea of how things should be and look. It didn't make it easy to get anything accomplished.

Nonetheless, somehow everything got done. The evening arrived, along with over one hundred of Mark's friends and family members, who welcomed him home, thanked him for serving our country in the name of freedom, and gave thanks that he was safe.

As with so many of his experiences over that past year, this too was surreal. He had agreed to the party. He had wanted it. But now that it was happening, he felt a bit awkward. All these people had come from near and far to see him. And just about all of them asked about Cinnamon.

"Hey, whatever happened to Cinnamon?" was a common question.

"Is she gonna make it home to the States?" was another.

And to each question, Mark gave an answer that downplayed what was going on. "Well, we'll see. We're still working on it. Still trying to get her home." He was trying to have fun at the party—and, truly, he did enjoy it. But the apprehension he felt over Cinnamon's not being home yet was still there. It continued to haunt him, and the questions lingered. What if she didn't make it? What if something terrible happened again and she became lost for good this time? It was bittersweet. Mark thought that it would have been fun if Cinnamon had made it home in time to be at the party with him.

He tried to relax. She was almost home. Her flight was booked. If all went well, she would be home in just a few days. Everyone was pulling for them. It was hard, though. With every person who asked about Cinnamon, Mark's heart ached, and the pictures of her in the slide show he had put together for the party made her not being there all the more difficult to handle.

But Mark was a trooper to the end of the night. He made the rounds of all his loved ones who had come to see him, and he made sure that everyone had a good time.

It was Saturday, July 15, thirty-seven days into Cinnamon's adventure.

Sunday morning, Mark received an e-mail from Chief Blake about Cinnamon's flight.

I have the ticket, and will call right after my dinner for the details.

That was it? Mark had hoped for more details. His nerves were raw. He knew the chief was doing a tremendous favor taking care of Cinnamon and getting her home, but it was just torturous waiting to hear from Chief Blake and then getting so few particulars when he did.

The chief never did call that night. They always had trouble contacting each other. It was hit-or-miss and depended on when and how they tried to do so. Because of the chief's limited Internet access, e-mail was slower, but it was definitely easier. It wasn't until after 9:00 P.M. that night, an interminable fourteen hours later, that Mark got word of Cinnamon's flight.

Dep Manas 0600 Jul 18

Flight: Aeroflot SU 315 (from Moscow)

Arrive JFK 18 Jul 1640

Michael Thomsen will meet you at the baggage carousel for
Flight Aeroflot SU315

It was short and to the point. Cinnamon would be departing
Bishkek at 8:00 P.M. EDT on Monday night, July 17. The flight
number from Moscow was all the information he needed to meet
her. She'd be arriving a little after 4:30 P.M. on Tuesday at JFK
airport in New York. Mark would drive up to meet her. It was
just four hours from home.

When we found out that Cinnamon would be flying that week,
we looked more closely at her itinerary. To our dismay, we found a
new reason to worry. Her flight would take her through Moscow,
where she'd have a four-hour layover. What if she did not make it
to her connecting flight? What if the ground crew didn't give her
any water or forgot to load her onto her flight to New York? What
if Michael Thomsen left Moscow without her? Yes, we worried.
We worried about anything and everything that could go wrong.
We had to consider and plan for every contingency or obstacle that
reared its head, threatening for her final journey home to go awry.

I went online and did some more research through the WSPA.
If they had a member society in Kyrgyzstan, surely they would
have one in Moscow. I'd contact them and see if they could help. I
got lucky yet again. Indeed, there wasn't just one but two animal-
welfare societies in Moscow. I typed up an e-mail and sent it to
both.

Subject: Puppy flying needs help in Moscow

I introduced myself and gave a brief summary of what had happened. Then, I dove in with my huge request.

I knew it wasn't as crucial an issue as when I first contacted
Yulia, but I hoped to ward off the possibility of anything going
wrong. We'd been burned before and didn't want to be again. I
hoped that they'd understand.

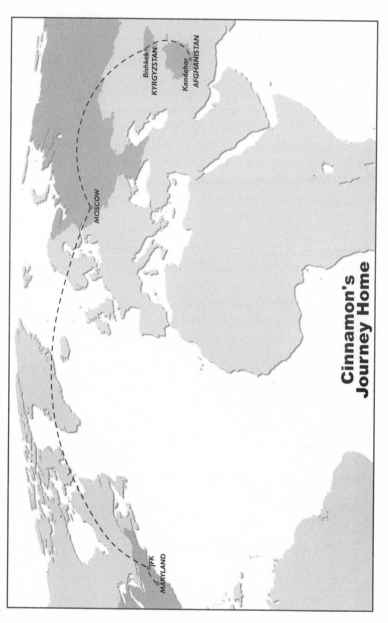

Cinnamon's
Journey Home

Once we received word that Cinnamon's flights were confirmed from
Bishkek, Kyrgyzstan through Moscow and on to the U.S., we were
newly concerned.

It took us about 3 weeks to find her and make her travel arrangements and we are now flying her home.

She is coming through Moscow on Tuesday, July 18, 2006 on Aeroflot and because she was lost once (not because of the airline) we want to be sure she flies through without any incident.

She must change planes in Moscow and continue on to New York. Is it possible that there could be someone from your organization at the airport to help her companion traveler (he does not speak your local language) just in case something unusual happens and/or she misses her connection?

I realize this is a big question to ask and am open to any suggestions you might have to prevent any incidents.

I thank you in advance for any assistance that you may offer. Please contact me as soon as you can. . . . . I await your reply.

While I had to admit that e-mail served its purpose in everyday life and in uniting those that helped me find Cinnamon, I still felt it had its limitations. It was too slow for my liking, and you never really know if someone has gotten your message. When I hadn't heard back the next day, I decided to call to see if I could get faster results.

I called Moscow in hopes of talking with someone from the Moscow Animal Rights Center. I reached a woman named Elena, the head of the group, on my first try.

"Hello, is this Elena?" I began, assuming she would understand me.

"Yes, this is Elena. What can I do for you?" She'd heard my English and responded in my language, notwithstanding her thick Russian accent.

I took a deep breath, then went on. "Elena, yes, my name is Christine Sullivan. I am from the United States and needed to ask your help. I sent you an e-mail but wasn't sure if you got it."

"Yes, I did receive your e-mail. I am not sure I can help you."

Hmmm. Not exactly the response I was hoping for, but I waited to see what she might say.

"You see, there are only three of us that work here at the society, and one of our volunteers is sick and not able to do anything right now. We are stretched very thin."

I wasn't surprised. This wasn't an emergency, and the issue of volunteer shortages was apparently a global one.

She continued. "Also, the airport is quite far, so it would be impossible for someone to get there on such short notice. I'm sorry I can't do more."

I understood, and I told her so. But I thought perhaps she could help in a different way, by giving us just a little peace of mind.

"Well," I continued, just a bit shaken up, "would it be okay if I gave the man traveling with the puppy your name and number in case he runs into any problems in Moscow? I don't expect that he will but just in case."

"Sure, that would be fine."

I thanked her, and we hung up. I also tried to reach the other group in Moscow, but no one there ever answered my call.

Well, that was it. We had tried to plan for the worst. Now, we hoped for the best.

It was Sunday, July 16. Cinnamon had been detoured for thirty-eight days, and she just might be home in two more.

Mike Thomsen awoke Monday morning. He'd be departing for home with Cinnamon in the wee hours of Tuesday morning. He had called his wife the day before to give her the news. He had wanted to surprise her, but, having tried that once before when he had been deployed with the Air National Guard, he thought better of it. He had gone through all the trouble keeping it a secret, but somehow she'd found out anyway.

He dialed home.

"Hey, Honey." He tried to sound casual. "Guess what?"

"What?" she asked.

"I might be coming home pretty soon," he baited her.

"Really? How soon?"

"Well, like Monday or Tuesday."

All Mike could hear on the other end of the phone was the sound of his wife crying.

To make things easier, Mike went to Manas and stayed on base after work that day. He'd have to go to the airport around 1:00 A.M. When he went to get Cinnamon and prepare to go to the airport, he was surprised by what took place. First, Cinnamon was not even in her kennel. As usual, someone had her out for a jaunt. Then, guys came out of nowhere to say good-bye to her—a lot of guys.

Up until then, Mike hadn't had the chance to meet Cinnamon. In fact, the first time he had even seen her was when he went to pick her up. Mike wasn't really a dog person. He had grown up with a dog as a young boy and enjoyed him, but he preferred cats. But when he finally met Cinnamon that night, he enjoyed being with her from the start. During those few moments when Mike and Chief Blake were getting Cinnamon ready to head to the airport, Mike saw what an energetic and sweet puppy she is. Seeing all the people who came out to say good-bye to her showed just how lovable she really is. He could see why so many people had helped find her and get her home. Mike even thought he saw Chief Blake shed a tear or two saying good-bye to Cinnamon.

Mike, Chief Blake, and Maria went in the back gate to the civilian airport. Being with Security Forces, Chief Blake had the access. They had one final detail to take care of before Cinnamon could fly. they had to have her paperwork filled out and approved by the veterinarian at the airport. Maria had made the arrangements for him to be there.

When the vet didn't show up as planned, they all got very nervous. The chief had him paged. Finally, he arrived, and without even looking in Cinnamon's direction, he filled out the paperwork. Chief Blake gave him the required fee, 100 som, the equivalent of $2.50 U.S.

Cinnamon was finally ready to fly home.

To thank me for finding Cinnamon, Mark and Alice alluded to doing all kinds of extravagant things for me, but I couldn't let them. I *wouldn't* let them. Having found Cinnamon was enough.

It was more than enough. Plus, having built an incredible bond and friendship with Mark, cherishing it every step of the way and hoping it would last eternally was a bonus. But they insisted on doing *something*, and so I went for what I considered the brass ring.

It was Maryland-blue-crab season, and Alice, having grown up in Maryland, was a connoisseur at picking them fresh from the boats. Her family had a deep-rooted history in crabbing. All I wanted by way of a thank-you was a blue-crab feast at the best crab place in town—Jimmy Cantler's Riverside Inn, or Cantler's, as I knew it. Mark and Alice had taken me there before. The crabs were fabulous. So, off we went.

Cinnamon was almost home. It was a little scary to celebrate, but I was headed home the next day. We wouldn't have another chance for this dinner for a long time. Maryland was not easy to get to by land, sea, or air from where I lived. And in the past twelve months, I had made enough trips down from Vermont to last me at least another five years.

Cantler's isn't quite one of those places where you sit down at a picnic table with a bunch of strangers alongside you, scream your conversation across the table trying to rise above the roar of the crowd, and drink cold beer to wash down your feast, although it is close. This time, it was just family at the table.

Alice conducted her usual interrogation of the wait staff about the size, quality, and price of the crabs. I'm from New York City and can't say I have ever witnessed anything like it, even from the most forward city slicker. She had it down. I'd seen it before. The best part is that it always results in the most tasty, succulent crabs of the season. Tonight was no different. I reveled in it all— the dinner, the company, the impending homecoming. I couldn't have been happier or having more fun, but silently we all still felt the anxiety running just underneath the surface. Cinnamon still wasn't home.

In the midst of dinner, Mark's cell phone rang.

"Hello?" we'd heard him say. "Can't hear you. We're at dinner. Hold on a sec." He sprang from the table, and out the backdoor he went. Who could it be? What was going on? Did this have anything to do with Cinnamon?

It was already Tuesday in Kyrgyzstan, and Cinnamon was due to board her flight anytime now. Did her journey take another unexpected twist? We could only wait for Mark to return to find out if the call even had anything to do with Cinnamon or not. The minutes ticked by. What could be taking so long? The crabs were getting cold.

As I peered toward the door, willing him to come back into the room, the door burst open. The look on Mark's face said it all, a grin as wide as the Mississippi.

"She's on her way. That was Michael Blake. They just put her on the plane. She'll be at JKF tomorrow afternoon."

I couldn't believe it. It was really true. Cinnamon would be here the next day. Just a few short weeks before, Mark's gut-wrenching e-mail had gone out. He had thought that he would never find her or know of her whereabouts again. Now, she was finally headed home. She'd be in the U.S. in about twenty-two hours.

Alice was elated that Cinnamon had boarded her flight home. It was an emotional time. She was still exhausted from planning Mark's party and entertaining the guests long into the night over the weekend. Cinnamon's journey had been long, and now she was almost home. It was very surreal for Alice. She was thrilled that her girl would soon be with them. She thought that Mark would be, too.

"Aren't you excited she's almost home?" she asked her husband later that night.

Adamantly, he replied, "I don't want to talk about it." Mark was afraid if he talked about Cinnamon's coming home, he would jinx it. It was very hard to be jubilant until she actually arrived.

Alice, on the other hand, prayed constantly. "It's gonna happen," she told Mark. "Regardless of all the bad things that have gone on, it's gonna happen."

Mike Thomsen knew how nervous everyone was about Cinnamon's making it home safely. When he landed in Moscow, he went to check on her. They had a long layover. He reached into

ve Left, Cinnamon's water bowl was often dirty or dried up so Mark gave
fresh water as often as possible. *Above Right,* Mark giving Cinnamon some
on for breakfast in the cement bunker that she often slept in overnight.
rtesy Scott Wells

w Left, Cinnamon with Katib Ridvanov's children at his home in Bishkek,
rgyzstan. Courtesy Katib Ridvanov Below Right, Yulia Ten, founder of the
imal Welfare Society of Kyrgyzstan, initiated the search for Cinnamon in
hkek. Courtesy Yulia Ten

Colonel Arnold Holcomb (standing) was on one of his many walks with Cinnamon when they visited with some of her other friends on Manas Air Force Base.
Courtesy James Kamrad

Mark and I joyfully welcomed Cinnamon home moments after she arrived at JFK airport, NY.
Courtesy Mark Feffer

No worse for the wear, Cinnamon eagerly loaded into Mark's car and seemed ready for the ride from JFK airport to her new home in Maryland.
Courtesy Mark Feffer

In the driveway of their home, Alice has an emotional moment meeting Cinnamon for the first time.
Courtesy Mark Feffer

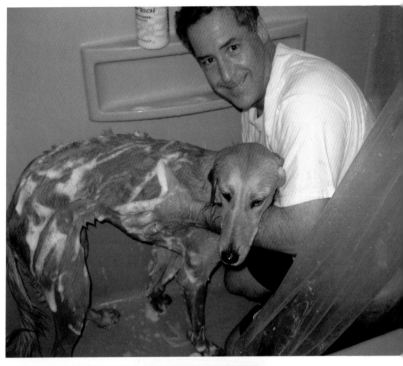

Still a young puppy, Cinnamon couldn't help messing her crate where she had spent twenty-six hours traveling on her way home. Mark gives Cinnamon her first bath ever, which she desperately needed.
Courtesy Mark Feffer

On her first day home, Cinnamon shows the telltale signs of undernourishment—her drawn face and protruding ribcage.
Courtesy Mark Feffer

Family photo showing
Cinnamon with Alice, Mark,
and Chibi (Baby).
Courtesy Mark Feffer

Cinnamon looking very regal at
the North Rim of the Grand
Canyon.
Courtesy Mark Feffer

Cinnamon gets comfortable
on the sofa, one of her favorite
places and positions.
Courtesy Mark Feffer

Mark gives Cinnamon a
special cupcake for her first
birthday in November 2006
Courtesy Mark Feffer

Mark with Jackson and Baby
(Chibi), who he tucked into
coat to keep warm.
January 2004
Courtesy Mark Feffer

...rk and Alice's growing pack of rescues, Pete, Cinnamon, and Elvis. April 2009
...rtesy Mark Feffer

...rk and Cinnamon visit with Grace Davidson at Armstrong Elementary, Res-
...,VA, for a school fundraiser supporting Operation Baghdad Pups. April 2008
...rtesy David Mathis

Chief Michael Blake and me when I finally h the chance to m him Stateside. January 2009
Courtesy Christine Sullivan

On a mission with Operation Baghdad Pups, fourteen-week-old Julian was one of several pups I accompanied from Baghdad to the U.S. The puppy climbed into my lap for comfort after our trip of more than thirty hours to the U.S. and her vet exam. February 2009
Courtesy Bev Westerman

his pocket and pulled out a piece of paper. He looked down at the name and number written on it. I had contacted the Moscow Animal Rights Center to see if they could help him in case anything went wrong. We'd given him the contact information for the head of the group. Mike hoped that he wouldn't need to call them.

The airport terminal in Moscow was all one building. Mike was up on the top floor, and he assumed Cinnamon was somewhere down below, with the baggage and cargo. He approached an airline employee to ask if he could go take care of Cinnamon. He explained the situation. He explained that she needed water and a break to stretch her legs.

"No, I am sorry," the employee told him, "without a Russian visa, you cannot go out of the terminal."

The employee tried to assure Mike that Cinnamon would be taken care of. He hoped she was right. He tried not to worry, but it was useless. In fact, Mike's worry worsened when they left Moscow. He hadn't been able to check on Cinnamon there. He agonized about her during the entire flight to New York. What if he got to JFK and she was dead? It was a possibility. The belly of these planes can get so cold. Sure, they were supposed to be heated, but who could guarantee it?

Mike just kept wondering what he would do. What would he tell Mark? It haunted him almost the whole way. Finally, Mike made a decision, a decision to trust that if God intended for him to get this far with Cinnamon, he wouldn't allow him to get there and have things be all wrong. He had to believe it. He had to put his mind at ease that everything would be all right. Mike tried to rest. They'd be in New York in a few more hours.

Mark, Alice, and I began the next phase of planning. Who would go to the airport to get Cinnamon? Who would watch Baby, Mark and Alice's older dog? She had been ailing recently and couldn't be left alone for very long. Could Mark and Alice go to JFK together? Alice had to meet the puppy with whom she'd already fallen in love. I wanted to go to the airport, too. I wanted to be there when she got off that plane. I just *had* to meet Cinnamon. Could we all go together?

Deciding on a plan was tough. As much as I wanted to go greet Cinnamon, I wanted Mark and Alice to go together more. Alice, however, felt that she had to stay home. Baby was sixteen years old and having seizures on a regular basis throughout the day. On top of that, she was mostly incontinent. As much as I wanted to go to JFK to be there when Cinnamon arrived, I offered to stay behind and watch Baby. My dad, too, had offered to watch Baby so the three of us could all go. Alice wouldn't hear of it, though. Baby required a level of care that Alice preferred to give herself. She insisted, so my dad decided to make the drive to JFK with Mark.

I, on the other hand, had to take the train back north. I had driven from Vermont to Connecticut, and then taken the train from there to Maryland for Mark's party. My car was still in Connecticut. I had to go back and get it, then drive to JFK airport on Long Island. The drive to JFK from Connecticut could be my undoing. The flight was due to arrive at 4:30 P.M. I'd have to navigate New York City traffic during the afternoon rush hour. It would be harrowing. I'd be cutting it close, but I had to do it. I had to be there.

It was tough on Alice. She desperately wanted to go to the airport with Mark, to be there for him and to meet Cinnamon. While he wouldn't admit it, Alice knew how nervous and worried he was. She was terribly disappointed not to be going, but she knew Mark would be okay and that she would see Cinnamon soon enough. She had waited this long. She could wait a little longer.

Given how badly I wanted to travel with Mark and my dad, being on the train and then in the car rubbed my nerves raw. To pass the time and stay connected, I kept in touch with Mark by cell phone. At one point while on the train, I knew I had traveled north of the airport on my way to Connecticut. By that time, Mark and my dad had already arrived at JFK. I still had to get to my car in Connecticut and then drive to the airport in New York. I was going mad. It was like running the last quarter mile of a marathon. The finish line was in sight, but I wasn't sure I would make it. The afternoon traffic on the Brooklyn-Queens Expressway just about did me in, but I had to keep going. Our girl was almost home.

We all met up at the airport, just as we had planned. Getting there for Mark and my dad had been no problem. We grew up in New York, and my dad knew the streets and highways better than the back of his hand. Now that we were finally at the airport, there was more waiting, but of course we couldn't *just* wait.

To pass the time, we did things that we thought would matter. Mark tried to find a gate agent to check if Cinnamon was on the manifest. There had been a layover in Moscow, and we worried perhaps she missed the flight or had been abandoned again. I hate to admit it, but the fear was real.

Trying to find a gate agent proved fruitless. We found out that the airline doesn't begin to service a flight until it is within about half an hour from the airport. We wouldn't know anything for another hour or two.

Next, we tried to find out how incoming animals were handled when they had to clear customs. It hadn't dawned on us before, but we now panicked. Michael Thomsen had a connecting domestic flight. When coming through customs, he'd have to claim his luggage and drag it through customs to be cleared for entry into the U.S. Suppose Mister Thomsen didn't know he had to claim Cinnamon. Suppose he didn't care, and he just left her to make his flight.

Mark tried to find out more. By then, we were all pacing. Rows and rows of people gathered where travelers would enter the terminal after clearing customs. There was a corral set up past the entry from customs, and it had two exits for travelers to filter through. Each exit was about one hundred feet and fifty or so bodies from the other. We had to have one of us posted at each, otherwise we might miss Michael and Cinnamon coming out. We assumed he would claim her and bring her through customs.

Mark had returned with two versions of what would happen to Cinnamon when the flight landed. One agent told him that animals would come out to a separate holding area, where Mark could claim her himself. Another assured us that Cinnamon had to be claimed by Michael Thomsen. We didn't know what to believe. The energy of the crowd grew. I tried to pass the time talking with a man and his parents. He was adopting two children from Russia, and his wife was on the plane with them. Apparently, she didn't speak Russian, and they didn't speak English. She had been alone with them for two weeks and now had been on a plane with them for over ten hours—and I thought we had it bad!

I tried to listen and be enthusiastic for him, but all I could do was wonder if Cinnamon was on the plane. Would she get through customs? My dad was stationed at the other end of the exit from where I stood. Mark paced back and forth between us. He couldn't decide which end to settle on. He tried to position himself so he could see both sides of the corral. Michael would come out one way or another, but we had no idea which end he'd wind up at.

Mike was relieved when they landed at JFK, but his relief was short-lived. His worry came barreling back. He had been able to find his bags pretty quickly, but he wasn't sure where he would pick up Cinnamon. He asked an employee.

The man pointed and said, "They'll be coming out those doors over there."

Mike looked over and saw a large set of double doors. He watched and he waited for what seemed like a long time. Then he asked again.

"Wait here," he was told, "I'll go check."

The man disappeared through another set of double doors at the opposite end of the room. He came back a short time later, but he didn't have Cinnamon. He just smiled at Mike and waved. Mike thought how odd it was. Then, the man disappeared again.

Finally, he came out with Cinnamon in her crate. Mike was so relieved and said a silent prayer of thanks. He had been waiting to get Cinnamon for what seemed like forever. At last, he was directed which way to head out. He still hadn't been through customs.

On his way through, it seemed to him that everyone in customs had been waiting for him and Cinnamon, that they all knew about her. Maybe it was just his imagination, but, without notice, another customs line opened up just for them. The customs agent looked briefly at his passport, waved him through, and that was it. They'd made it. Now, he just had to find Mark.

The passengers started to filter out, and like the New Yorker I have always been—although I hadn't lived in New York for a single day in over twenty years—I went after what I had come for. I stopped about every fifth person that came out of customs.

"Excuse me. What flight were you on?"

"Holland."

"Thanks."

Again, "Excuse me. What flight did you come off of?"

"Switzerland."

Finally, "What flight did you say you were on? Moscow?"

"Yes."

"Okay, thanks."

Then, I riveted my eyes on the people that filtered out. The energy continued to grow. I watched the door beyond the corral. It was the only way passengers would be exiting customs. Then, I looked up. Where'd Mark go? I didn't see him. And then I saw what I was waiting for, a crate on a luggage cart. It didn't seem real. Was that our girl? How many dog crates would be coming through customs at just that time, when Cinnamon was due to arrive? As I realized it had to be her, I started jumping. I jumped up and down. People were staring. I kept jumping, and then I started screaming.

"She's here! She's here! She's here!"

Why wasn't anyone else screaming? Wasn't anyone else as excited to see their loved ones as I was to see that crate rolling through that door?

People kept staring. *What in the world was this lady screaming about?* I didn't care. I just kept jumping and just kept screaming. Seeing that baby come through those doors felt like the most exciting moment of my life.

I looked around again. Where was the man meeting his new children? I had wanted to wish him well, but I didn't see him. He had disappeared in the crowd. Oh well, all that mattered to me was that Cinnamon had arrived, and still I kept jumping.

Mark charged forward to try to intercept them, but he couldn't tell which way Michael would go through the corral. It was only moments before the rolling crate reached me. Mark was nowhere. I felt bad for him but couldn't contain my excitement.

I exclaimed my greeting to Michael: "You probably figured I'm Mark's sister, Christine. I can't tell you how glad I am to see you." He grinned. He probably thought I had lost my mind. I didn't blame him. I couldn't stop jumping.

Michael didn't say much, at least I don't think so. I was trying to get a glimpse of Cinnamon inside the crate at the same time I was trying to get out of the way of the people that continued to stream into the terminal from customs.

In the meantime, Mark and Dad showed up from across the corral. We made our way as close to the exit as we could get but didn't make it outside before Mark opened the crate. Out popped a weary, lanky puppy. For a split second, Mark looked closely to see if it was really Cinnamon. Then, she stretched, peed, and then she peed some more. Then, she lathered my brother's face with kisses.

Sweet victory.

EIGHTEEN

IN THE FEW moments after we let Cinnamon out of her crate, we assessed how she had fared. Her crate was soiled, and she tracked the mess across the terminal floor before we could get her outside. Then, she headed out the door with Mark for some fresh air.

After cleaning the mess, we realized that, for having spent twenty-four hours in a crate, soiled and with no blanket, Cinnamon seemed no worse for the wear. She was breathtaking to see. The smile on Mark's face was priceless. After all his anxiety, the obstacles we'd faced, and the waiting, Mark finally had Cinnamon home. His relief was evident yet indescribable. It seemed he could finally breathe easy. I only wished that Alice could have been there to greet Cinnamon, but her other baby, Baby, needed her.

We snapped several dozen pictures. Then, we finally managed to have a conversation with Mike Thomsen. We thanked him profusely. It had worked out well for all of us. We made our way to our cars, including Mike, whose connecting flight home was not until the next day. We'd agreed I'd give Mike a ride to his hotel. During this time we tried to take in everything about Cinnamon. We wanted to hug her and hold her as much as we could—maybe to try to make up for everything she had been through, maybe to just make sure the moment was real. Either way, she was a puppy who only wanted to sniff anything and everything she could get her nose on, and as far as we were concerned, that was quite all right.

———

Alice tried her best not to be anxious about the waiting, but it was hard. Cinnamon was on the last leg of her journey, and Alice hoped nothing would go wrong. She focused on Baby, who required her constant care.

Finally, Alice's phone rang. "Hello?"

"Hey, it's us. She's here!" Mark bellowed into the phone.

"Oh, my gosh! I can't believe it! How does she look?" Alice ached not being there.

"Well, aside from the fact that she messed her crate, she doesn't look too bad. She hadn't been let out of her crate in Moscow, so no one can blame her."

"Oh, that's fantastic. Mark, I'm so happy." Alice breathed a full breath for the first time in days. Her new baby was finally in safe hands. The emotions she felt overwhelmed her. "I can't wait to meet her."

"We'll be home as soon as we can. We're gonna try to get her cleaned up, then we'll hit the road."

Alice knew that she had done the right thing by staying home to care for Baby. It would be tough waiting another four hours to meet Cinnamon, but she had waited this long. She could wait just a little while longer. *My little girl, whom I haven't met yet, is safe and sound,* she thought to herself. *She's been through the worst. It will only get better for her from here.*

Alice said a silent prayer of thanks.

Mark wanted to give Cinnamon a break from being cooped up before he loaded her in his car to head home. Her crate needed a good cleaning as well. We lacked running water and were standing in the middle of the parking garage at JFK airport, so cleaning her crate wasn't that easy to do. We used the napkins, baby wipes, and bottled water that we had in our cars, and did the best we could. It would have to suffice until Mark arrived home. In the grand scheme of things, we had conquered greater mountains. This was small potatoes.

When Mark, my dad, and Cinnamon left the airport and headed

south, I left and headed north toward Vermont. I said good-bye, knowing that the puppy I helped bring home belonged to my brother. During the time we searched for her, it felt as if she were my baby, but now I had to let her go. She'd live with Mark and Alice in Maryland. I'd have to settle for being her aunt. It was difficult to face. I loved her before I met her, and I had welcomed her home. Now I had said good-bye. It happened just too fast.

Cinnamon's four-hour car ride home was uneventful, since she slept most of the way. It paled in comparison to the twenty-four-hour plane ride through the former Soviet Union in a cramped, dark, and soiled crate. At least during the car ride, she got a potty break now and again.

Initially, my dad drove while Mark sat in the back with Cinnamon. Mark felt like he was caring for a new baby. He was overwhelmed with tenderness for her as she fell into a long, deep sleep. He had an incredible sense of relief and disbelief all at once for what they'd been through, for what we'd accomplished. Mark finally felt his anxiety and fears slip away, and as Cinnamon slept, he made a silent commitment to her that nothing like this would ever happen to her again.

On the way home, Mark called Alice every hour to let her know what her new baby was doing and how close they were to home. They stopped briefly to get something to eat and to let Cinnamon out, but all she wanted to do was sleep. Driving down the road leading to their house, Mark called Alice one more time.

"We just passed the firehouse," he teased Alice. They'd be home in seconds.

Alice tried to be calm as she waited, but the anticipation was too great. She paced, and as she waited, she talked to Baby, "You're not gonna like your new sister too much." Baby was old and sickly. She couldn't be bothered with much these days—and certainly not a new puppy in the house. Alice paused just a moment to look back on everything it took to get Cinnamon home. It had been a trying journey.

Our mom had come over to wait with Alice. She had as many "granddogs" as she had grandchildren. As was typical for her, she welcomed each and every one. When she got to Alice's house, she was loaded with presents for Cinnamon.

Mark finally pulled in the driveway. It was late and it was dark. Alice quickly turned the front lights on and went out to greet her new girl. Mark opened the car door and Cinnamon jumped right out. She wiggled and she waggled as she greeted her new mom and her grammy.

My dad beamed. "She slept on my lap on the way home," he bragged.

Baby, on the other hand, was not all that happy to meet Cinnamon. In fact, fireworks broke out when they took Cinnamon inside to meet her. Cinnamon defended herself and went back at Baby. Mark and Alice quickly separated the two.

The next order of business was to get Cinnamon a bath. Mark had cleaned her at the airport as best he could, but she didn't smell all that great. Mark felt bad putting her through the ordeal, but he got her in the tub right away. He had no choice.

Once Mark was finished and got her mostly dry, they pulled out Jackson's old bed. It seemed fitting for Cinnamon to sleep in it now. They put her on the big, blue bed and wrapped her in a fluffy towel. Her coat was still a bit damp, and they didn't want her to be cold in the air conditioning that ran all night. They tucked her in and said good night, and then Cinnamon closed her eyes and slept, it seemed, like she hadn't in weeks.

The next day, the fun began. Cinnamon acclimated to her new playground. Mark described it in an e-mail that he sent out.

> She had a good first day today. She loves the big fenced yard and runs around like a crazy person. She's very intrigued with the crows, seagulls, and squirrels. . . . She also went swimming off our pier several times. I think she's overwhelmed with all the new and exciting people, places, things and smells.

Being the puppy she was, Cinnamon explored her new home. It seemed that she was on sensory overload. Everything she encountered—sights, sounds, and smells—were new to her. She took it all in. She had never seen a large body of water before, but her new home was on a river which Cinnamon waded into. The yard was full of birds and squirrels. Cinnamon took full advantage and gave them chase. While the squirrels were faster than the chickens she had captured in Bishkek, she still was a hunter at heart. It took less than twenty-four hours in her new home for Cinnamon to catch her first squirrel—much to Alice's horror. It paled only in comparison to the day that she regurgitated one at Alice's feet.

Mark and Alice understood why Cinnamon hunted. She was just doing what she was built for and had learned to do. She was just trying to survive. Cinnamon didn't yet know that for the rest of her life she would be provided for. They did their best to deter her, even putting bells on her collar so the squirrels might hear her coming. It helped some, but hunting was in Cinnamon's genes.

While Cinnamon investigated her new home and played in her safe, fenced yard, I was back in Vermont. I was gratified that our adventures had a happy ending. I typed one last e-mail to everyone who had been rooting for Cinnamon and pulling together to find her and bring her home.

Subject: CINNAMON—WE DID IT!!!

Thanks to all your prayers and support we welcomed Cinnamon home at JFK airport on Tuesday! In spite of 26 hours in her crate, she seemed no worse for the wear. It was an amazingly joyful homecoming . . . she is now exploring her new home in MD.

There were many people involved in the 'search and rescue' mission along the way. Each one contributed and we could not have done it without them.

Thank you all so much,
Chris

It was short and to the point. I thought perhaps people's interest in the story had died off. I wanted to let those who cared know without burdening those who didn't with a long, driveling message.

I had been wrong, though. People did still care, and they told us so through their e-mails, congratulating and wishing us well. It was touching to see how many people followed Cinnamon's story and to read their sentiments about her homecoming.

Oh Chris, am SO DELIGHTED. Burst out crying! Answered Prayers! Am so glad she's home safe and sound, what a very special puppy!

WooHoo. . . . You give this puppy a big ass hug for me I am just so thrilled.

That's brilliant, well done! she looks so happy, bless her.

This is such an amazing story . . . [when you said she had] "Jackson's eyes" [that] really got me. She was there to watch over him and now she's safe where they can watch over her. People who don't understand loving a dog and don't understand faith would have to be swayed by this series of events. I LOVE answered Prayers!

I am so happy to hear the good news. It's really refreshing to see/hear something good and nice these days.

What a wonderful story and happy ending, we are so thrilled for Cinnamon, your brother and your family.

That is JUST AWESOME . . . we prayed for all of you!

Terrific!! I'm so happy for you and her and her new family!! Get a big sloppy doggy kiss for me :-)

Welcome home Cinnamon. . . . Thank you for sharing the journey. Our four legged friends are so amazing.

wow, what a lucky dog Cinnamon is. . . . she sure has lots of
people who love her and will treat her right.

GREAT PICTURES. CINNAMON IS PRECIOUS. SHE LOVES
ME!! LOL [From her Grammy who had met her the night she
came home.]

We were all incredibly grateful and relieved when Cinnamon
finally arrived home safely on Tuesday, July 18. Cinnamon had
been missing for forty days following her abandonment. Her trip
home lasted an unbelievable forty-four days from the time she departed Kandahar Air Field in Afghanistan to the time she arrived
in the United States.

In the first week that Cinnamon was home, she had difficulty ad-
justing to the heat and humidity of the mid-Atlantic. Alice took
her to the park and on trail walks, but she could not walk for more
than a few minutes at a time. She would stop and lie down in the
cool grass every few feet. She had arrived dehydrated and under-
nourished. A short quarter-mile stroll was a struggle. Although
she had been a desert dog in Afghanistan, Cinnamon had spent
most of her hot, dusty days there curled up under a desk in the air-
conditioned offices of her military friends.

After Cinnamon settled in to her new home and family, she
went with Mark, Alice, and Baby on a three-week, cross-country
RV trip. They explored the Western states and several national
parks. After the initial tussle that Cinnamon and Baby got into on
Cinnamon's first night home, they learned to tolerate each other.
Cinnamon reveled in relaxing, traveling, and exploring with her
new family. Each morning she seemed to ask, "So, where are we
going today?"

Baby, on the other hand, had continued her slow decline. Before Mark came home, she'd had a difficult time getting around.
Alice had purchased a dog sling to carry her in, and Baby loved
it. Alice had often coaxed Baby, "You have to hold on 'til your
daddy gets home." Alice was thrilled that Baby did just that.
While she could barely see, Baby followed Mark around his first

few days home. She barked and jumped on him like she had in her youth. But the trip out West was hard on her. She seemed to have difficulty breathing and panted hard.

A trip to a vet in Nebraska revealed that Baby was suffering from pulmonary disease. The lack of oxygen at the high altitudes they'd been to had caused Baby to pass out several times. They decided it best to cut their trip short and head home.

In the next few weeks, Alice tended to Baby day and night. When the time came to let Baby go, Mark and Alice prepared for Baby's final trip to the vet's office, but Baby never made it. She died in Mark's arms on their way to the hospital, happy to have spent her final days with her daddy.

Just a few months after Cinnamon came to live with Mark and Alice, they added another pup to the pack, "Telegraph" Pete. He had been found on Telegraph Road and brought to the local pound. He was scheduled to be euthanized in just hours, when Mark came looking for a new family member and playmate for Cinnamon. Pete is likely a Labrador/Pit Bull mix and is an exuberant, oversized baby. It took Mark just minutes to decide to rescue Pete. Another miracle. This time, it was Pete who had won the lottery.

Then, in 2008, Alice had just gotten off the train near home and was headed for her car when she noticed a police officer holding a dog on a leash fashioned out of an electrical cord. The sight caught her attention, so she approached the officer and asked him about the dog. It turned out that the dog was a stray, and the officer was about to bring him to the local pound. Alice was concerned about the black dog, who looked like a Labrador/hound mix. He was dirty and underweight, and he smelled terrible. He had likely been alone on the streets for several weeks. After talking with the officer for a few minutes, Alice was able to convince him to let her care for the dog. So she coaxed the dog into the backseat of her car, where he instantly curled up and fell fast asleep. Alice took him to their vet to ensure he was healthy, and then directly to a local dog wash, where he patiently allowed her to bathe him.

Over the next few weeks, Alice tried to find the dog's family by calling nearby animal shelters and searching the Internet for postings about him. It was all to no avail. In the meantime, New Dog, as they had come to call him, followed Alice everywhere, as if expressing his thanks with unbridled devotion. It got harder and harder for her to think of him being reclaimed. Alice had fallen for another pup! New Dog's easygoing nature fit in well with Cinnamon and Pete. As New Dog's personality emerged, and since he had jet-black hair and constantly howled, they decided to call him Elvis, as in "nothin' but a hound dog." Once that happened, we all knew he was there to stay.

The Feffer family now lives happily as a thriving pack. Mark has settled back into civilian life and has renewed his career in technology sales. Alice is considering a career in animal care and exploring a variety of options.

Pete and Cinnamon have become the best of friends, and Pete gives Cinnamon a run for her money. They run and play together all day long, and Elvis too joins in the fun. The three entertain other four-legged friends on a regular basis. The neighborhood dogs often come by for play dates, so all the dogs are well socialized and exercised. Finally accustomed to spending long hours outside, Cinnamon has so much energy that Pete and Elvis often must come inside to take a break while she continues to frolic in the yard.

Cinnamon has grown to be a strong, healthy girl. With her independent start in life, she still prefers to be outside on her own instead of cuddled up inside with her family. But each night after they all go for an evening walk to close out their day. Cinnamon nestles in for another night of puppy dreams. Looking at her now, you'd never know of the long journey this scrappy camp dog from Afghanistan took to find her way home.

EPILOGUE

I HAVE NO way of knowing just how many people prayed for Cinnamon's rescue and safe return. I'm sure it was at least a couple of hundred. I sent the original e-mail to almost eighty people, asking for them to pray that we would find Cinnamon when she was first abandoned. At least one person I know sent it on to eighty-seven of her friends and family members. Another soldier had his family in Japan following the story. Dozens sent notes wishing us well and expressing hope that we would find Cinnamon and that somehow she would be returned home to my brother. Still others offered money when we tried to arrange her transportation. This was just the people we knew about.

It was a miracle that we found Cinnamon after she disappeared in Kyrgyzstan. It was miracle upon miracle, but I knew from the beginning that we would find her. I knew like you know the flowers will bloom again in the spring. You don't know exactly when, and you certainly don't know how, but you know they will. I believed in this more than I had ever believed in anything before. One friend even suggested that her own faith had been renewed through Cinnamon's miracle.

How many other lives had Cinnamon's life, plight, and rescue touched? We'll never know for sure. But during the interviews I did for this book, I got a sense of the goodwill that Cinnamon spread. Cinnamon had lived on two military bases during her brief time in the Middle East. When I phoned Major Mark Anarumo for his interview, he summed up the feeling that people got from being with Cinnamon: first he chuckled, and then the first words out of his mouth were "Cinnamon rides again!" He expressed, as did most others I talked with, how astounded he was at what had happened to her, how much loving goodwill she spread, how she boosted the morale of everyone who knew her, and how incredible it was that she had been found after being abandoned at the airport.

Mark reports that, still to this day, in the quiet moments when Cinnamon is sleeping, he'll often gaze at her in disbelief. He marvels that she made it home, and he gives thanks for his blessings. Cinnamon's journey was, and still is, surreal for both him and Alice. It's hard for them to believe—even having lived through it—all that we went through to bring Cinnamon home. They are thrilled for her as she continues to play and learn and explore. They are thankful that she is alive. Several people who cared for Cinnamon in Kandahar were convinced that she wouldn't be if Mark and Alice hadn't adopted her.

Alice believes that Cinnamon's breed is either a Sloughi or Saluki, or perhaps a mixture of both. Both breeds are ancient hounds that originated in Africa and Egypt and were raised to be proficient hunters—surely this explains Cinnamon's ability to catch chickens and squirrels. Although in the Middle East most dogs are considered dirty and unfit to live with human beings, the Sloughi and Saluki dogs are prized by the Bedouins. Alice was moved when she learned that many of these prized animals display a white blaze on their forehead or chest, which the Bedouin people believe is the "Kiss of Allah." Considering Cinnamon's miraculous journey home, no one was surprised to learn that her coat displays this distinguished marking.

From the time we searched for Cinnamon and brought her home, we all understood that Katib Ridvanov and Anna Soloviova were relatives. I found out very late in production of this book that this, however, is not true. Katib and Anna are not related. Because this fact does not affect the story, and it is what we knew at the time, I have left all references to their being related as originally experienced. Fortunately for Mark and Cinnamon, Anna knew that Katib loves animals, especially dogs, and that he would not turn a blind eye to the trouble that befell Cinnamon.

Katib continues to be an ambassador for the animals at the

Bishkek airport. Not long after Cinnamon came home, Yulia e-mailed me with a report of his most recent efforts to assist a stranded traveler.

> By the way—Katib helped me again—we were sending a cat to the USA and one of the custom officers didn't want to let her go even though all papers were done properly and we had all permissions etc.—he was looking for a bribe or so. Katib was on duty that night fortunately and helped us to solve the situation.

Yulia Ten is an angel sent from above. Without Yulia, it is unlikely that we would have found Cinnamon or been able to secure her return. She acted despite feeling that the situation was hopeless. We owe her a tremendous amount of gratitude for responding as quickly as she did and working tirelessly on behalf of Cinnamon. It is a debt that can never truly be repaid.

Yulia continues her work with the Animal Welfare Society of Kyrgyzstan. She is frustrated that in the short time since I first contacted her the stray population in Kyrgyzstan has gotten much worse. She believes that educating the country's youth is the best way to encourage better care for animals. She provides animal-education programs in schools and intends to institute a program throughout all the schools. Her hope is to eventually influence the animal-cruelty laws, promote responsible pet ownership, and reduce the stray overpopulation through spay and neuter programs.

Michael Blake was another savior in Cinnamon's plight. His diligent efforts and resourcefulness ensured that Cinnamon was well cared for and transported safely to the U.S. Like Mark, he has settled back into civilian and family life. He continues to fight crime as a police officer in his hometown in Florida. Sadly, his dog Ginger passed away at twelve years old, not long after Mike returned from his deployment. The Blake family marvels at Cinnamon's story and the part Mike played in helping her get back home. They all, even their other dogs, Sprinkles and Tinkerbelle, hoped to meet her sometime soon. Personally, I looked forward to meeting Mike, and in January 2009 I had the opportunity to do so. Meeting your hero and being in his company is a fun and exciting experience that I recommend for everyone!

In 2006, Terri Crisp crossed paths with a philanthropist who wanted to extend his charity to animals. Together, they founded SPCA International, and the organization almost immediately received a request from a soldier in Baghdad who needed help getting a puppy home. Knowing the details of Cinnamon's odyssey, Terri recognized the need for a program to assist soldiers in successfully bringing their furry companions to the U.S. SPCA International's program, which is named Operation Baghdad Pups, was partly inspired by Cinnamon's story. As of this writing, the program, which is funded through public donations, has brought more than one hundred companion animals, including dogs and cats, to loving, permanent homes in the U.S. with their soldier moms and dads. The staff is even working to rehome a donkey

After a two-week vacation at home, Mike Thomsen returned to Kyrgyzstan to finish out his contract. After seven long months away from his family, Mike decided he couldn't justify being away another year, so he took a job that would allow him to be home. In 2008, Mike bumped into a friend who was surrendering his new puppy to the local shelter. The friend's wife had become allergic to the young dog soon after they had brought him home as a stray. Although Mike proclaimed to prefer cats to dogs, he didn't hesitate to step in and take the pup for himself. Jack, a miniature Black Labrador Retriever, who was only eight weeks old at the time, fit in perfectly with Mike's family and now has his forever home.

Dave Simpson was transferred to Japan after his tour in Afghanistan ended. His love for Cinnamon was strong enough that, when he was in the Maryland area in 2008, he contacted Mark to arrange a visit with him and Cinnamon. When Dave arrived at Mark's house, Cinnamon was out in the yard playing. He quickly called to her, "Cinny, Cinny, Cinny," and the moment she heard the familiar voice, she yelped as if she recognized the sound of Dave's voice and bolted in to greet him. The two enjoyed a happy and heartfelt reunion.

Mark and I are often asked about the dog handler who abandoned Cinnamon. People want to know if we ever had the opportunity to ask him about his choices, if he satisfactorily explained his reasons for what he had done, and if he has ever apologized. To each of these questions, the answer is no.

At the time Mark looked for Cinnamon, Matthew Roberts eventually gave Mark details of what happened at the Bishkek airport. Given that Roberts had the opportunity to contact Mark or take Cinnamon back to Manas but didn't do either, his explanation seemed unlikely. But the information Roberts provided to Mark became the point where Chief Blake, and then Yulia, began to search for Cinnamon. Because we had to pour our efforts into finding Cinnamon before it was too late, we couldn't afford the time it would take to pursue additional information from Roberts. Just moments after Mark sent his e-mail informing us that he believed Cinnamon was gone for good, he e-mailed Matthew Roberts expressing his frustration and disdain for Roberts's choices. Roberts sent back the money and phone card that Mark had given him for his trip but otherwise did not reply.

Shortly thereafter, Alice convinced Mark to contact the company that Roberts worked for and let them know what Roberts had done. Initially, Mark received a brief reply from Roberts's supervisor, Henry Carson, who apologized for what had happened—but not without admonishing Mark for writing to the chief operating officer [COO] of his company, which Mark did, to share the details of what had taken place and express his dissatisfaction over Roberts's actions.

As a result of Mark's e-mails, however, two brief investigations ensued. One was within Roberts's company. Mark was told that they would look into the matter but did not receive any followup about the inquiry after his first contact with the COO.

We learned much later that the other investigation was conducted by the military's liaison officer who handled the contract with Roberts's company. I found out from Roberts himself what had happened.

During my research, I had contacted Roberts to ask if I could interview him. In an e-mail, he expressed concern about participating in my "project" until he knew more about my "thesis and motivation." Until that point, he did not know of my relationship to Mark or involvement in Cinnamon's rescue. I had planned to disclose this to him before beginning his interview, but after writing back and acknowledging his unease, I did not hear from him again. He had, however, already related to me that he nearly lost his job for "trying to do the right thing" and that his company had considered making him reimburse the military for his flight to the U.S. Additionally, the military liaison officer to his company had said he should no longer be involved with animals or their lives. Roberts claimed, however, that he tried to do the right thing and even attempted to buy an additional seat for Cinnamon. In the end, Roberts expressed some strong opinions about Mark, by writing that Mark "tried to defraud the government" through him . . . and "took advantage of [his] goodwill and desire to help" and then "because of [Mark's] rank" . . . there were "no consequences [for Mark]."

When I interviewed Chief Blake, he informed me that when Roberts returned to Manas Air Base shortly after Cinnamon made it home, he sought the chief out looking to make amends. According to Chief Blake, Roberts did not earn any goodwill that day, and few were happy to see him.

As I continued writing Cinnamon's story down, I felt it was for the best that Roberts had not contacted me again. It was more important to me that I share our tale to inspire others. I intended to write a book about love, hope, perseverance, and triumph—the very things that helped shape our happy ending. The book would include the miracles and unlikely coincidences that took place and the generosity of everyone who was involved in Cinnamon's search and rescue. I knew that Cinnamon was safe and for me that was enough.

To this day I often think about what we went through to find Cinnamon and get her home. I am continually astounded by what took place. We were confronted with innumerable obstacles that we had to overcome. There was an amazing string of events, which began long before Mark ever met Cinnamon, and these events had to occur in a precise order for us to have succeeded in even finding Cinnamon.

One of the most astounding coincidences is that Mark even met Cinnamon in the first place. As previously described, Mark had been in and out of the Navy Reserves several times since his commission and had to persuade navy personnel to let him back in during 2004. Then, his personnel status had been designated in a way that led to his deployment to Afghanistan. Because Mark got back into the reserves and did not get the assignment of his choice, he was in Kandahar and met Cinnamon. What would have happened to Cinnamon if Mark had not adopted her? Looking back and considering the many "coincidences" that occurred, I firmly believe that it was all meant to be—Cinnamon was meant to have a new life in the United States and she and her story were meant to enhance countless lives near and far.

Another pivotal event was my meeting Terri Crisp. Animal disaster relief is something I had neither done before nor ever thought about until I had seen the images of Katrina's animal victims. I am convinced that my being in Louisiana and meeting Terri in 2005 set the stage for me to help find Cinnamon the following year. I often wonder, had I volunteered with a different rescue group and never met Terri, would I have been of any use in finding Cinnamon. After all, Terri connected me to Yulia when I didn't know where to begin my search, and my contacting Yulia essentially was the starting point of Cinnamon's rescue. But regardless how it came to be that we were able to bring Cinnamon home, every ounce of effort and every moment of anguish was worth seeing her come through the doors at JFK airport. I am humbled and extremely grateful to know that Cinnamon's life is already better and will be longer than the one she started out with because of what we accomplished.

I never imagined I would write and publish a book, but once Cinnamon's story settled in with me, I felt it needed to be told. I found that when I talked to people about what happened, the story did for others what it did for me—it made them believe that just about anything is possible. Because of that, I felt more people needed to hear what happened. When I initially put pen to paper, the words just spilled out. The book that you are now holding was a labor of love, much like finding Cinnamon had been. Once I started, I just couldn't stop.

I am extremely grateful that, by telling Cinnamon's story, I have been able to help other animals in need. But I also recognize that there are many, many animals who are not so fortunate. While at the time of Cinnamon's disappearance our efforts were focused on finding her and getting her home, Mark, Alice, and I were and continue to be aware that millions of animals in the United States and worldwide wait in vain for their rescuers. Whether they live hardened lives as strays on the streets or wait endlessly at shelters without love or a family to call their own, too many die alone or are euthanized by a rescue and adoption system that is too overwhelmed to save them all. We have many critics who feel our exorbitant expenditure of time, effort, and money may have been better spent on saving multiple dogs here at home. I understand and can empathize with that position. I would save all the animals if I could. We all would. Tragically, however, we cannot. And leaving Cinnamon behind would not have changed that. Saving the world's homeless animals is a monumental undertaking, but I firmly believe that, just as in Cinnamon's search and rescue, everyone must do their part, no matter how big or how small. And if each and every one of us follows his or her heart and takes action, then we can make a difference for animals everywhere, just as we did for Cinnamon.

In 2007, I traveled to Bartlesville, Oklahoma, following the flooding that had taken place there. With Terri Crisp and a handful of other volunteers, I helped provide animal disaster relief for the Washington County SPCA (WCSPCA). Their physical shelter was under four feet of water, and their operations were relocated to the local fairgrounds, along with the resident 150 dogs, cats, and horses. It was there, again, that I experienced the deep rewards of caring directly for animals in need. I also met my newest rescue, a black Labrador/Chesapeake Bay retriever mix, named Smiley. Whenever I would approach Smiley in his run, he would wag his tail in celebration and curl his lips in a nervous, submissive smile—thus the name he'd been given. His run was positioned such that every morning when I would arrive, I could immediately see him staring at me and wagging his tail. I spent extra time with him, and soon it was as if he awaited my return each morning. Two months after I got home, I checked the WCSPCA's Web site and learned that Smiley was still lingering at the shelter. It broke my heart. When I inquired why he still had not been adopted, I was told that he was exhibiting undesirable behaviors common to dogs that are in shelters for extended periods. These behavioral issues had made him nearly impossible to place, and Smiley had been at the shelter for seven months. Feeling that his days were numbered, I instantly decided to adopt him and was lucky to find two volunteers who offered to drive him 1,500 miles to a town near my home. While he was in transport, I found the perfect name for my new boy—Brunswick. The name is taken from the motto for New Brunswick, Canada—*spem reduxit*—which is Latin for Hope Restored. It was just the right name to signify his new beginning.

Of the more unusual and exciting things I've done since finding Cinnamon early in 2009, I traveled to Baghdad with Operation Baghdad Pups to escort several military companion animals to the U.S. for the soldiers who had adopted them. And, while it seems extravagant, even wasteful perhaps, to travel 14,000 miles in a week to transport a few dogs and cats, I can attest to the rewards of doing so. When I took Julian, a fourteen-week-old puppy who made the long journey back with me, for her health exam after arriving in the States, without prompting she climbed into my lap and snuggled up inside my coat. In that moment, I knew that helping to bring her to the U.S. was the right thing to do. Having provided love and comfort to a soldier in his time of need, Julian will now live out her days being loved and comforted in return by that very same soldier.

Other than that, my e-mails have become boring again. I don't get phone calls from the former Soviet Union anymore. I also don't get to see Cinnamon very often, but I check in with Mark and Alice fairly regularly to see how Cinnamon, Pete, and Elvis are faring. They happily give me updates of Cinnamon's latest antics and how she, Pete, and Elvis romp in the yard together. I can hear the pride of parenthood in their voices.

I don't talk with Mark and Alice as much as I did when we searched for Cinnamon, and with them still twelve hours away and all of us settling back into our own routines, that probably won't change much anytime soon. But the journey that we all shared is one I will never forget.

Cinnamon is now a local celebrity in Maryland. There were several news stories done about her adventures when she and Mark finally made it back to Maryland. When Mark and Alice walk down the street with her, Pete, and Elvis, it is not uncommon for a stranger to smile at them and say, "That's Cinnamon, isn't it?" She still spreads goodwill wherever she goes. And while Pete and Elvis are a bit overshadowed by their famous sister, they don't mind because their rescues were assured the day Cinnamon was found.

> Saving one animal will not change the world,
> but surely the world will change
> for that one animal.
>
> —Unknown

ACKNOWLEDGMENTS

THERE ARE SO many people to thank who helped make Cinnamon's homecoming, and thereby this book possible. First, thank you to those who cared for Cinnamon at Shir Zai, including Dave Simpson, Dave Schlosser, and everyone from the 4-1 Kandak. I am incredibly grateful to the leadership at Manas Air Base, including Major Mark Anarumo, Colonel Arnold Holcomb, and the Wing Commander, for accommodating the search for Cinnamon and her care when they didn't necessarily have to. For the countless others at KAF, Shir Zai, and Manas who walked, watered, fed, played with, watched out for, and otherwise cared for Cinnamon so that she ultimately made it home.

A vast amount of gratitude goes to Anna Soloviova, for her compassion for Cinnamon and her quick thinking in saving her and to Katib Ridvanov and his family, for taking Cinnamon in when there was nowhere else for her to go.

I am particularly grateful to Terri Crisp and to the World Society for Protection of Animals, including Stephanie Dawes, for the pivotal roles they played as I began my search for Cinnamon.

I will always be indebted to Yulia Ten, whose compassion and generosity changed the ending of this story. Without Yulia's involvement it's unlikely we would have found Cinnamon. Heartfelt thanks go to Michael Blake and Jim Kamrad, for their empathy for Cinnamon and Mark's plight, and for their selflessness and perseverance in helping get Cinnamon home.

Thank you to Maria Onisenko; Daniel, the interpreter for Mark's team; Dr. Frank Cerfogli, DVM; the army veterinarian; and the

Afghan veterinarian (not named for security purposes), for their invaluable help. Thank you also to Lola and Paul Michaud and Bob Gielarowski, for their willingness to help with Cinnamon's Stateside logistics and transportation. Thank you to Michael Thomsen for trusting that he was meant to be a part of this journey and for successfully delivering Cinnamon safe and sound.

Tremendous thanks go to Mark and Alice, for the countless hours they spent with me while I probed into their memories, emotions, and lives and for their help to ensure the accuracy of dates, times, places, and events, and also for Mark's help in navigating the road to being published.

Thanks to my friends who supported and encouraged me from the moment I first thought about writing this book. I am grateful to Stephanie Scroggs-Scott of SPCA International/Operation Baghdad Pups, for her generosity in time spent mentoring me in the world of media relations, which initially helped launch our story. Thanks also to Alanna Ramirez, for helping me find a publisher for this book.

I am especially grateful to my editor, Daniela Rapp, of St. Martin's Press, for seeing the heart and soul in my story, for her outstanding editorial skill, and for thoughtfully guiding me in delivering a book that was even better than when she received it. Thank you also to all those at St. Martin's who worked on and embraced this book.

I am especially grateful to my niece, Christine Llano, who cheered me on and kept me going at times I needed encouragement the most. Thank you to my mom, Ada Marie Feffer, for much more than I could recount here, but particularly for the writing genes that she passed along and for being the very best promoter an author could ask for. I have tremendous gratitude for my dad, Richard Feffer, for so many reasons, but especially that he shared with me his spirit of adventure, which continues to shape who I am today. And also that, with few but important words, he taught me to throw caution to the wind and follow my heart. Regretfully, my dad passed away in 2008, but he made sure I knew how proud he was of me and for that I am eternally grateful.

I would also like to thank Spirit and Brunswick, for their interminable patience while I worked on this book when I knew they'd much rather have been out hiking, running, or chasing little critters. And thank you to Billy, for always encouraging me to follow my heart and my dreams.